Thanks for
support Simon.

Jeremy

Domestic Extremism and the Case
of the Toronto 18

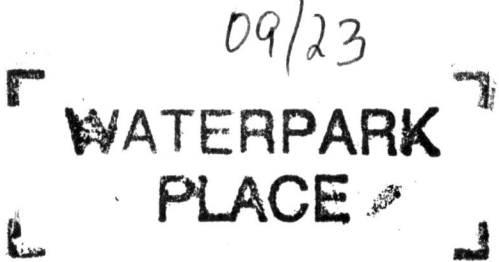

WATERPARK
PLACE

Jeremy Kowalski

Domestic Extremism and the Case of the Toronto 18

Jeremy Kowalski
Waterloo, Ontario, Canada

ISBN 978-1-349-94959-5   ISBN 978-1-349-94960-1 (eBook)
DOI 10.1057/978-1-349-94960-1

Library of Congress Control Number: 2016940556

© The Editor(s) (if applicable) and The Author(s) 2016
This work is subject to copyright. All rights are solely and exclusively licensed by the Publisher, whether the whole or part of the material is concerned, specifically the rights of translation, reprinting, reuse of illustrations, recitation, broadcasting, reproduction on microfilms or in any other physical way, and transmission or information storage and retrieval, electronic adaptation, computer software, or by similar or dissimilar methodology now known or hereafter developed.
The use of general descriptive names, registered names, trademarks, service marks, etc. in this publication does not imply, even in the absence of a specific statement, that such names are exempt from the relevant protective laws and regulations and therefore free for general use.
The publisher, the authors and the editors are safe to assume that the advice and information in this book are believed to be true and accurate at the date of publication. Neither the publisher nor the authors or the editors give a warranty, express or implied, with respect to the material contained herein or for any errors or omissions that may have been made.

Cover image © Eugene Sergeev / Alamy Stock Photo

Printed on acid-free paper

This Palgrave Macmillan imprint is published by Springer Nature
The registered company is Nature America Inc. New York

For my good friend James Eldin Reed
13 March 1945–5 April 2012

Prologue

And this place our forefathers made for man!
This is the process of our love and wisdom
To each poor brother who offends against us;
Most innocent, perhaps—and what if guilty?
Is this the only cure, merciful God?
Each pore and natural outlet shriveled up
By ignorance and parching poverty,
His energies role back upon his heart
And stagnate and corrupt; till, changed to poison,
They break out on him like a loathsome plague-spot.
Then we call in our pampered mountebanks
And this is their best cure: uncomforted
And friendless solitude, groaning and tears
And savage faces at the clanking hour,
Seen through the steams and vapour of his dungeon,
By the lamp's dismal twilight. So he lies
Circled with evil, till his very soul
Unmoulds its essence, hopelessly deformed
By sights of every more deformity![1]

On 2 June 2006, approximately 400 police officers[2] from various jurisdictions across the province of Ontario—codenamed operation O-Sage by the Royal Canadian Mounted Police (RCMP)—were involved in the concerted arrests of seventeen individuals living in the Greater Toronto Area (GTA).[3] The individuals who were arrested were detained under provisions enshrined in Bill C-36,[4] the Anti-terrorism Act (ATA) ratified by Canadian parliament in December 2001. The individuals arrested were described in one newspaper article in the following terms: "sources say the arrests involve a 'homegrown' terrorism cell—Western youths who have never set foot in Afghanistan but allegedly were radicalized here, and who are thought to be potentially as dangerous as the cells that once took orders from Osama bin Laden."[5] In another newspaper article, Luc Portelance, who at the time was the assistant operations director in the Canadian Security Intelligence Service (CSIS), is quoted as describing the individuals arrested as "people who 'have become adherents of a violent ideology inspired by al-Qaeda.'"[6] These individuals would later become codified by the Canadian corporate media as the *Toronto 18*. The arrest and subsequent trials of these individuals are judicially significant as this was the first time a group had been charged with terrorism-related offenses in contravention of the Canadian Criminal Code, and only the second time anti-terrorism laws had been used to prosecute a person in Canada.[7]

On 1 April 2008, approximately 22 months after various Canadian and international media[8] descended upon the Superior Courthouse in the city of Brampton, Ontario, to report on the arraignment of the initial seventeen individuals[9] arrested under Canada's anti-terror legislation, and after those in attendance and those following the media coverage were witness to a securitized spectacle of steel barricades, rooftop positioned snipers, dozens of tactical law enforcement officers from the Regional Municipality of Peel armed with sub-machine guns, bomb-sniffing dogs, and an orbiting helicopter,[10] I entered the same courthouse to begin observing the pre-trial proceedings of the first alleged member (a youth at the time of arrest) of the group to stand trial for purported terrorism-related offenses. Throughout those proceedings and those of the other accused, I had the opportunity to observe the details of not only the activities of the Toronto 18 but also those of the Canadian law enforcement and security apparatuses as they emerged. The remainder of the prologue provides a synopsis of those activities.

According to an article in the *Toronto Star*, the investigation of various individuals in the group was initiated by CSIS in 2004 as a result of the "fundamentalist views" various individuals were expressing on particular Internet sites. On 17 November 2005, CSIS sent an *advisory letter* to the RCMP apprising them of the criminal activity of one member of the group.[11] As a result of receiving the advisory letter, the RCMP initiated its own investigation of the individual identified in the document and this individual's associates. The aegis of the investigation fell under the Integrated National Security Enforcement Team (INSET).[12] In the context of Toronto, the INSET responsible was "O Division."

While CSIS and the RCMP were coordinating their surveillance activities, on 27 November 2005, CSIS requested that a "directed source"[13] attend a town hall meeting where the controversial Canadian Security Certificate Program was being discussed at the Taj Banquet Hall in the City of Toronto. According to testimony given by the "directed source" at the first trial I observed in June 2006, he was tasked with attending the function to initiate contact with members of the nascent group to obtain information regarding their future activities. After initiating contact with the principal actors in the group, one of the actors "began to recruit the agent by indoctrinating him with emotional arguments about the oppression of Muslims."[14] After establishing a degree of trust, which was partially achieved through the directed source indicating that he had previously received military training, one of the principal figures divulged to the directed source that several areas had been scouted for "training." As indicated in the same document, the principal actor suggested that the directed source may fulfill a role in the training given his previous exposure to military training.[15] Approximately three weeks later, the directed source, who had by this time become a confidential informant/police agent for the RCMP, accompanied approximately twelve individuals as they traveled north from the GTA to Washago, Ontario (a rural town in Ramara Township), to participate in what would be later described by prosecutors and subsequently reported by the Canadian media as a training camp.

On 18 December 2005, various members of the Toronto 18 engaged in a variety of outdoor exercises, including using paintball to simulate combat activities, running an obstacle course, shooting a 9 mm firearm, marching with a flag of the declaration of faith (white writing on a black background), and participating in three *halaqah* (formal sessions of discussion used by one of the principal figures on two separate occasions to impart his ideology and concomitant convictions to the participants at the camp). According to testimony delivered under cross-examination by the confidential informer on 16 June 2008, the Washago training camp was used by the principal actors to screen potential "jihadis" or "soldiers" for their group. However, as this witness indicated in his testimony, several of the attendees were unaware of the actual purpose of the training camp. Several of the attendees understood that the training camp was a religious retreat and an opportunity to learn outdoor survival skills. As the witness later suggested in his testimony, it is arguably during the second *halaqah* that the genuine intentions of the training camp were revealed to all of the attendees.[16] Indeed, one of the principal figures of the group is recorded at the training camp as stating the following in a speech to the participants at the camp:

> Our mission is here. This is where we come back at the end of the day. We all got our missions, which we gotta fulfill. We all know what we gotta do when we go back whether its like enroll in school and be patient and this and that but at the end of the day, but especially the young guys... I don't how, how involved we'll be able to get you guys again and how often but this is the hearts. This is where the hearts are okay [.] [...] Our mission's greater, whether we get arrested, whether we killed, we get tortured, our mission's greater than just individuals. It's not about you or I or this Amir or that Amir, it's not about that. It's about the fact that this has to get done. Rome has to be defeated. And we have to be the one's that do it, no holding back, whether it's one man that survives, you have to do it. This is what the Covenant's all about, you have to do it. And God willing we will do it. God willing we will get the victory.[17]

Although one could argue that this piece of audio does to a certain degree reveal the stated objectives of the speaker in abstraction, the directed source/confidential informer stated in his testimony that the youths in the group were being manipulated and exploited and were, ultimately, being led down the wrong path.[18] The participants in the training camp returned to the GTA on 30 December 2005.[19]

As outlined in an "Agreed Statement of Facts" for one of the accused, on 4 February 2006, the confidential informant departed the GTA with one of the principal figures and two other members of the group for Opasatika, Ontario. The purpose of this journey was to see a piece of real estate that the two principal figures of the group had identified as a potential safe house and base of operations. According to the document, the confidential informer/police agent recalled that the principal actor he was traveling with described the surveillance he had performed on Parliament Hill in Ottawa, Ontario, and his plans to infiltrate by force the Canadian House of Commons and begin executing hostages until the Canadian government agreed to withdraw its troops from Afghanistan.[20] It is during this journey that the musings of beheading the Prime Minister of Canada were intercepted by the surveillance equipment that had been placed in the confidential informer's/police agent's vehicle.[21] Shortly after returning from performing reconnaissance in Opasatika, one of the principal actors revealed to the other that he had successfully built a remote detonator that was effective to a range of 30 feet. However, the objective of the principal actor in charge of building the detonator was to develop a device with a range of 300 meters (a seized video recording of the testing of the detonator was presented and submitted into evidence in court).

During the eight weeks following the journey to Opasatika, there was growing tension between the two principal figures in the group as a result of the impatience one of the principal figures was experiencing due to the perceived lack of material progress and inaction of the other principal figure. According to one media report, one of the principal figures "wanted to slow down and craft an attack designed for maximum impact," whereas the other principal figure "wanted to attack as soon as possible."[22] After mounting tensions, one court document indicates that on 28 March 2006 the frustrated principal figure contacted the other principal figure and left the following message: "everybody in Mississauga, we just quit everything, totally."[23] This action resulted in the fracturing of the group into two distinct factions: the Mississauga group and the Scarborough group.

Following the severing of the group into two distinct factions, the principal figure in the Mississauga group continued orchestrating his plans to conduct an attack in downtown Toronto using manufactured fertilizer-based explosives. It is around this time—early April 2006—that a second police agent assumed a role of paramount importance for the security and law enforcement apparatuses investigating this case. This individual would facilitate and broker the purchase of specific chemical compounds for the Mississauga group. As one journalist reports, this individual is "portrayed in court documents as playing a crucial, clandestine role in thwarting the high profile plot, yet has received almost no attention to date. He claims that he so thoroughly infiltrated an inner circle of radicalized youths that he was given envelopes of cash and shopping lists of chemicals, as he was asked to help attack Toronto with fertilizer bombs."[24] It is during the months of April and May that the bomb plot unfolded.

On 7 April 2006, the police agent referred to above met the principal actor of the Mississauga group and another individual to discuss the details of the plan. As indicated in one court document, this is the date on which the principal actor divulged the targets of the attack and the month in which the attack would commence. In mid-November 2006 (however, according to a report in the *National Post*, one of the co-conspirators had expressed an interest in detonating the bombs on 11 September 2006 "so the date would be remembered forever"),[25] the Mississauga group was planning to rent three U-Haul trucks, pack the trucks with fertilizer-based explosives (a mixture of ammonium nitrate and nitric acid—the same compound used in the Oklahoma City bombings of 19 April 1995), and detonate the bombs using the remote-controlled trigger mechanisms designed by the principal figure of the group at the following locations: the Toronto office of CSIS, the Toronto Stock Exchange (TSE), and an unnamed military base between Toronto and Ottawa (presumably Canadian Forces Base (CFB Trenton)). According to the same court document, on a later date during an exchange between one of the individuals involved in the bomb plot and the police agent, the magnitude of the bombs was compared to that of the bombing of housing compounds in Riyadh, Saudi Arabia, on 12 May 2003 and the London transit bombings on 7 July 2005. Ultimately, after various meetings, exchanges, and changed plans throughout the months of April and May, it was arranged that the chemicals would be delivered on 2 June 2006 to an industrial storage unit located at 1228 Gorham Street, unit #6, Newmarket, Ontario.[26] As a result of the second agent's cooperation and participation in the apprehension of the group, this individual was paid approximately four million dollars (CAD) by the RCMP and, upon the arrest of the group, was relocated with his family under the auspices of the witness protection program.[27]

While the Mississauga faction was in the midst of planning and solidifying the logistics for their desired objectives, the Scarborough group held a second "training" camp at the Rockwood Conservation Area, near Guelph, Ontario, from 20 to 22 May 2006. At this camp, approximately eight individuals participated in what could be construed as benign recreational activities, including swimming, hiking, rowing in an inflatable dingy, and sitting around a campfire. As argued in court, the apparent incriminating evidence of the nefarious intent of the Rockwood training camp was a video recovered by law enforcement officials of the group concealing their identities while holding swords on either side of a flag of the declaration of faith. Within two weeks of the Rockwood training camp, members of both the Mississauga group and the Scarborough group were arrested. These arrests were coordinated to coincide with the delivery of the chemicals on 2 June 2006. On 3 June 2006, the following two headlines appeared in two out of the three largest Toronto-based newspapers:

"Never mind foreign terrorists, why is Canada growing its own extremists?" (*National Post*) and "Terror Cops Swoop GTA" (*Toronto Star*).[28]

Using the case of the Toronto 18, this book attempts to identify and deconstruct the conditions that make the emergence of particular types of extremist actors probable in place-specific contexts. Although to date myriad explanations from a range of academic disciplines have emerged attempting to illuminate with varying degrees of effectiveness the causes of the social phenomenon popularly referred to as "homegrown terrorism," many of these modes of analysis are constrained and limited by the manacles of state intellectualism. As a consequence, this area of research is being threatened by an analytical ossification that has the potential to lead those that follow these lines of inquiry into *The Dungeon* Samuel Taylor Coleridge poetically describes. Therefore, if these manacles are to be broken, much more critical and reflective forms of interpretation and analysis need to be employed in order to help escape from the epistemological and ideological narrowing engendered by dominant discourses and authorized narratives.

Introduction

On 3 June 2006, the day following the arrests of the alleged members of the group that would be later codified as the Toronto 18, the acting Deputy Director of Operations for CSIS, Jack Hooper, described this nascent threat facing Canadians in the following terms: "We have a bifurcated threat at this point," Mr. Hooper testified. "The threat that comes to Canada from outside as well as a homegrown threat, and the homegrown variants look to Canada to execute their targeting." "We must be vigilant on two fronts," he added, "that which is coming to us from the outside environment and, increasingly, that which is growing up in our communities."[29] This characterization of a "homegrown" threat emerging in Canada found popular expression in an editorial cartoon that appeared in the *National Post* newspaper on 6 June 2006 entitled "Homegrown." This editorial cartoon depicts a flower pot emblazoned with a Canadian maple leaf with a plant sprouting beside a sign that reads terror with a picture of a bomb. Indeed, the arrests of these individuals appeared to have situated Canada among the constellation of Western countries that have experienced "homegrown" threats/attacks: the 2 November 2004 murder of Theo Van Gogh in Amsterdam, the Netherlands; the 7 July 2005 transit bombings in London, England; the arrests of alleged terrorist cells in Germany (5 September 2007) and Denmark (October 2005 and September 2007); and the Charlie Hebdo attack in France (7 January 2015). Although the utilization of this "homegrown" terminology to characterize the alleged nascent threat could certainly be construed as value neutral, the implications of deploying this terminology are actually quite significant.

First, the "homegrown" terminology signals a spatial shift in the securitized gaze from a constructed Other external to the nation space, to a constructed Other internal to the nation space—the enemy within or a fifth column. Secondly, the "homegrown" terminology connotes the existence of an organic Other that naturally grows in particular communities—an organic and natural enemy. In an op-ed piece entitled "Knowing the enemy within," Wesley Wark, a visiting professor in the University of Ottawa's Graduate School of Public and International Affairs, galvanizes these sentiments: "the arrests of 17 alleged terrorists in the Toronto area have illuminated one of the greatest challenges to face Western democracies and their intelligence services: the challenge presented by so-called second generation or homegrown terrorist groups in our midst."[30] He goes on to state, "homegrown terrorist groups are the most difficult target imaginable for intelligence services. They have an invisibility that is a product of the fact they operate in a democratic society protective of their rights and they blend into that society as individuals."[31] In the context of the arrests in Toronto, the deployment of the "homegrown" descriptor effectively renders particular communities and groups as suspect, thereby producing repositories of fear, anger, and resentment directed at communities and groups problematically and irresponsibly identified as being connected to the individuals arrested. For example, shortly after the arrests in the Toronto case, the International Muslims Organization of Toronto, a mosque located in the GTA, was vandalized by unknown assailants.[32] A mosque in Hamilton, Ontario, also became the object of vandalism following these same arrests.[33] Therefore, not only is it necessary to enact a terminological break from characterizations that (in)advertently implicate various communities and groups as being complicit in the activities of specific actors, but it is necessary to identify fenestrae that enable the penetration of a complex social phenomenon that largely remains opaque.

Since the macabre spectacle of 11 September 2001 figuratively and literally caused the subject of extremism to forcefully enter the consciousness of Western states, a veritable cornucopia of academic journal articles and books has emerged in the social sciences and humanities—political science, sociology, history, anthropology, psychology, geography, computer science, philosophy, literary studies, communication studies, law—attempting to interpret, explain, and ultimately demystify particular types of extremism. However, as John Horgan notes, "in spite of this mass of data, or even perhaps because of it, it is ironic then that even now a sound understanding of terrorism continues to elude us. It still surprises us that just because there is more information on terrorism than ever before, it does not necessarily follow that we understand it any better."[34] Yonah Alexander's observation about the amount of material produced in the aftermath of 11 September 2001 and his questioning of the quality of material available reinforces Horgan's comment. According to Alexander, approximately 150 books on terrorism were produced within a year after the attacks on the World Trade Center and the Pentagon. Although this volume of publishing has continued, Alexander accurately questioned whether or not the quality of the majority of books in print would stand the test of time.[35] Consequently, as Brian Jenkins asserts, "we are deluged with material but still know too little."[36] As a result, enormous knowledge gaps continue to pervade the corpus of research and literature on the subject of terrorism.

To date, much of the research on terrorism has explored and focused on the effects of terrorism on wider society and/or on the direct impact of terrorist events on victims.[37] A considerable amount of literature also analyzes the relationship between the media and terrorism.[38] However, as Andrew Silke argues, "surprisingly little research of scientific merit has been conducted on the perpetrators of terrorist violence. The activities of terrorist groups, and the nature of their membership, have by and large been studiously ignored by social scientists."[39] He goes on to state that "very few published attempts have been made to systematically study terrorists outside of a prison setting or to study in a systematic manner the actual activities carried out as part of the terrorist campaigns."[40] In effect, as one moves analytically closer to the actual actors involved in a terrorist campaign, the quality of the research significantly diminishes. These analytical shortfalls are compounded by the relatively marginal position of terrorism studies as a field of academic inquiry.

Prior to the events of 11 September 2001, the marginal status of terrorism studies was well documented. For instance, in the mid-1980s Paul Wilkinson observed that terrorism research is "small scale, and even peripheral, in most universities and research institutions. Apart from the research groups working in a few well-known major centers... most scholars working in this field are working alone, or at most with one or two colleagues in a larger academic institution."[41] These comments became more poignant when one surveyed the amount of doctoral and graduate research being conducted at universities. According to a study conducted by Avishag Gordon on English language theses indexes, between 1960 and 1997 only 278 theses (cumulative number of both MA and PhD) on the subject of terrorism were produced.[42] However, as noted by Gordon, the growth trend of the theses on the subject of terrorism was encouraging: "the classification by decade records three indexed in the 1960s and 12 indexed in the 1970s, but 122 in the 1980s, which apparently shows that the 'take off' years for literature on terrorism were the 1980s. The 1990s, up to 1996, provided 126 items, thus demonstrating continuous, even accelerated, literature growth in this subject area."[43] If the field of terrorism studies was relatively slow to mature in the period prior to 11 September 2001, its growth following that date has been unprecedented leading some scholars to refer to the present period as "a golden age" for research on the subject of terrorism.[44]

According to a review conducted by Richard Jackson, "A study from 2006, for example, found that 14, 006 articles about terrorism had been published between 1971 and 2002, with 54% of the articles published in 2001 and 2002. Another study found that 2, 281 non-fiction with the term terrorism in the title has been published between September 2001 and June 2008; in comparison, only 1, 310 such books had been published in the entire period prior to 2001."[45] As Jackson continues, "Fueling this veritable explosion of terrorism literature is a vast network of both new and old terrorism research centers, think tanks, postgraduate and doctoral programs in universities, private and government-funded research programs, terrorism research consortiums and associations, regular seminars and conferences, new data bases, and a great many other scholarly activities."[46] However, despite the significant growth and expansion of the field of terrorism studies, several problems that were evident in the period prior to the events of 11 September 2001 continue to haunt this body of research.[47]

As Gordon identifies, the majority of the research conducted on the subject of terrorism from the 1970s to the 1990s focused on trend analysis rather than on specific case studies or context-specific analysis of the terrorism phenomenon.[48] Similarly, this high-level focus on the subject of terrorism has persisted and forms the basis of a considerable amount of the terrorism literature produced in the period following the 11 September 2001 attacks. As Richard Jackson observes, in mainstream approaches to the subject of terrorism, there is a prevailing tendency to provide decontextualized and ahistorical analyses of this social phenomenon.[49] As a consequence, the majority of the dominant literature on the subject of terrorism is analytically superficial: "Trying to understand terrorism without detailed knowledge of the history and context in which it emerges, or the way in which terrorism as a strategy has evolved and developed over previous centuries, can only result in surface-level forms of knowledge and highly dubious and ideological distortions (such as the notion of 'new terrorism')."[50] Therefore, in order to develop a more comprehensive and robust understanding of the social phenomenon of terrorism, it is imperative to engage in context-specific and/or place-specific forms of analyses. Although engaging in this type of analysis is not unique to a singular academic discipline, the social science of geography is certainly well positioned to make significant contributions in this regard. Indeed, as the phenomenon of terrorism in all of its expressions is inherently geographical as much as it is political, one would reasonably expect geographers to have a much stronger presence in this area of research. However, to date, the relatively limited contribution to the corpus of terrorism literature by geographers is noteworthy.

In a post-11 September 2001 context, the academic literature that explores the intersection of geography and terrorism is oriented on two analytical trajectories. These two trajectories can be characterized by what Robert Cox refers to as the "problem-solving" approach and the "critical" approach.[51] Cox characterizes the problem-solving approach in the following terms:

> It takes the world as it finds it, with the prevailing social and power relationships and the institutions to which they are organized, as the given framework for action. The general aim of problem solving is to make these relationships and institutions work smoothly by dealing effectively with particular sources of trouble. Since the general pattern of institutions and relationships is not called into question, particular problems can be considered in relation to the specialized areas of activity in which they arise.

Conversely, Cox characterizes the critical approach in the following terms:

> Critical theory, unlike problem-solving theory, does not take institutions and social and power relations for granted but calls them into question by concerning itself with their origins and how and whether they might be in the process of changing. It is directed toward an appraisal of the very framework of action, or problematic, which problem-solving theory accepts as its parameters.

Using the two theoretical approaches identified by Cox as a framework, Jeroen Gunning describes the distinction between these two types of approaches vis-à-vis research on the social phenomenon of terrorism. According to Gunning,

> [...] a 'problem solving' approach does not question its framework of reference, its categories, its origins or the power relations that enable the production of these categories. It is state-centric, takes security to mean the security of the state rather than that of human beings, on the assumption that the former implies the latter, and sees security in narrow military or law-and-order terms [...].

As Gunning continues,

> It is ahistorical and ignores social and historical contexts; if it did not, it would have to account for the historical trajectory of the state, which would undermine the state's claim to being uniquely legitimate. The problem-solving approach is positivist and objectivist, and seeks to explain the 'terrorist other' form within state-centric paradigms rather than to understand the 'other' inter-subjectively using interpretive or ethnographic methods. It divides the world sharply into dichotomies (for instance, between legitimate and 'good' state, and the illegitimate and 'evil' terrorists). It posits assumptions based on these dichotomies, often without adequately exploring whether these assumptions are borne out in practice.[52]

On the other hand, the critical approach to the study of the social phenomenon of terrorism decenters the state as the singular legitimate referent and analyzes the effects of (counter-)terrorism on individuals and society operating on multiple scales including: the local, the regional, the national, and the international. Furthermore, the critical approach analyzes the relationship between state violence and the (re-)production of oppositional violence and seeks to historicize and contextualize violent events and/or conflicts. It challenges taken-for-granted assumptions and categories and analyzes how terrorism discourses are used to not only discredit and target oppositional groups but justify state violence as a necessary corollary of national security.[53] Although, as Gunning suggests, traditional approaches to the subject of terrorism predominantly follow a problem-solving mode of engagement, the majority of contributions to this area of inquiry from the geographic discipline follow a critical mode of engagement.

The most salient contribution from the geographical literature on the subject of terrorism and the war *of* terror is found in the geographical sub-discipline of critical geopolitics and its sub-field popular geopolitics. However, rather than (in)directly focusing on or functioning in support of state-centric agendas and policy initiatives,[54] critical geopolitical research not only provides an analysis of the multiscalar spatialities of state violence and terror that have resulted from the geopolitical policies and practices of the war *of* terror but provides an analysis of how popular culture is utilized to influence, (re-)produce, and/or reinforce geopolitical imaginings that help to both support and justify those same policies and practices. These critical geopolitical modes of analyses are an important dimension in understanding the contemporary manifestation of particular types of terrorism because the state and its various modalities of violence have been, and continue to be, integral in creating the conditions in which specific forms of oppositional violence become probable. As John Horgan states:

> States and governments have been responsible for equally and often far more reprehensible acts of violence on scales unreachable by conventional terrorist organizations: this point is blatantly obvious, yet we choose both to derogate and label as terrorism violence that appears to bubble up from 'below', rather than imposed from 'above'.[55]

In effect, this shift from "below" to "above" exposes to varying degrees the culpability of states in maintaining and sustaining oppositional campaigns of violence.

Some examples of the multiscalar spatialities of state violence engendered by the war *of* terror and its "coalition of the willing" find expression in the following works. For instance, Stuart Elden provides an examination of the war *of* terror and its international impact on the connection between sovereignty and territory. As a result, Elden demonstrates how the sovereignty of nation-states is routinely violated to protect the sovereignty and related interests of more powerful states.[56] This violation of the state sovereignty and territorial integrity of various nation-states on an international scale is further explicated through four different analyses provided by Simon Dalby, Derek Gregory, Jim Glassman, and David Harvey. For example, Dalby describes how geopolitical reasoning predicated on a system of autonomous states and territorial responsibilities precludes the possibility of a response that does not involve mobilizing for war.[57] Gregory provides a post-colonial cultural critique of the political, military, and economic modalities of power in three places, Afghanistan, Iraq, and Palestine, and explains how an Orientalist geographical imaginary is used to justify and legitimate the occupation of these territories.[58] Similarly, Glassman reveals how the US government uses Orientalist reductionism to characterize countries, such as the Philippines, Indonesia, and Thailand, as sources of

Islamic terrorism in order to exercise its influence in regions like Southeast Asia.[59] On the other hand, Harvey argues that the war *of* terror serves as a pretense for the USA to substantiate the requirement for international interventions in order to engage in predatory capital accumulation and ultimately secure its own geostrategic interests.[60] Other expressions of the spatialities of state violence at the international scale can be found in the literature that discusses the production of an archipelago of extrajudicial and extraterritorialized spaces for the detention and torture of individuals apprehended in the war *of* terror. For example, Gregory interrogates the complex geographies that make the operation of places of exceptional violence like Guantanamo Bay and Abu Ghraib possible.[61] Additionally, Trevor Paglen attempts to illuminate and map the covert and top-secret spaces that not only support the global projection of American military power but support the execution of the war *of* terror both nationally and internationally.[62] While the international spatialities of state violence associated with the war *of* terror are an important dimension of critical geopolitical research and analysis, the manifestation of state violence at the national scale is another important aspect of the critical geopolitical literature.

According to Stephen Graham, "As global violence telescopes within and through local places, so new physical, social, and psychological barriers are being constructed and enacted. In many contexts, militarized discourses of 'homeland security' are infiltrating, and starting to reshape, previously civil societies, spaces, and policy debates."[63] As a consequence, these militarized discourses and the national security imperative they portend began to manifest materially in a variety of forms. For instance, Louise Amoore provides an analysis of the emergence of the "biometric border" and the increased use of technology in managing, encoding, and filtering the movement of bodies at the border crossings of the USA.[64] Similarly, Benjamin Muller provides an analysis of the ways in which borders and the bodies that traverse them are being re-imagined as a result of the increased securitization of border spaces as sites of risk management.[65] Stephen Graham, Peter Marcuse, Mitchell Gray, and Elvin Wyly offer analyses that move beyond the border and illuminate the transformative impact that the events of 11 September 2001 and subsequent counter-terrorism policies and practices have had on cities and urban life throughout the USA. For example, Graham demonstrates how the supposed war on terror is predicated on "dialectical constructions of urban place" and the "constitutive representation of 'homeland' and 'target' cities."[66] Furthermore, Graham analyzes not only the increasing militarization of cities and urban life but discusses how metropolitan areas are increasingly being treated and managed as battle spaces where "enemies" of the state must be neutralized through various forms of state interdiction.[67] Similarly, Marcuse provides an analysis of the "citadelization" of the urban form following 11 September 2001 and the downgrading of urban life and erosion of democracy being justified as a necessary corollary of the war on terror.[68] As a result of the militarization and citadelization of both the urban form and urban life in various cities across the USA, Gray and Wyly have re-imagined the urban space of American cities through, what they term, "The Terror City Hypothesis." According to Gray and Wyly, "the terror city is a construct that redefines the urban by portraying all cities in terms of their *vulnerability* to terrorism or their *propensity to breed and harbor terrorists*."[69] Consequently, they argue, "in American cities, more and more aspects of everyday life and death now *take place* in the shadow of horror and fear, sustained by the manufactured certainty of uncertainty in an endless American war on terror. A culture of intensified (yet routine and almost mundane) militarization now pervades daily life in America's roster of world cities."[70] As Matthew Hannah argues, a corollary of the suffusion of the landscapes of everyday life with a high level of fear and risk is the willingness of the national body to condone counter-terrorism policies and practices like the use of torture because of the misapprehension that these brutal methods actually mitigate risk.[71] However, the critical geopolitical analysis of the spatialities of state violence associated with the war *of* terror extends beyond the international and national and examines the embodied experiences of these geopolitical forces, processes, and practices.

The approach to the study of the geopolitical at the scale of the body is indicative of a feminist approach to critical geopolitics advanced by Lorraine Dowler, Joanne Sharpe, and Jennifer Hyndman.[72] For example, in the article entitled, Richelle Bernazzoli and Colin Flint attempt to assess "the extent to which the goals and practices of the elite have been successful in embedding militarism in the fabric of society."[73] Furthermore, Hyndman analyzes the embodied effects of the war *of* terror through providing an examination of Afghani and Iraqi civilian death tolls, which are usually purposefully underrepresented or unreported, as state-sponsored murder, euphemistically disguised under the adage "collateral damage," is considered counter-productive to the interests of the countries involved in these forms of atrocities.[74]

Whereas critical geopolitical research and analysis has documented the multiscalar spatialities of state violence that have occurred, and continue to occur, as a result of the war *of* terror, the sub-field of popular geopolitics has made important contributions to developing an understanding of how popular culture (re-)produces and supports the dominant narratives and geopolitical imaginings necessary to justify and legitimate the execution of the war *of* terror. However, before continuing, it is necessary to briefly define popular geopolitics and identify its object of study. According to Jason Dittmer, "popular geopolitics refers to the everyday geopolitical discourse that citizens are immersed in every day."[75] As such, to access these everyday geopolitical discourses, popular geopolitics studies the mass media in all of its forms, such as television programs, cinema, literature, comic books, newspapers, televised news networks, music, the Internet, and other cultural artifacts, to deconstruct the ideological assumptions, genre and narrative conventions, visual and linguistic tropes, and rhetorical devices that consciously or unconsciously inform and reinforce particular abstracted geopolitical imaginings and by extension support concrete geopolitical policies and practices.[76]

Although the evaluation and analysis of several of the media identified above appear in the popular geopolitical literature, the cinematic and filmic response to and/or representation of the war *of* terror has received the most attention by scholars who operate in this sub-field. As Klaus Dodds indicates, "From the Second World War onwards Hollywood has had a long and profitable relationship with various government bodies including the Department of Defense and intelligence agencies such as the CIA and NSA."[77] However, while Hollywood has profited from this relationship, the US government and its various apparatuses have assuredly benefitted as well: throughout periods of war and/or other forms of crisis, cinema and film become powerful propagandistic spaces and tools that are utilized to indoctrinate the public with specific threats, dangers, and fears.[78] In effect, as Mark Lacy explains: "The cinema becomes a space where 'common sense' ideas about global politics and history are (re)produced and where stories about what is acceptable behavior from states and individuals are naturalized and legitimated."[79] Indeed, the strength of the co-relationship between Hollywood and the US government is evinced through the former White House Deputy Chief of Staff, Karl Rove, approaching Hollywood writers, directors, and producers on behalf of the Bush Administration to not only solicit their opinions regarding potential future threats but to enlist their help in supporting and propagating the war *of* terror.[80] For example, Jason Dittmer provides an analysis of the proliferation of the superhero genre of film and attempts to demonstrate how superheroes not only become figures that represent the anthropomorphization of American values and beliefs but serve as characters that "articulate a particularly American geopolitical vision and sense of self, which is often shorthanded as American exceptionalism."[81] Similarly, Simon Dalby illustrates how films that represent war and conflict seemingly unrelated to the war *of* terror, such as *Gladiator*, *Black Hawk Down*, and *The Kingdom of Heaven*, obliquely support it through reinforcing a warrior ethos of foreign intervention characterized by morality, virtue, and the defense of human rights.[82] Alternatively, Sean Carter and Klaus Dodds demonstrate how the action-thriller genre of film, which takes the war *of* terror as its subject matter, can be utilized to advance and legitimate a "Jacksonian" form of US foreign policy and practice: the uncompromising and overwhelming unilateral response toward enemies in order to secure the physical safety and economic viability of the domestic population.[83] As these examples illustrate, the transmission and consumption of geopolitical discourse through popular cultural mediums are a powerful propagandistic tool where fictional storytelling is used to help inform and shape the geopolitical reality of the war *of* terror.[84]

A review of the critical geographic/geopolitical literature that has emerged following the events of 11 September 2001 and the ensuing war *of* terror reveals both the important contributions and the current limits of these approaches to analyzing the relationship between geography and (counter)terrorism. One of the most significant contributions of this literature is its analysis and documentation of the multiscalar spatialities of state violence precipitated by the war *of* terror and its related popular cultural diffusion. Through identifying, deconstructing, and illuminating these manifestations of the war *of* terror, this literature reveals how the violence of the state, masquerading under the auspices of counter-terrorism, is happening everywhere and to us all. However, as previously stated, the contributions of this literature also expose its current limits.

The limits of the available critical literature on the relationship between political geography/geopolitics and (counter)terrorism emerge in two forms: First, there are a relatively small amount of academic voices that can be found operating in these areas of research. As a consequence, the full range of benefits a political geographical/geopolitical sensibility and analytical framework can offer this subject area remains under explored and somewhat muted. Second, the predominant focus of the critical political geographic/geopolitical literature tends to emphasize a deconstruction of state violence that has emerged as a result of the war *of* terror and its supporting dominant narratives and propagandistic elements. Although this emphasis is by no means misplaced and is certainly of paramount importance if an understanding of how place, space, landscape, and the social are implicated by the state violence engendered by the war *of* terror, very little attention has explicitly focused on what is popularly codified as Islamist extremism. Furthermore, when one looks to the available political geographic/geopolitical literature on Islamist extremism in a Canadian context, virtually nothing has been produced. However, arguably, a critical political geographic/geopolitical analysis of Islamist extremism is uniquely positioned to further develop and enhance our understanding of this social phenomenon.

To date, the political geographer Colin Flint has been the most vocal proponent of the importance of political geography in developing an understanding of the phenomenon of extremism. According to Flint, "a political-geography approach to terrorism explores the spatial manifestations of power that intertwine to cause contexts of action and reaction, and the means to commit terrorism and enact counterterrorism."[85] Whereas current social scientific analysis of the phenomenon of Islamist extremism is relatively good at answering questions related to *who*, *what*, *when*, and *where*, this same research has been very weak at answering the questions of *why* and *how* beyond an Orientalist explanation. As such, the political geographic approach as explicated by Flint would seem to offer an important avenue for answering the underexamined questions of the *why* and *how* of Islamist extremism. For, as Flint states, "no other discipline is better suited to synthesize the multiple causes of conflict, understand and give voice to place-based perceptions that both lead to confrontation and define the path towards peace, and how peace at the local scale and global structures are linked."[86] Flint goes on to state that "political geographers have the responsibility to offer 'geographical imaginations' that investigate not only the specificities of place that can provoke terrorism, but also the vertical and horizontal linkages that implicate us all in the causes and consequences of terrorism."[87] In an effort to answer the questions of the *why* and the *how* of extremism and to subsequently help fill the knowledge gaps that continue to pervade formal, practical, and popular understandings of Islamist extremism, this book utilizes a critical political geographic mode of analysis to deconstruct the conditions and relations that make the emergence of this social phenomenon in a place-specific context probable.[88]

As the assassination of Theo Van Gogh in Amsterdam (2004), the transit bombings in London (2005), the apprehension of the Toronto 18 (2006), the Boston Marathon bombings (2013), the killing of a British soldier in the streets of London (2013), the shooting death of a Canadian soldier and the subsequent violation of the Canadian Parliament in Ottawa (2014), and the Charlie Hebdo attacks in Paris (2015) to varying degrees illustrate, domestic extremism of the *Islamitic*[89] type is a social phenomenon that condenses in particular places as a result of a constellation of moments unique to each context. Although domestic extremism is not a new phenomenon, the current expression of the Islamitic type represents a departure from the conventional motivations of past and present Islamitic movements. Whereas many Islamitic movements were and are motivated by a mixture of secessionist, irredentist, and/or nationalist objectives, the contemporary manifestation of Domestic Islamitic Extremism is motivated by a conjuncture of influences that are simultaneously local, national, and transnational in character and exceed the limits of any one particular geopolitical unit or territory.

Certainly all instances of Domestic Islamitic Extremism are intriguing and warrant academic investigation. Moreover, a comparison of each incident and its broader political and socio-spatial context could potentially proffer a significant amount of fertile information that could be used to identify, analyze, and establish the commonalities and differences of each case. However, although this approach is appealing, a rush to a comparative engagement of alleged incidences of Domestic Islamitic Extremism to establish an ideal typical profile of the actors/groups involved is analytically and methodologically premature, superficial, and potentially counterfactual. As Andrew Silke states:

> [extremism] is not a homogeneous activity. There is a wide variation both in terms of the actors and in terms of the activities they engage in. Such variation means that any attempt to study all [extremist] activity under one rubric must inevitably end in frustration. If it is to be fruitful, research which is concerned particularly with the behaviour of [extremists] must have an applied focus. Fundamentally, it should not try to consider all [extremist] activity under all situations. Rather the circumstances should be select, such as considering just one type of activity.[90]

Therefore, if one is to avoid the analytical and methodological problematics that underpin this broad and all-encompassing approach to understanding the social phenomenon of Domestic Islamitic Extremism, one should arguably enact a place-specific analysis of each case and/or event. For, as H.H.A Cooper argues, "we can never attempt to treat [extremism] as a discrete subject, somehow distinct or outside of the political, social, and economic context in which it occurs. It is, as Cooper states, 'a creature of its own time and place.'"[91] Although it is not explicitly stated in the preceding quote, the reference to "place" suggests that there is a definite and definable geographical and/or spatial dimension of extremism. Therefore, geographical considerations, such as the concepts of place and scale, should be added to the list of factors to be considered when assessing the contexts of extremist activity. Furthermore, if one accepts that extremism is inherently and inescapably a geographical phenomenon, then a place-specific analysis should proceed from a geographically informed perspective.

A place-specific analysis of extremism enables one to examine, identify, and reveal the particular context, circumstances, processes, forces, and motivations unique to each incarnation of this phenomenon. Furthermore, a place-specific analysis implicitly acknowledges the complexity and heterogeneity of the phenomenon and helps one to circumvent the reductive and essentializing tendencies of abstracted modes of analysis. Donna Haraway captures these sentiments in her assertion that "The only way to find a larger vision is to be somewhere in particular."[92] However, as reinforced by the position of Erik Swyngedouw,[93] I am not suggesting that specific places are disconnected from other places and that the influences felt in one place are not evident in others. Certainly, place-specific structures and systems are a product of, and are linked to, other place-specific systems and structures whether at the local, regional, national, or global scales. Rather, I am suggesting that "an understanding of place as a local setting for everyday life in which problems are experienced, made sense of, and acted upon is a key concept."[94] This conceptualization of the specificity of place initiates an inductive process of knowledge production that moves from the ground upward, from the local to the global, from the material to the abstract, and/or from the empirical to the theoretical. In effect, an in situ examination of domestic extremism provides the foundation necessary for one to begin to interpret the particularities of other place-specific events. Following this interpretation of other cases, comparative analyses can proceed in an attempt to identify potential commonalities, which could eventually lead to the development of an ideal typical understanding of the processes, conditions, and contexts in which and through which domestic Islamitic extremist actors emerge.

The place-specific context and focus of this book is the Greater Toronto Area (GTA), Ontario, Canada. I have chosen to focus on the GTA because of the apprehension of an alleged Domestic Islamitic Extremist group in June 2006, which was described in the Canadian corporate media as the "Toronto 18." In effect, this case serves as the point of departure for this analysis and provides the contextual framework for an examination of this particular incarnation of domestic extremism.

Before continuing, it is important to mention that Canada has a history of domestic extremism. In fact, one can trace Canadian acts of domestic extremism back to the nineteenth century, when Louis Riel lead the Red River Rebellion, also known as the Red River Resistance, for *Metis* national self-determination in 1869. Several members of Riel's group were executed by firing squad, and Riel himself was executed at the gallows. Three additional examples can be identified from the more recent past. The first can be traced to the 1950s when a Doukhobor sect known as the "Sons of Freedom" engaged in a campaign of arson that targeted publically funded schools designed for Doukhobor children. The motivations for these acts of arson were to protest government interference in the lives of the Doukhobor community. The second dates from 1962 to 1973 when the *Front de Liberation de Quebec* (FLQ) carried out a domestic extremist campaign against the Canadian government. This campaign was motivated by Quebec nationalist/secessionist objectives. In October 1970, the Canadian government invoked the War Measures Act and effectively dismantled the FLQ.[95] The third example refers to the bombing of an Air India flight in 1985, perpetrated by Sikh extremists in British Columbia. The attack was motivated by nationalist/secessionist objectives—national self-determination and autonomous governance of the Punjab province in India. Although the contemporary manifestation of Domestic Islamitic Extremism is associated with what David Rapoport problematically designates as the "religious wave" of terrorism,[96] this type of extremism is not a departure from what Canada has experienced in the past. In actuality, Domestic Islamitic Extremism is a continuance of the genealogy of domestic extremism in Canada as it engenders politically motivated actions and practices.

As previously stated, the following analysis draws upon various dimensions of the case of the "Toronto 18." Although this case has received very little treatment in formal literature to date,[97] presumably due in large part to the absence of an actual violent event, this case is empirically important due in large measure to the length of time this group was under surveillance by Canadian security and law enforcement apparatuses. As a result, there is a comprehensive documentary record that details the activities and subsequent transformation of the actors involved in the group over a relatively long period of time. The benefit of this is that one is afforded the opportunity to assess a rich empirical manifold and identify and analyze the factors that contributed to the ideological conditioning and subsequent political transformation of the group. In this respect, the case of the Toronto 18 is uniquely positioned to significantly contribute to our understanding of the complex transformational processes associated with domestic extremism of the Islamitic type.

To access the documentary record and empirical manifold relating to the case of the "Toronto 18," I spent approximately 2.5 years attending the court cases of the various members of the group who stood trial for terrorism-related offenses contrary to the Criminal Code of Canada. As a participant observer, I was given the opportunity to not only witness and record the testimony of various state and non-state actors involved in this case but review the evidence submitted throughout the trials. It included voluminous wiretaps of conversations between the various actors involved in the group and digital videos and documents retrieved from the computers of the accused. Although conducting research in a courtroom environment can be very productive and rewarding, this form of research certainly presents many challenges. (There is a more detailed discussion of, and reflection on, conducting research in a courtroom setting in the conclusion of this book.)

The overall objective of this book is to analyze and develop a more comprehensive understanding of the intersectionality of place, scale, and the process of extremization in a particular time-space conjuncture. To accomplish this objective, my theoretical approach is guided by an understanding of the state, ideology, and discourse as advanced by Nicos Poulantzas, Antonio Gramsci, Louis Althusser, and Michel Foucault. First, Poulantzas' conceptualization of the state: the material condensation of a relationship of social forces in particular localities is significant because Poulantzas argues for moving beyond functionalist conceptions of the state and instead approaches the state as a social relation that is expressed, felt, experienced, sanctioned, contested, and reproduced in the everyday practices of civil society.[98] In effect, the state does not exist as an entity outside of, or in contradistinction to, the social but is rather deeply enmeshed and entangled within it.[99] This understanding of the state is important as the state becomes intrinsic to the formation of a social actor. Second, my theoretical approach is informed by a Gramscian and Althusserian conceptualization of ideology. Although the concept of ideology as advanced by literary and cultural theorists like Terry Eagleton and Raymond Williams is influenced and informed by Althusserian thought, this work generally approaches ideology as a linguistic social relation that manifests, for instance, in textual forms. However, according to Gramsci and Althusser, ideology is a material social relation that manifests in institutional and individual actions and practices. This conceptualization of ideology is crucial as ideology as a material social relation becomes integral to the formation of a subject. In this sense, a subject is produced by and reproduces ideology through material actions and practices. Third, my approach is informed by Foucault's conceptualization of discourse. For Foucault, discourse is a social relation of power through which knowledge is (re)produced institutionally. This understanding of discourse calls attention to the power relations that shape and authorize particular forms of institutionalized knowledge. This understanding of discourse is valuable as it enables one to identify the relationship between power and knowledge and its societal effects. Using these conceptualizations of the state, ideology, and discourse as a theoretical foundation, I analyze the relationships between three independent yet interrelated and mutually reinforcing *spheres of influence* that serve a role in producing the conditions that make the development of an extremist actor probable in a place-specific context. I have designated these spheres of influence as: the Transnational Sphere of Influence, the State Sphere of Influence, and the Group Sphere of Influence.

The significance of these *spheres of influence* is that they facilitate an analytical engagement with an undertheorized and underexamined aspect of the extremization process: the macro-social relations and structures that make the emergence of Islamitic extremist subjectivities probable. In many respects, these *spheres* and the type of analytical engagement they inform represent a departure from the vast majority of the research and literature on the processes of extremization. For instance, much of the current literature on extremization is produced within the narrow disciplinary spectrum of psychology and/or social psychology and tends to overly subjectivize this process by focusing on micro-social relations and structures, e.g. behavior, personality, identity, kinship, and peer group. As a result, the broader conditions that make particular extremist subjectivities probable are generally neglected or are treated as tangential to the formation of an extremist actor. However, macro-social relations and structures are not incidental to the process of extremization but are integral to it. Therefore, the terms of engagement need to be modified in order to not only avoid the potential for analytical atrophy and ossification but to actually advance our understanding of the process of extremization.

To engage in my analysis of Domestic Islamitic Extremism, I utilize the conceptualizations of geographers Tim Cresswell (1996) and Kevin Cox (1998) as key building blocks for my theoretical approach. Blending these literatures has enabled me to situate my research within a context-sensitive, multiscalar framework whereby specific spheres of influence occupied by Islamic social actors in the GTA may be identified, interpreted, and analyzed. To examine the emergence and development of domestic extremism of the Islamitic type, I find Cresswell's geographical conceptualization and theory of *In Place/Out of Place* particularly useful for developing an understanding of the dynamics of place and the (re)production and (re)constitution of ideology. According to Cresswell, the signifier *place* extends beyond a material spatial referent and refers to expectations of behavior: "in this sense 'place' combines the spatial with the social—it is 'social space.' Insofar as these expectations serve the interests of those at the top of social hierarchies, they can be described as ideological."[100] As Cresswell goes on to state, "expectations about behavior in place are important components in the construction, maintenance, and evolution of ideological values."[101] Furthermore, expectations of behavior can be either enshrined in law or have become so socially "normalized" and "naturalized" that behavioral expectations are taken for granted and remain unstated.[102] Conversely, being out of place or being codified as such connotes the crossing of a boundary. A boundary that delineates the point where expectations, values, mores, sensibilities, social conventions, and/or laws of a particular "place" and dominant ideological system have been transgressed and subsequently violated. Boundary crossings can potentially spark intense social, political, and legal reactions to support and/or reinforce ideological positions. The reactions of a hegemonic group, whether socially, politically, and/or legally, or a combination thereof, are of course contingent upon the perceived severity of the transgression in question. For Cresswell, as for myself, the concept of *transgression* is particularly important because not only does *transgression* "foreground the mapping of ideology onto space and place,"[103] thereby enabling the construction, representation, and defense of being "in place" versus "out of place," but the concept of *transgression* embodies a particular form of subversive politics and behavior. As the concept of *transgression* is central to my analysis, it is necessary to establish an understanding of this term.

The term "transgression" literally means crossing a boundary. In the Cresswellian sense of the term, the boundary being transgressed can be material, ideological, or both. As Cresswell asserts, "to have *transgressed* means to have been judged to have crossed some line that was not meant to have been crossed."[104] Therefore, as Cresswell goes on to state, "transgressive acts are the acts judged to be 'out of place' by dominant institutions and actors (the press, the law, the government)."[105] Moreover, "intentional transgression is a form of resistance that creates a response from the establishment—an act that draws the lines on a battlefield and defines the terrain on which contestation occurs."[106] In effect, the act of transgression becomes an act that disorders and disrupts what was once a normalized and naturalized "order of things"[107]: "these deviations from the dominant ideological norms serve to confuse and disorientate. In doing so they temporarily reveal the historical and mutable nature of that which is usually considered 'the way things are.' The way the world is defined, categorized, segmented, and classified is rendered problematic."[108] As a consequence, the dominant is forced to acknowledge the existence of an "other" order not without but within, an alternative internal order that resists and challenges the dominant's claim to a singular, coherent, and immutable ideological system. The reaction by the dominant to such transgressions is, according to Cresswell, "evidence of the relationship between place and ideology."[109] So, how does Cresswell's conceptual apparatus provide an interpretive lens through which to analyze the phenomenon of Domestic Islamitic Extremism in a place-specific context like the GTA.

I conceptualize Cresswell's "in place" and "out of place" as two competing discursive formations: "in place" represents a dominant discursive formation whereas "out of place" represents a subversive discursive formation. Conceptualizing these two competing discursive formations with respect to Islamitic extremism in the GTA is useful as I believe these two discursive formations are constantly acting upon elements of particular communities. Given the dominant forces that I conceptualize acting upon particular social actors, Cresswell's theory of transgression is important as the act of transgression represents a decisive moment: the crossing of an ideological boundary and, in this case, the occupation of a subversive discursive formation. Through analyzing the case of the "Toronto 18," one can begin to identify and examine the forces that create the conditions necessary to facilitate an act of transgression.

To understand how the forces that I have identified above conflate, combine, and intertwine to influence a transgression, I utilize Kevin Cox's (1998) concepts of "spaces of dependence" and "spaces of engagement" to conceptualize a network of *scales* and its role in domestic extremism of the Islamitic type. I believe that this conceptualization of a network of scales is important to developing an understanding of domestic extremism as it illuminates how social actors at the local scale are constructed by, and actively construct, a network of scales that can both facilitate and support social and political activity in a particular place.

Cox delineates two distinct yet interrelated processes inherent to the social production of scale: "spaces of dependence" and "spaces of engagement."[110] Cox defines "spaces of dependence" in the following terms:

> those more-or-less localized social relations upon which we depend for the realization of essential interests and for which there are no substitutes elsewhere; they define place-specific conditions for our material well being and our sense of significance. These spaces are inserted in broader sets of relationships of a more global character and these constantly threaten to undermine or dissolve them. People, firms, state agencies, etc., organize in order to secure the conditions for the continued existence of their spaces of dependence but in so doing they have to engage with other centers of social power: local government, the national press, perhaps the international press, for example.[111]

Engagement with other centers of social power to ensure the continued existence of spaces of dependence generates a space of engagement: "space in which the politics of securing a space of dependence unfolds."[112] Although these "spaces" are distinct from one another, they are interrelated as the space of dependence relies upon the space of engagement to realize and secure various interests and objectives.

Cox conceptualizes both spaces as constituting a network of associations through which scale is produced and material interests are actualized and realized. Although the material interests are place specific and local, spaces of dependence and spaces of engagement may rely upon a network of associations that exist simultaneously at multiple scales (the local, the regional, the national, and the global).[113] As Cox states, "local politics appears as metropolitan, regional, national, or even international as different organizations try to secure those networks of associations through which respective projects can be realized."[114] However, these networks of associations and their concomitant spatial forms are entirely contingent and provisional and depend upon the social actors involved. For example, the spaces of dependence and engagement and the network of associations the Canadian government and its security apparatuses operating in the GTA construct for their counter-terrorism initiatives and practices will be different than the spaces of dependence and engagement and the network of associations Islamitic social actors operating in the GTA construct to achieve their objectives. Moreover, as the objectives of actors shift, so too will their networks of association and the scales at which the networks operate. In effect, the construction by social actors of networks of associations and their spatial and scalar form is dynamic, fluid, and amorphous, rather than static, rigid, and nested. Therefore, spaces of dependence and engagement must be recognized as being provisional and entirely contingent upon the objectives of the social actors involved.

In the context of this argument, the spaces of dependence and engagement are significant as they illuminate the fact that the network of scales produced through these spaces embodies and expresses the social struggle for power and control of particular groups within particular settings.[115] Furthermore, the construction of particular networks of scales in one place can be of eminent magnitude as specific networks—organizational, ideological, doctrinal, political, social, and technological—and their concomitant material manifestations can have an immensely transformative impact on the ways in which various actors act and/or behave in particular places.[116] For example, the various Islamitic social actors involved in the "Toronto 18" constructed, and were constructed by, a particular network of associations/scales (local, national, and international) in order for the ideological conditioning and political transformation of the group to occur.

Cox's conceptualization of a network of scales is important for understanding the process of extremization as it provides the analytical tools to not only understand how specific spheres of influence conflate and condense in the local but how a particular ideological position is supported and maintained in a place-specific context. When combined, Cresswell's concept of *place* and Cox's conceptualization of a *network of scales* form a potent theoretical framework through which to identify, interpret, and analyze the conditions that make the ideological conditioning and political transformation of extremist actors probable. Therefore, I intend to demonstrate how particular spheres of influence conflate and condense in a particular time-space conjuncture, thereby creating the conditions through which some Islamitic social actors undergo a political transformation and transgress from a dominant discursive formation and related mode of activity to a subversive discursive formation and related mode of activity.

My argument is composed of six chapters. As a point of departure into my analysis, the first chapter attempts to critically examine the commonly held assumption that domestic extremism of the Islamitic type is related to the Islamic religion or purely to Islamist movements. Although these assumptions may appear to be common sense and certainly have become deeply enmeshed in formal, practical, and popular discourse, the efficacy and veracity of these assumptions become highly problematic when subjected to critical scrutiny. The second chapter seeks to identify and trace the extradiscursive moments—post-Cold War, immigration trends in GTA and Canada from Muslim-majority countries, the events of 11 September 2001, and the war in Afghanistan—that make the emergence of particular dominant and subversive discursive formations possible. This type of genealogy is important as discourses do not emerge in a vacuum and possess long histories. The third chapter seeks to construct the dominant and subversive discursive formations and ideological positions acting upon and shaping the various members of the Toronto 18 and foreshadows my discussion of how the various spheres of influence I have identified created the conditions through which the transgression from one formation to another is made probable.

Cumulatively, the fourth, fifth, and sixth chapters of this book provide an empirical analysis of the specific spheres of influence that I have identified in the case of the Toronto 18. The fourth chapter offers an examination of the role transnational information flows and ideational connectivities served in the ideological conditioning and political transformation of the members of the group. The fifth chapter examines the role of the policies and practices of the Canadian state in contributing to the conditions that made the development of an extremist actor probable. The sixth chapter describes the actions and practices of the "Toronto 18" and examines how these actions and practices contributed to the ideological conditioning and political transformation of various members of that group. In the concluding chapter, not only is the process of extremization explained as animated by the conflation of the spheres of influence discussed in the preceding chapters, but, as previously indicated, a reflexive analysis of performing participant observer research in a courtroom environment is provided. Finally, as a coda to my analysis, the epilogue outlines the outcomes of the criminal proceedings against the various members of the "Toronto 18."

Notes

1. An excerpt from the Samuel Taylor Coleridge poem, "The Dungeon."
2. Shepard, Bhattacharya & Josey, "Men attended 'training camps,'" A1.
3. See, for example, Blanchfield, Mike & Woods, Alan. (2006, June 5). "Arrest tally will grow, insiders say." *National Post*, A3, for an article citing sources indicating that more arrests relating to this case were anticipated. Approximately two months after the initial arrests of the seventeen suspects, an eighteenth was arrested. Hence, the codification of the group as the so-called Toronto 18.
4. See http://www2.parl.gc.ca/HousePublications/Publication.aspx?DocId=2330951&Language=e&Mode=1 for a web-based copy of Bill C-36 (last accessed on 20 February 2010).
5. Shephard, "Threat on the home front: How Internet monitoring sparked a CSIS investigation into what authorities allege is a homegrown Canadian terror cell," A1, A14.
6. Appleby & Freeze, "Complex operation leading to arrests of alleged terrorists shrouded in secrecy," A1, A4.
7. The first person to be charged under the anti-terrorism legislation introduced into the Canadian Criminal Code in December 2001 was Mohammad Momin Khawaja. In March 2009, Khawaja was found guilty of participating in, contributing, financing, facilitating terror, and developing and possessing an explosive device. Although Khawaja is a Canadian citizen, the charges related to his connections to and involvement with a British group that were planning to target various locations in London in 2004. For a description of the Khawaja case, see Freeze, Colin. (2006, June 5). "British case sheds light on current one." *Globe and Mail*, A7.
8. See, for example, Leong, Melissa. (2006, June 7). "World's media descend on Brampton court." *Toronto Star*, p. A3; and *Globe and Mail* (2006, June 4). "Arrests make headlines around the world." As well see Bhattacharya, Surya. (2006, June 7). "Relatives overwhelmed by intense media crush." *Toronto Star*, A1, A8.
9. An eighteenth individual was arrested in connection with the group approximately two months following the initial set of arrests.
10. See, for example, Leeder, Jessica, Levy, Harold & Josey, Stan. (2006, June 4). "Sharp shooters, bomb dogs, tears." *Toronto Star*, A4; Bell, Stewart & Humphreys, Adrian. (2006, June 6). "Truck bomb in Toronto, shots on crowd." *National Post*, A1, A4; and see Diebel, Linda (2006, June 5). "Big show, a very careful tell." *Toronto Star*, A3, for a description of the theatricality of the arrests and subsequent press conferences.

11. Shephard, "Threat on the home front: How Internet monitoring sparked a CSIS investigation into what authorities allege is a homegrown Canadian terror cell," A1, A14.
12. According to the RCMP website, INSETs were developed to "increase the capacity for the collection, sharing and analysis of intelligence among partners with respect to individuals and entities that are a threat to national security and; create an enhanced investigative capacity to bring such individuals and entities to justice; and enhance partner agencies collective ability to combat national security threats and meet all specific mandate responsibilities, consistent with the laws of Canada and the Charter of Rights and Freedoms. INSETs are made up of representatives of the RCMP, federal partners and agencies such as Canada Border Services Agency (CBSA), Canadian Security Intelligence Service (CSIS), and provincial and municipal police services. INSETs exist in Vancouver, Toronto, Ottawa and Montreal" (http://www.rcmp-grc.gc.ca/secur/insets-eisn-eng.htm).
13. In December 2005, CSIS requested that the "directed source" contact the RCMP and begin working with them. It is around this time that this directed source began operating in the capacity of a confidential informer. However, according to one court document, in February 2006 this individual entered an agreement with RCMP INSET and officially became a police agent. As well, see Friscolanti, Michael. (2008, August). "2.4 Million Raise? Toronto 18 informant Mubin Shaikh ups his price." *Maclean's*, 18–19, for a brief description of this key witness and his involvement in this case both before and after the arrests of the various members of the group.
14. R.v. AD, "Agreed Statement of Facts," 1.
15. Ibid., 1.
16. Author's notes, June 2006.
17. Transcript of Training Camp Audio. RCMP: Author. This transcript was submitted by the prosecution as part of the evidence against various members of the group. For a more elaborate discussion of this speech, see Chap. 6.
18. Author's notes, June 2006.
19. For media commentary on the training camp and the participants, see Blatchford, Christie. (2008, June 8). "Suspects believed they'd be left alone to train at Christmas." *Globe and Mail*, A1, A13. As well see Walkom, Thomas. (2006, June 7). "If these are terrorists, they are second rate." *Toronto Star*, A1, A6.
20. R.v. AD, "Agreed Statement of Facts," 8.

21. Although the principal figure of the Scarborough group discussed this plan, there was no real evidence submitted in court that demonstrates that this plan was being prepared in concrete form.
22. McArthur & Friesen, "From soccer field to schism to arrests." A7.
23. R.v. SK, "Agreed Statement of Facts," 3.
24. Freeze, "How a police agent cracked a terror cell," A4.
25. Laidlaw, "Details of alleged Toronto 18 bomb plot revealed," on-line edition: last accessed 21 March 2010.
26. R.v. ZA, "Agreed Statement of Facts," 32.
27. Author's notes, January 2010.
28. The *Globe and Mail* did not lead their 3 June 2006 edition with any reference to the arrests. The following article entitled "Terrorism raids sweep Toronto" appeared on page A2.
29. Bell, "Nevermind foreign terrorists, why is Canada growing it own extremists?" A8.
30. Wark, "Knowing the enemy within," A17.
31. Ibid., A17.
32. For coverage of this incident, see Howlett, Karen. (2006, June 8). "Citizens warned of potential backlash." *Globe and Mail*, A8.
33. Incidentally, the same Hamilton-area mosque was vandalized following the events of 11 September 2001.
34. Horgan, *The Psychology of Terrorism*, xxi.
35. Alexander quoted in Silke, *Research on Terrorism*, 25.
36. Jenkins quoted in Silke, "The Organization Men: Anatomy of a Terrorist Attack," 1.
37. Silke, "Introduction to Research on Terrorism," 9.
38. See, for example, Dobkin, Bethami (1992). *Tales of Terror: Television News and the Construction of the Terrorist Threat*. New York: Praeger; Nacos, Brigitte. (2002). *Mass Mediated Terrorism*. New York: Rowman & Littlefield Publishers; Norris, Pippa, Kern, Montague & Just, Marion. (2003). *Framing Terrorism*. New York: Routledge; and Poole, Elizabeth & Richardson, John. (Eds). (2006). *Muslims and the News Media*. London: I.B Tauris.
39. Silke, "Introduction to Research on Terrorism," 9.
40. Ibid., 9.
41. Wilkinson quoted in Horgan, *The Psychology of Terrorism*, 26.
42. Gordon, "Terrorism Dissertations and the Evolution of a Specialty: An Analysis of Meta-Information," 141.
43. Ibid., 146. This analysis refers to research across the social sciences and humanities that specifically name terrorism as the subject matter of the material. However, presumably, a much broader corpus of research exists that engages the study of "conflict" in a variety of forms and contexts.

Although for analytical purposes the differentiation between the study of terrorism and the study of conflict may be methodologically convenient, the study of terrorism and the study of conflict per se should not be uncoupled nor understood as mutually exclusive as many forms of conflict should not be perceived as residing outside of the province of terrorism.

44. Jackson, "The Study of Terrorism 10 Years After 9/11," 4.
45. Ibid., 2.
46. Ibid., 2.
47. For an analysis of the problems associated with research on the subject of terrorism, see Gunning, Jeroen. (2007). "A Case for Critical Terrorism Studies." *Government and Opposition*, 42 (3): 363–393; and Silke, Andrew. (2001). "The Devil You Know: Continuing Problems With Research On Terrorism." *Terrorism and Political Violence*, 13 (4): 1–14.
48. Gordon, "Terrorism Dissertations and the Evolution of a Specialty," 148.
49. Jackson, "The Study of Terrorism 10 Years After 9/11," 8.
50. Ibid., 8–9.
51. Cox, "Social Forces, States and World Orders: Beyond International Relations Theory," 130.
52. Gunning, "A Case for Critical Terrorism Studies," 371–372.
53. Ibid., 376–377.
54. Dodds, "Screening terror: Hollywood, the United States and the construction of danger," 229.
55. Horgan, *The Psychology of Terrorism*, p. 2. For an excellent analysis of state-sponsored terrorism, *see* Chomsky, Noam. (1988). *Culture of Terrorism*. Boston: South End Press.
56. For a more elaborate review and analysis of Elden's argument, see Kowalski, Jeremy. (2011). *Terror and Territory: The Spatial Extent of Sovereignty* by Stewart Elden. *The Canadian Geographer*, 55: 518–520.
57. See Dalby, Simon. (2003). "Calling 911: geopolitics, security, and America's new war." *Geopolitics*, 8 (3): 61–86.
58. See Gregory, Derek. (2004). *The Colonial Present*. Oxford: Blackwell Publishing.
59. See Glassman, Jim. (2007). "Imperialism Imposed and Invited." In Derek Gregory & Allan Pred (Eds.), *Violent Geographies: Fear, Terror, and Political Violence* (93–110). New York: Routledge.
60. See Harvey, David. (2003). *The New Imperialism*. Oxford: Oxford University Press.
61. See Gregory, Derek. (2007). "Vanishing Points." In Derek Gregory & Allan Pred (Eds.), *Violent Geographies: Fear, Terror, and Political Violence*, (93–110). New York: Routledge.

62. See Paglen, Trevor. (2009). *Blank Spots on the Map: The Dark Geography of the Pentagon's Secret World*. New York: Dutton.
63. Graham, "Introduction: Cities, Warfare, and States of Emergency," 11.
64. See Amoore, Louise. (2006). "Biometric borders: Governing mobilities in the war of terror." *Political Geography*, 25: 336–351.
65. See Muller, Benjamin. (2011). "Risking it all at the biometric border: Mobility, Limits, and the Persistence of Securitisation." *Geopolitics*, 16 (1): 91–106.
66. Graham, "Cities and the 'War on Terror,'" 271.
67. See Graham, Stephen. (2010). *Cities Under Siege*. London: Verso.
68. Marcuse, "The "War on Terrorism" and Life in Cities after September 11, 2001," 264.
69. Gray and Wyly, "The Terror City Hypothesis," 331.
70. Ibid., 330. It is important to mention that the originality of Gray and Wyly's hypothesis comes from their conceptualization of the changing urban form in an American context, for the militarization of urban space is certainly not new as evidenced, for example, in the urban spaces of Northern Ireland, Israel, and Sri Lanka. See, also, Pain, Rachal & Smith, Susan. (Eds.). (2008). *Fear: Critical Geopolitics and Everyday Life*. Hampshire, England: Ashgate Publishing Limited., for a collection of essays that provide an analysis of the lived experiences of fear, including these experiences precipitated by the war *of* terror.
71. Hannah, "Torture and the Ticking Bomb: The War on Terrorism as a Geographical Imagination of Power/Knowledge," 623.
72. See, for example, Lorraine, Dowler and Jennifer Sharpe. (2001). "A Feminist Geopolitics?" *Space and Polity*, 5 (3): 165–176; and Hyndman, Jennifer. (2001). "Towards a Feminist Geopolitics." *The Canadian Geographer*, 45 (2): 210–222.
73. Bernazolli and Flint, "Embodying the garrison state? Everyday geographies of militarization in American society," 157.
74. See Hyndman, Jennifer. (2003). "Beyond Either/Or: A Feminist Critique of September 11". *Acme: An International E-Journal for Critical Geographies*. 2 (1): 1–13., and Hyndman, Jennifer. (2007). "Feminist Geopolitics Revisited: Body Counts in Iraq." *The Professional Geographer*. 59 (1): p. 35–46. For other examples of Feminist critiques of the events of 11 September 2001 and subsequent war *of* terror, see: Hannah, Matthew. (2005). "Virility and Violation in the US "War on Terrorism." In Lise Nelson & Joni Seager. (Eds.), *A Companion to Feminist Geography*, (550–564). Malden, MA: Blackwell Publishing., and Hyndman, Jennifer. (2005). "Feminist Geopolitics and September 11." In Lise Nelson & Joni Seager. (Eds.), *A Companion to Feminist Geography*, (565–577). Malden, MA: Blackwell Publishing.

75. Dittmer, *Popular Culture, Geopolitics & Identity*, 14.
76. Ibid., 15.
77. Dodds, "Screening terror: Hollywood, the United States and the construction of danger," 228.
78. Ibid., 230.
79. Lacy quoted in Dodds, "Screening terror: Hollywood, the United States and the construction of danger," 231.
80. Carter & Dodds, "Hollywood and the 'war on terror': genre-geopolitics and 'Jacksonianism' in the Kingdom," 101.
81. Dittmer, "American exceptionalism, visual effects, and the post-9/11 cinematic superhero boom," 114.
82. Dalby, "Warrior geopolitics: Gladiator, Black Hawk Down and the Kingdom of Heaven," 439.
83. Cater & Dodds, "Hollywood and the 'war on terror': genre-geopolitics and 'Jacksonianism' in the Kingdom," 109.
84. For further analysis of the relationship between cinema and geopolitics, see: Shapiro, Michael. (2009). *Cinematic Geopolitics*. Routledge: New York.
85. Flint, "Terrorism and Counterterrorism: Geographic Research Questions and Agendas," p. 161.
86. Ibid., 167.
87. Ibid., 167.
88. The concept of *place* is elaborated in Chap. 3.
89. The author elaborates on the use of this terminology in Chap. 1.
90. Silke, *Research on Terrorism*, 12.
91. Cooper quoted in Horgan, *The Psychology of Terrorism*, 31.
92. Haraway, *Simians, Cyborgs, and Women: The Reinvention of Nature*, 196.
93. See Swyngedouw, Erik. (1997). "Neither Global nor Local: "Glocalization" and the Politics of Scale." In Kevin Cox (Ed.), *spaces of globalization: reasserting the power of the local*, 137–166. New York: The Guilford Press.
94. Flint, "Terrorism and Counterterrorism: Geographic Research Questions and Agendas," 163.
95. Parker, "Fighting an Antaean Enemy: How Democratic States Unintentionally Sustain the Terrorist Movements They Oppose," 169.
96. Rapoport, "The Fourth Wave: September 11 in the History of Terrorism," 421.
97. For an example of some of the scholarly literature that has emerged regarding this case, see: Smolash, Wendy. (2009). "Mark of Cain(ada): Racialized Security Discourse in Canada's National News Papers." *University of Toronto Quarterly*, 78 (2): 745–763; Molloy, Patricia. (2010). "Terror Time in Toronto: A Response to the Response of the

Arrests of the Toronto 17." In Stephens, Angharad & Vaughan-Williams, Nick. (Eds.). *Terrorism and the Politics of Response*. New York: Routledge; and Kowalski, Jeremy. (2013). "Framing the Toronto 18: Government Experts, Corporate Media, and the Orientalizing of the Other." In Hennebry, Jenna & Momani, Bessma. (Eds.). *Targeted Transnationals: The State, the Media, and Arab Canadians*. Vancouver: UBC Press.
98. Poulantzas, *State, Power, Socialism*, 132.
99. Ibid., 39–40.
100. Cresswell, *In Place/Out of Place*, 3.
101. Ibid., 4.
102. Ibid., 3. See Bourdieu, Pierre. (1984), *Distinction: A Social Critique of the Judgement of Taste*, Cambridge, Massachusetts: Harvard University Press, for a comprehensive discussion of the normalization and naturalization of behavior, social mores, and class-based cultural currency.
103. Cresswell, *In Place/Out of Place*, 9.
104. Ibid., 23.
105. Ibid., 23.
106. Ibid., 23.
107. See Foucault, Michel. (2003). *The Order of Things*. New York: Routledge.
108. Cresswell, *In Place/Out of Place*, 26.
109. Ibid., 27.
110. Cox, "Spaces of dependence, spaces of engagement," 2.
111. Ibid., 2.
112. Ibid., 2.
113. Ibid., 7.
114. Ibid., 19.
115. Swyngedouw, "Neither Global nor Local: Glocalization and the Politics of Scale," 140.
116. Flint, "Terrorism and Counterterrorism: Geographic Research Questions and Agendas," 164.

Contents

1 Islamic, Islamist, Islamitic:
   From Conceptual Violence to a Conceptual Break   1

2 Displacement and Condensation:
   The Internationalization of the *Clash*
   and the Construction of the *Homo Terrorismus*   37

3 Through a Looking Glass Darkly: The Symmetry
   of Competing Discursive Formations   85

4 A Condition of Transgression:
   The Transnational Sphere of Influence   129

5 A Condition of Transgression:
   The State Sphere of Influence   153

6 A Condition of Transgression:
   The Group Sphere of Influence   183

Conclusion	207
Epilogue	223
Bibliography	229
Index	243

Acknowledgments

In one of his Memorable Fancies in "The Marriage of Heaven and Hell," William Blake states, "I was in a Printing house in Hell & saw the method in which knowledge is transmitted from generation to generation." Any piece of academic work does not materialize through the intellectual labors of a solitary author but through interactions and exchanges with a multitude of individuals. As such, I would like to take this opportunity to identify some of the individuals that ultimately helped bring this project to fruition. First, I would like to thank my doctoral supervisor and committee members for their unwavering support, sage insight, and sophisticated intellectual guidance. William Jenkins, Sabah Alnasseri, and Valerie Preston were an honor to work with and to them I will remain forever indebted. Second, I would like to thank the Madame Registrar at the Brampton County Courthouse who, throughout the various trials of the Toronto 18, always helped to ensure that I had access to the documents I needed. Similarly, I would like to thank Isabel Teotonio, a reporter for the *Toronto Star*, who generously engaged in knowledge exchanges with me during the trials and helped to fill in the gaps when needed. Third, I would like to thank all of the individuals that participated in interviews for this project and shared their valuable insights with me on various dimensions of the subjects discussed in this book. In this respect, I would like to specifically thank Mubin Shaikh for discussing with me on several occasions not only the details of the activities of the members of the Toronto 18 but his experiences interacting with the group from initial contact to arrest. My exchanges with him were very illuminating and assisted me greatly in understanding the many nuances of this case. Fourth, I would like to thank my parents, Dave and Karen Kowalski, for their enduring love and support throughout my development as an academic. Without them many of my achievements would not have been possible. Furthermore, I would like to thank my wife, Alicia, and my son, Tristan, for their deep love and devotion. The endless joy they bring into my life helps to keep the melancholy at a manageable distance. Lastly, I would like to sincerely thank Sarah Roughley, Alexandra Dauler, Elaine Fan, and Chris Robinson at Palgrave Macmillan for facilitating the publishing process and bringing this project to print form.

List of Figures

Fig. 1.1	South Toronto maple leafs (Globe and Mail, 10 June 2006)	6
Fig. 2.1	"In Other News Today" (Although this political cartoon satirizes the media coverage following the arrests of the various members of the Toronto 18, the cartoon accurately captures the fear that has been inculcated into Canadian citizens by various state officials and institutions and the corporate media.) (*Globe and Mail*, 6 June 2006)	73
Fig. 3.1	"Dominant/transgression/subversive model"	90
Fig. 3.2	"Young Man/Old Man" (Botwinick, "Husband and Father-In-Law: A Reversible Figure," 312–313)	90
Fig. 3.3	"Dominant discursive formation"	99
Fig. 3.4	"Subversive discursive formation"	109
Fig. 5.1	"The Canadian Security Regime" (For a more elaborate description of the roles of various Canadian governmental entities involved in the national security of Canada, see the Canadian Department of Justice website at: http://www.justice.gc.ca/eng/cj-jp/ns-sn/role.html)	164

CHAPTER 1

Islamic, Islamist, Islamitic: From Conceptual Violence to a Conceptual Break

Since the tragic spectacle of 11 September 2001, attempting to neutralize the threat of terrorism has become one of the primary preoccupations of North American and Western European nation-states. Various states have deployed a variety of strategies to reorder space at multiple scales both discursively and materially in order to produce an expansive field of disciplinarity in which and through which the placing, identification, and categorization of bodies by the state as either benign and subordinate or threatening and subversive have been made possible. For example, this multiscalar reordering of space to align with the war *of* terror finds expression in and is evinced through the following:

- The instrumental and ambiguous "Either you are with us, or you are with the terrorists" bifurcated worldview promulgated by President George W. Bush on 20 September 2001 to a Joint Session of Congress at which time the geographical imagination of the "war on terror" was officially inaugurated and operationalized.
- The current war in Afghanistan and the occupation of Iraq.
- The expansion of the war *of* terror into Pakistan, Yemen, and North Africa vis-à-vis US drone strikes and/or special forces operations.
- The development of a transnational prison archipelago and its attendant transportation network, whose geography is punctuated by Abu Ghraib (Iraq), Guantanamo Bay (Cuba),[1] Bagram Prison (Afghanistan), shifting black sites (unofficial and secret prisons and torture facilities), e.g. the "Salt Pit" in Afghanistan,[2] the island of

Diego Garcia,[3] and the complex flight paths of "ghost planes" circumnavigating the globe.[4]
- The militarization and citadelification of the urban environment in an attempt to mitigate risk and vulnerability.[5]
- The incremental increase in the securitization of borders[6] and airports[7] as sites not only of surveillance, interpolation, and interdiction but as sites of degradation, humiliation, and indignity, as demonstrated by passengers at airports standing in supine repose as an image of their naked body is scrutinized by airport security personnel.
- The furtive and systematic eradication of any meaningful distinction between the public and private domains and the consequent elimination of the privacy and anonymity of citizenry throughout the globe through the development of signals intelligence programs and networks that gather and store virtually all communications that rely upon advanced communications infrastructure, e.g. the "Five Eyes" signals intelligence network comprised of the following partners: Australia, Canada, England, New Zealand, and the USA.

As Elias Canetti states, "there is nothing man fears more than the touch of the unknown. He wants to see what is reaching towards him, and to be able to recognize or at least classify it."[8] However, under the auspices of the threat of terrorism, the power of the state to discipline bodies that move in and through particular spaces and inscribe them with specific identities and subjectivities has produced devastating results.

The power of the state to discipline and inscribe bodies is demonstrated through the litany of abuses experienced by those who have been placed in what Paddy Hillyard terms a "suspect community."[9] These abuses encompass a variety of state security actions and practices that include but are not limited to: targeted harassment and screening; extrajuridical detention, illegal transfer, false imprisonment, and torture; and the targeted killing of innocent individuals suspected of being militants. Some examples of these aforementioned abuses are illustrated through the following:

- The thousands of South Asian and Southwest Asian men arrested, detained, and incarcerated for months in the New York City area following 11 September 2001 without charge or access to legal counsel.[10]
- The hundreds of (innocent) individuals being held and tortured in Guantanamo Bay; the degradation, dehumanization, and torture of

detainees, including children, in Afghanistan (Bagram and Kandahar) and Iraq (Abu Ghraib).[11]
- The many documented and undocumented individuals who have been forcibly disappeared under the auspices of the "Extraordinary Rendition" program, such as the Canadian citizens Maher Arar (2002) and Ahmad About El Maati (2001), the Italian citizen Abu Omar (2003), and the German citizen Khaled el-Masri (2003).
- The five men (Hassan Almeri, Adil Charkaoui, Mohamed Harkat, Mahmoud Jaballah, and Mohammad Mahjoub) imprisoned for years in Canada under the controversial "Security Certificate" legislation contained within the Immigration and Refugee Protection Act.
- The murder of Jean Charles de Menezes, a Brazilian electrician working in London in July 2005, who, after an investigation, was found to be on his way to work.[12]
- The arrest of Rizwaan Sabir—a graduate student who was arrested at the University of Nottingham in May 2008 under suspicion of being a terrorist for downloading a copy of the al-Qaeda training manual from the US Department of Justice website. Incidentally, Rizwaan Sabir was released after spending six days in detention after it became clear to the law enforcement services involved that the material was being used for legitimate research for his master's thesis on radical Islamic groups.[13]

Certainly, the implications of the examples provided are manifold and include racial profiling and other forms of state racism, human rights violations, the suspension of habeas corpus and other national and international laws, the use of *reverse onus* to be exonerated of guilt, the use of state-sanctioned violence under odious circumstances, and the erosion of academic freedom. However, the examples of abuses and the implications cited above should not be understood as simply isolated incidents and/or unfortunate circumstances arising from specific North American and Western European counter-terrorism policies and practices. Instead, these individual abuses and their related implications cumulatively form a constellation of crisis points that brings into focus the materialization of what Henry Giroux codifies as a "culture of cruelty."[14] According to Giroux, "the culture of cruelty that emerges in this context speaks not merely to the death of public values or to a society that is politically adrift but more importantly to the demise of democracy itself."[15] Indeed, a question that becomes of paramount importance as a result of the appearance of these crisis points is: how is it possible for a culture of cruelty to emerge where the bodies of the innocent become sites of state discipline and inscription? Although the answer to this question is very complex, this chapter offers an examination of one element of the answer: the conceptual confusion and imprecision that appear to pervade the dominant representation of the contemporary phenomenon of domestic extremism of the al-Qaeda-inspired type that has emerged in a North American and/or a Western European context.

Given the ubiquitous presence of the subject of terrorism over the last decade in scholarly analysis, security and public policy discussions, and corporate media coverage and commentary, a point of departure into an examination of the conceptual confusion and imprecision redolent of domestic extremism of the al-Qaeda-inspired type must proceed with an analysis of the efficacy of particular typologies of terrorism as a mode of categorization and description.

Dispersing the Conceptual Fog: The Problematics of Categorizing and Representing the "New" Terrorism

As Alex Schmid and Albert Jongman observe in their seminal text on the subject of political terrorism, "in the literature one finds a multitude of *fundamenta divisionis*, or principles of distinction."[16] Some examples of the typologies of terrorism Schmid and Jongman outline and describe include: actor-based, victim-based, motivation-based, demand-based, and political-orientation-based. These typologies can then be further subdivided into different categories. For example, the sub-types under the political-orientation-based typology can include, as advanced varyingly by Brian Crozier and Davidson Smith: "ethnic, religious, or nationalist groups," "anarchist groups," "Marxist-Leninist groups," "state and state-sponsored," "ideological," and so on.[17] Indeed, several of these sub-types of terrorism as well as others are utilized to varying degrees by a variety of security and law enforcement apparatuses to assist them in framing, profiling, and ultimately countering the threats posed by these different actors. Furthermore, several scholars have begun to move beyond political, cultural, and social categories of terrorist analyses and are considering the potential psychological factors (psychopathology, personality traits, individual and group behavior, etc.) associated with the social actors involved with this phenomenon.[18]

Certainly, the development of typologies of terrorism is important as categorizing helps to enable an analysis of the commonalities, differences, connectivities, and relationships within and between various forms of terrorism. Moreover, typologies are important because, as Matthew Waxman states, "categorization influences the way we think about terrorism in terms of strategy, law, and institutions."[19] Given the importance of terrorism typologies not only for supporting academic analysis but for informing the policies and practices of various state apparatuses and institutions, the conceptual precision of typological categories is paramount. Conversely, conceptual imprecision can lead to scholarship that not only perpetuates inaccuracies regarding particular phenomena but can support and/or inform misguided state policies and practices resulting in the flagrant abuses referenced above. Therefore, it is imperative that the typological categorizations that suffuse the interconnected corpus of formal, practical, and popular discourse on the subject of terrorism be subjected to nuance and refinement so that the homogeneous and presumptive character of terrorism typologies does not obfuscate the empirical reality of particular phenomena:

> The most common terrorism typology includes 'nationalist,' 'ideological,' 'religious fanatical,' 'single issue,' and 'state-sponsored,' other varieties of terror encompass the 'psychotic,' 'criminal,' 'endemic,' 'authorized,' 'vigilante,' and 'revolutionary.' The objection that terrorism may be a fake category is in fact mentioned and then quickly dismissed in the literature. That wars, killings, and violence of various kinds are endemic to the human condition is obvious; the real issue concerns the wisdom of describing all (or many) such events as the work of 'terrorism.' Does this concept better clarify the facts, or is it, as with so many other historical constructs, a hypostatized creation of learned and lay people alike that is a certain path to self-deception?[20]

As Zulaika and Douglas assert, "myopia and self-deception are the almost certain outcomes of the politics of terrorist labeling."[21] Indeed, the "myopia" and "self-deception" to which the preceding quotations refer appear to have befallen a sub-category of the religious typology widely used in terrorism discourse: the sub-category of Islamic/Islamist terrorism, which is commonly used to codify the incarnation of contemporary terrorist groups of the al-Qaeda or the al-Qaeda-inspired type.

In a post-11 September 2001 context, the usage of the signifier "terrorism" by representatives of various western states, government experts, state intellectuals, and the popular media has become inexorably associated with a distinct, identifiable, and efficacious category of actors popularly characterized and encapsulated by the following visual representation (Fig. 1.1):

Fig. 1.1 South Toronto maple leafs (Globe and Mail, 10 June 2006)

This political cartoon appeared approximately one week after the arrests of the suspects believed to be members of the so-called Toronto 18. This cartoon was a satirical response to comments made by US Republican Congressman John Hostettler who reportedly described "South Toronto" as a "breeding ground for Islamic terrorists."[22] In effect, this image and the specific visual tropes that are utilized to construct the image (i.e. the Kalashnikov AK-47, the Arab *keffiyeh*, the small and dark menacing eyes, and the timepiece with wires denoting a suicide belt or other form of explosive) serve as a powerful visual metaphor for the signified of terrorism that has come to predominate not only many Western hegemonic constructions of terrorism but the Western popular imagination in states like Canada and the USA. As Peter Gottschalk and Gabriel Greenberg argue, images like the one depicted above are significant as they express the latent sensibilities, widely disseminated attitudes, and normalized stereotypes of terrorism in non-Muslim society.[23] Consequently, this normalized image of contemporary terrorism can now, as James Der Derian asserts, do double duty as an airport security profile, featuring the checkered *keffiyeh* of Arafat, the aquiline nose of Osama bin Laden, the hollowed face of John Walker Lindh, the maniacal grin of Saddam Hussein, the piercing eyes of Abu Musab Zarqawi ('He could direct his men simply by moving his eyes,' said Basil Abu Sabha, his Jordanian prison doctor).[24]

Der Derian goes on to state, "The historicity, specificity and even the comprehensibility of terrorism have been transmogrified by the new holy and media wars into a single physiognomy of global terrorism."[25] Indeed, "evil now has a face"[26] and is embodied to varying degrees by the image depicted above. However, it is precisely through the ensemble of visual tropes in the image represented above that one can begin to deconstruct the conceptual imprecision that leads to the myopia and self-deception inherent to the typological category of Islamic terrorism.

The assemblage of the following visual tropes: the Kalashnikov AK-47, the timepiece with wires denoting a suicide belt or other form of explosive, and the Arab *keffiyeh*, has the effect of equating Islam/Muslims/Arabs not only with violence and/or violent tendencies but with particular forms of violent activities. This equation finds expression in and is reinforced through popular discursive constructions which are used to codify terrorist actors of the al-Qaeda or al-Qaeda-inspired type. For example, following the initial arrests of the alleged members of the Toronto 18 and throughout the subsequent judicial process, the Toronto-based corporate media[27] varyingly described the actors involved in the group and/or their activities using the following popular geopolitical terminology: "militant Islam,"[28] "radical Islam," "Islamic terrorism," "Islamic extremism," "Muslim terrorism," "Muslim extremists"[29] "Generation jihad,"[30] "Jihadist generation,"[31] "Canadian jihad," "the jihadization of Western Muslim youths," "Western jihadist youth counter-culture," "global jihadi movement," "global jihadi terrorist counter-culture," and the pejorative "Canadian *jihadi*-land."[32] The influence of this type of mistaken, reductionist, and essentialist conflation of Islam/Muslims/Arabs with violence is illustrated through the following question proffered by a columnist commenting on the case of the Toronto 18:

> How [...] do we determine which young man, confused and inwardly aggressive but outwardly passive, is on track to become a killer because of religious reasons? [and] above all, how do we combat the conviction that seems to have taken hold on a scale for which there's no historical precedent—that mass murder can be a legitimate act, indeed a holy one?[33]

It is this erroneous conflation that leads one editorialist to make the following observation regarding the arrests of the alleged co-conspirators involved in the Toronto 18: "recent articles in the *Globe and Mail* and elsewhere imply that Islam is inherently violent. It must be, they insist, because some Muslims carry out violence in its name."[34] Although this conflation of Islam/Muslims/Arabs with violence is highly problematic, it is a construct that, arguably, has become deeply entrenched in the popular imagination of non-Muslim groups living in Canada, the USA, and other western European countries. As a consequence, adherents of Islam or those believed to be adherents of Islam become not only stigmatized as potential agents of violence, but particular religious and/or cultural markers that are (mistakenly) associated with Islam and/or all Muslims become indexical of the potentiality to violence and by extension extremism.

The use of the Arab *keffiyeh* as a visual trope in Fig. 1.1 exemplifies how a cultural marker is used not only to represent an Islamic/Muslim identity but is used to establish a correlation between an Islamic/Muslim identity and violence. In effect, the Arab *keffiyeh* becomes a stereotypical cultural marker for all Muslims—the presupposition being that the majority of Muslims are Arabs and all Arabs are Muslims. Therefore, Arab cultural markers become symbolic of an all-encompassing cultural marker for Muslims in general. However, this stereotypical representation of Arabs as Muslims and Muslims as Arabs undermines the inherent geographical, social, political, cultural, religious, ethnic, economic, and linguistic diversity of the groups who self-identify as Arabs and/or Muslims. For instance, according to Gottschalk and Greenberg,

> only 20 percent of all Muslims in the world identify themselves as Arab. The nations with the largest Muslim populations are Indonesia, Pakistan, India, and Bangladesh—very few of whose Muslims consider themselves Arab. Meanwhile, significant amounts of Arabs identify as Christian. Nevertheless, the persistence of the Arab caricature in [Western] stereotypes of Muslims leads to a confusing collapse of difference between the two somewhat overlapping groups.[35]

As a result, Arabs and Muslims are represented as a unitary, coherent, and monolithic entity. Indeed, as Natasha Bakht asserts, Muslims are not a homogeneous and monolithic whole as it is widely represented in Western society and popular culture.[36] However, the Western construction of the term Muslim as a category that has been reduced to a cultural/religious moment negates these empirical realities. Nonetheless, the homogenization of Islam and Muslims is demonstrated through the popular representation of Arab groups. As Paul Eid contends:

> In Western representations, Arab and Muslim categories are frequently amalgamated to a point where they are sometimes used interchangeably, especially in mass media. Indeed, the Arab category framed by the majority group is to a large extent imbued with Islamic symbols and images. In other words, Islam serves as a primary signifier giving shape and content to the Western notion of Arabness.[37]

The consequence of this categorical elision is that the Arab population becomes inextricably linked to Islam and by extension Muslims, which creates the impression that all Arabs are Muslim. This fallacious representation of Arabs effectively renders the inherent differences of these groups invisible.

The conceptualization of a single, unitary Muslim population is also exemplified by the following formulation: "Muslim community." This type of phraseology appears regularly throughout the coverage of the Toronto 18. Although this construction appears rather banal and prosaic, it actually is quite powerful as it essentializes and oversimplifies a very diverse and heterogeneous "community of communities."[38] Consequently, certain characteristics of some members of a Muslim population become representative of the whole. As Tasneem Jamal observes, in the context of Canada, "many Canadians [...] believe they know a Muslim when they see one. Muslims have names like Mohammed, they have Taliban-like beards and their women are draped in *Burkas*."[39] The following statement made by the columnist Christie Blatchford during her coverage of the Toronto 18 exemplifies this assertion:

> Even before I knew for sure that they're all Muslims, I suspected as much from what I saw on the tube, perhaps because I am a trained observer, or you know, because I have eyes.

> The accused men are mostly young and mostly bearded in the Taliban fashion. They have first names like Mohammed, middle names like Mohammed and last names like Mohammed. Some of their female relatives at the Brampton courthouse who were there in their support wore back head-to-toe *burkas*

(now there's a sight to gladden the Canadian female heart: homegrown *burka*-wearers darting about just as they do in Afghanistan), which is not a getup I have ever seen on anyone but Muslim women.[40]

Additionally, this stereotypical representation of Muslim groups was certainly reified by the multitude of photographs of the family members and/or supporters of the accused, which, incidentally, were almost exclusively of a woman or women wearing a *niqab* or *chador*—convenient cultural markers that, when represented in the context of the trial, could mistakenly be interpreted as being indicative of the violent tendencies of the "community" they are understood to represent.[41] The consequence of reproducing these stereotypical representations of Muslims is that the Canadian populace is provided with a very limited and myopic perspective on and representation of Islam, Muslims, and Arabs. Moreover, this perspective and representation, illustrated by the visual tropes used in the image above, effectively equates the whole of Islam, the entirety of Muslims, and all Arabs with violence:

> The conflation of Islamic and Arabic cultures on the one hand and extremism and fanaticism on the other becomes "natural" once political domination and socioeconomic inequalities have been dismissed as potential explanatory factors for armed conflict and violence. [...] [Furthermore] these omissions help to fuel Westerners' simplistic tendency to associate all Arabs and Muslims with religious fanaticism and terrorism.[42]

The (un)intended result of these ridiculously inaccurate associations is the collectivized punishment, vilification, and demonization of all Muslims and those believed to be adherents of the religion of Islam.[43]

According to Ceri Peach, the perception of Muslim groups as an undifferentiated and homogeneous entity arises from two popular perceptions of Islam.[44] The first perception arises from the Islamic concept of the *Ummah*—the global community of Muslims unified by religion irrespective of race, ethnicity, language, nationality, and so on. The second perception arises from the construction of Islam as a unified category of analysis. However, in actuality, Islam is not a unified category but is a reified category, "superimposed upon an ethnically fragmented grouping."[45] As Peach goes on to state, "there are, of course, specific issues which Muslims take a common stance: Iraq and Afghanistan, for example. However, being different from non-Muslims is not the same as all Muslims being alike."[46] Although Peach identifies two prevailing perceptions in popular Western discourse that perpetuate the perception of Islam, Muslims, and Arabs as a monolithic entity, a crucial dimension to understanding how not only the perception of a homogeneous entity is made possible but how the equation of Islam with violence is made possible is to excavate the roots of the "mode of apprehension"[47] that informs these particular representations and constructions.

THE ORIENTALIST IMAGINATION AND THE CONSTRUCTION OF TERRORISM

As the decoding of the visual image represented above serves to illuminate, there is a propensity in popular geopolitical discourse to utilize reductionist logic to apprehend the contemporary phenomenon of extremism of the al-Qaeda-inspired type by reducing the phenomenon to both a religious and/or cultural moment—a reduction embedded within the Islamic terrorism typology. This mode of apprehension is indicative of what Bryan Turner identifies as the persistence of Orientalist discourse and its damaging legacy,[48] which is apparent in the conceptualization and production of the Islamic Other in the war *of* terror. Although the reduction of this phenomenon to a religious and/or cultural moment has become what Antonio Gramsci would describe as "common sense,"[49] the common sensicality of this reduction is in actuality the product of a deeply naturalized Orientalist mode of apprehension that has come to predominate the popular non-Muslim Western imagination vis-à-vis Islam. Therefore, as Turner suggests:

> One way into these conceptual puzzles may be to recognize that our contemporary views of other religions, such as Islam, are part of an established tradition of talking about alien cultures. We understand other cultures by slotting them into a pre-existing code or discourse which renders their oddity intelligible. We are, in practice, able to overcome the philosophical difficulties of translation by drawing upon various forms of accounting which highlight differences in characteristics between 'us' and 'them.'[50]

The established tradition to which Turner refers is what Edward Said codified in his seminal work as Orientalism. According to Said, "Orientalism is a style of thought based upon an ontological and epistemological distinction made between "the Orient" and (most of the time) the Occident."[51] Said goes on to state, "Orientalism can be discussed and analyzed as the corporate institution for dealing with the Orient—dealing with it by making statements about it, authorizing views of it, describing it, teaching it, settling it, ruling over it: in short, Orientalism as a western style for dominating, restructuring, and having authority over the Orient."[52] In effect, Orientalism is a Western discourse predicated on constructing, solidifying, and continually reifying difference. Subsequently, the Orient[53] and its various human and physical geographies when refracted through an Orientalist prism become objects of Western exoticism, primitivism, and racism. As a result, a very particular hermeneutic of the Oriental emerges in the popular collective Western imagination: an Oriental Other interpreted and characterized as antediluvian, barbaric, dangerous, mysterious, sensuous, devious, effeminate, irrational, and indolent. In the case of Islam in the Orientalist imaginary, previous Western fascination—albeit mired in condescension, conceit, and self-aggrandizement—with Islam and its concomitant historical, cultural, political, economic, sociological, and geographical formations shifted to fear and even dread through a combination of internal Western state-institutional, most notably US, processes and forces and external encounters between Western states and Islam.

The internal state-institutional processes and forces that catalyzed the abovementioned shift can be traced historically to the advent of the Cold War and the ascendancy of the USA as the preeminent global power.[54] As a result of the Cold War and its associated reordering of global space, the US government, operating in conjunction with various post-secondary institutions, initiated a capacity building program to develop a comprehensive and robust power/knowledge economy that supported its geopolitical and/or geostrategic interests in various regions of the world, and a region of particular focus was Southwest Asia.[55] As Zachary Lockman states:

> For just as the evolution of nineteenth century academic Orientalism was linked with the extension of European power into Muslim lands, so too was the development of Middle East studies as an academic field closely connected with the emergence of the United States as a global superpower and its deepening involvement in the Middle East.[56]

Subsequently, the USA witnessed a proliferation of Middle East Studies departments in various universities around the country. However, the orientation of these departments marked a paradigmatic departure from previously established classical/European Oriental Studies departments. Whereas the classical/European Oriental Studies departments primarily utilized a philological method to apprehend the Oriental object, the US variant of Oriental Studies advocated and advanced the utilization of both the philological and social scientific methods to apprehend the Oriental object in order to develop a power/knowledge capacity that could be more readily instrumentalized by the US state and its various apparatuses: "one important service which scholars rendered the state during the era of the Cold War was to provide intellectual frameworks which policymakers could use to make sense of what was going on in the world and formulate policy accordingly."[57] Indeed, this shift in the analytical orientation of North American Oriental Studies departments coincides with the broader shift in the analysis of regional geography. As Trevor Barnes and Matthew Farish explain:

> The traditional notion of science held by geographers arrived from natural history, which was field-based, descriptive, and rested on scrupulously recorded observations of a lone scholar, and tended toward classification, even the encyclopedic. Regions were portrayed correspondingly. During the Second World War and afterward, however, a different model of science emerged, one produced in the crucible of war, both hot and cold, and forged through interaction among scientists, the military, industry, and the state. This science happened at the lab bench or at the writing desk, involved large sums of money and a team of researchers ("big science"), was theoretically abstract, mathematical, model- and machine- based, and geared towards meeting specific ends. [...] Accordingly, it produced a very different idea of region, conceived now as explanatory, theoretical, and instrumental, a tool to achieve functional objectives.[58]

As a result of this state-institutional arrangement and the marriage of the practical (policy) and formal (elite) spheres of analyses and engagement, the frameworks that were developed by what Antonio Gramsci describes as "state intellectuals"[59] were ultimately designed to reinforce and strengthen the positions of policymakers and practitioners vis-à-vis different regions of the world considered to be of geostrategic importance to the USA, including Southwest Asia. Ultimately, the positions taken by policymakers and practitioners cultivated a cultural ontology and epistemology that situated US political, economic, and social systems on the vanguard of modernity where "other cultures appear not merely as other, but as contrary."[60] In the case of the region of Southwest Asia, these intellectual frameworks and correlative policy positions were given further credence as a result of the external encounters between the USA and Islam throughout the Cold War period.

The external encounters that helped to precipitate the shift from fascination to fear and dread of Islam were a result of myriad political maneuverings and activities in Southwest Asia, e.g. OPEC Oil Crisis (1973), Iranian Revolution and Hostage Crisis (1979), PLO activities throughout the 1970s and early 1980s, and the bombing of the US Marine Barracks in Lebanon (1983), and so on, that undermined US and other Western interests. As a result of these external encounters, the subject of Islam began to congeal and further solidify as an object of Western-centric analysis, jingoistic policy,[61] and propagandistic reportage and commentary,[62] which were framed and supported by the internal state-institutional mechanisms of power/knowledge. As a consequence of these mutually reinforcing internal and external conditions, Islam became increasingly characterized as and associated with "a powerful enemy; an exotic and deviant growth of the Near East; a semi-inert, introverted mass; a failed civilization in need of restoration and revision; a mission field; and a fanatical, even suicidal, reaction against the trends of modern times."[63] These characterizations and associations became incrementally entrenched in the popular North American imagination after a succession of moments throughout the 1990s: the first Gulf War (1990–1991); the dissolution of the Soviet Union (1991) (see Chap. 2); the first World Trade Center bombing (1993); the bombings of the US embassies in Nairobi, Kenya, and Dar es Salaam, Tanzania (1998); and the bombing of the USS Cole in Yemen (2000). However, arguably, these same characterizations and associations assumed a position of permanence in the popular imaginary following the events of 11 September 2001[64] and have been reinforced by subsequent incidents involving groups of the al-Qaeda type in various jurisdictions around the world.

The lasting ontological and epistemological effect of the historical conjuncture of internal state-institutional processes and forces and external encounters between the USA and Islam has been the perpetuation of an Orientalist hermeneutic that enables contemporary phenomena, such as extremism of the al-Qaeda-inspired type, to be apprehended through a litany of ambiguous, but nonetheless evaluative and antagonistic binaries: "the West versus the Islamic world, extremists versus moderates, violent versus peaceful, democratic versus totalitarian, religious versus secular, medieval versus modern and savage versus civilized."[65] As a consequence, the specificity of the actors involved in extremism of the al-Qaeda-inspired type and their emergence in particular contexts are rendered opaque by reductionist constructions that conceal much more than they reveal about not only the motivations that animate social actors but the conditions that make the emergence of these types of actors probable. Instead, the reification of Orientalist binaries evident in the framing and interpretation of this phenomenon enables constructions like "Islamic terrorism" and the deeply embedded problematics inherent to this construction (as discussed above) to become a legitimate and authoritative typological category in dominant discourse. Moreover, as Aziz Al-Azmeh suggests in modification, the Islamic terrorism construction itself becomes the empirical manifold of contemporary Orientalist discourse and serves as a reaffirmation of the propositions, statements, and topos of the West/Islam dyad.[66] Therefore, to avoid both the discursive and empirical problematics associated with the Islamic terrorism typology, and to mitigate the material and embodied consequences for those wrongfully rendered suspect as a result of this fallacious typology, a typological departure from the dominant modes of categorization is required so that the conceptual confusion that imbues the phenomenon of extremism of the al-Qaeda-inspired type is afforded more clarity.

Although the term "Islamist," which is also referred to varyingly as "Islamism" or "Political Islam," is widely deployed in formal, practical, and popular discourse in North America and beyond as a discursive mechanism that is meant to delineate a distinct belief system that stands in opposition to the religion of Islam, as Ladan Boroumand and Roya Boroumand assert, "these beliefs are properly called "Islamist" rather than "Islamic" because they are actually in conflict with Islam—a conflict that we must not allow to be obscured by the 'terrorists' habit of commandeering Islamic religious terminology and injecting it with their own distorted content,"[67] this term is also problematic.[68] Indeed, unlike the use of the adjective "Islamic" to modify the noun "terrorism," the use of the adjective "Islamist" does facilitate a rupture within terrorism discourse that attempts to differentiate the religion of Islam from, as Bassam Tibi states, "the political concepts developed on the grounds of the politicization of Islam."[69] For, as Tibi goes on to observe, "it is not the substance of religion that is of interest of the exponents of political Islam; not spirituality, but religious symbolism employed in the pursuit of political ends is their concern."[70] However, the problematic of the term "Islamist" is not in its attempt to rupture and delineate, which is certainly an important, if not an imperative, initiative, but its usage in dominant discourse.

Terminologically, the term "Islamist" has become an overdetermined signifier that is conflated, to varying degrees and in differing analytical contexts, with fundamentalism, reformism and revivalism, radicalization, extremism, militancy, jihad, the Middle East, Arabs, anti-Western sentimentality, and ideological and physical violence. However, as Jonathan Taylor and Chris Jasparo identify, "Not all Islamists are terrorists [...] and vice versa." Nonetheless, as they continue, "Those who consider Islamism the chief explanation for the 11 September attacks [...] find the links between terrorism and Islamism incontrovertible and argue that Islamism is an inherently threatening and destabilizing ideology which has set itself up against modernity, secularism, the West or democracy."[71] As such, it has become an expansive and nebulous catch-all term which in deployment erroneously equates the individual phenomena outlined above with violence and/or extremism. As Valentina Bartolucci argues, "such semantic mixes and assumptions not only hamper a detached understanding of the phenomena, but also have important political implications. From such understandings Islamists, 'radical' or not, end up being considered as 'potential terrorists.'"[72] Consequently, while the term Islamist implicitly recognizes the active politicization of Islam by various types of actors and groups, in the dominant discourse the term Islamist maintains a tacit linkage between particular types of extremism and (a version of) Islam. As a result, the religion of Islam is still implicated as the centripetal force of extremism. Therefore, the efficacy of "Islamist" as a social scientific term and category is called into question as its associations and implications in dominant usage appear to reaffirm not only the equation of extremism with Muslims and Islam but more broadly the West/Islam dyad and its inherent Western-centric evaluations and judgments.[73]

Departing from Dominant Discourse and the Recasting of Extremism

Given the problematic terminological and typological nature of the Islamic/Islamist constructions discussed above and the consistent utilization of these designations in dominant discourse, a "technique of defamiliarization"[74] is required so that the actors involved in these particular movements can be reconceptualized in order to provide a different perspective that both reshapes and illuminates the contours of the appropriate political phenomena.[75] Following the progressive and innovative analysis of Sabah Alnasseri in his German-language scholarship on the Muslim Brotherhood, the technique of defamiliarization and the attendant reconceptualization required for these political movements can be enacted through the introduction of the following neologism: *Islamitic*. As Alnasseri suggests, the introduction of the neologism Islamitic not only signals a terminological departure from dominant discourse and analysis but signals that one is conceptually dealing with something new.[76] However, whereas Alnasseri offers more of an unstable[77] treatment of what is meant by the term Islamitic, further elaboration of the Islamitic term is required to develop it into a more stable and coherent concept.

The most important characteristic and defining feature of the Islamitic concept is that it offers a critical engagement with particular phenomena, for instance, the phenomenon of terrorism of the al-Qaeda or al-Qaeda-inspired type, which extricates the religion of Islam from this phenomenon and reveals the political and secular orientation of the social actors under consideration. This extrication is significant as it requires one to accept a hermeneutic shift that situates this phenomenon in modern political formations rather than modern religious formations. Although this assertion may be considered contentious in dominant opinion, or appear to be misguided, the political and secular orientation of these actors is demonstrated when one analyzes the socio-structural, intellectual, and organizational dimensions of the phenomena.[78]

Contrary to dominant sentiment regarding the socio-structural characteristics of the actors who either support or directly participate in the political activity of Islamitic groups (both constitutional and non-constitutional), a sentiment which characterizes these actors as subaltern (rural or the fringe urban poor and undereducated), the vast majority of these actors live in urban environments and come from relatively advantaged economic backgrounds (middle to upper class).[79] According to an extensive study conducted by Graeme Blair et al. on attitudes toward and/or participation in militant groups in Pakistan, rigorous empirical analysis revealed that "the perpetrators of militant violence are predominantly from middle class or wealthy families."[80] Furthermore, as Blair et al. go on to assert, "there is no reliable link between poverty and support for specific terrorist tactics."[81] In actuality, based upon the findings of their study, "the poor in Pakistan hold militant groups in much lower regard than do middle-class Pakistanis, challenging the conventional wisdom that expanding the size of the middle class via economic development will decrease violence."[82] Similar socio-structural characteristics can be found when one assesses the profiles of other actors involved in violent Islamitic groups operating in other countries, such as al-Qaeda-affiliated or al-Qaeda-inspired groups.

In the case of the Toronto 18, which one of the primary figures described as an al-Qaeda-inspired group that adheres to the tenets of "jihad" espoused by Osama bin Laden and al-Qaeda,[83] all of the actors lived in the Greater Toronto Area (GTA), primarily in Mississauga and Scarborough, and the vast majority came from middle-class backgrounds. Moreover, just as two-thirds of the nineteen actors involved in the 11 September 2001 atrocities had pursued formal academic training,[84] four of which were recruited from a university in Hamburg, Germany,[85] six of the adult actors, including the leader of the Mississauga Group, were, at one time or another, enrolled in universities in the GTA and beyond, including the University of Toronto, Ryerson University (Toronto), and McMaster University (Hamilton).[86] Indeed, the fact that many of the actors who support al-Qaeda or al-Qaeda-inspired Islamitic groups and/or movements are middle class and have attended post-secondary institutions undermines socio-economic explanations of North American and/or Western European domestic Islamitic extremism: that the actors involved come from economically disadvantaged backgrounds and have received very little if any formal education. In many respects their socio-structural backgrounds (urban and middle to upper class) serve as a precondition for the pursuance of and accessibility to formal academic education and knowledge. Therefore, what becomes abundantly clear, given the socio-structural characteristics of these actors, is that these actors do not emerge from the margins of society but, rather, emerge from its center.

The second dimension which illuminates the political and secular orientation of Islamitic actors and groups is the intellectual tradition of the ideologues that inform the worldview and practices of many of these same actors and groups. When one traces the genealogy of thought that informs many Islamitic actors, especially those of the al-Qaeda or al-Qaeda-inspired type, what comes into focus is an intellectual tradition that is secular and not religious in nature. For example, the contemporary ideological framework of al-Qaeda and by extension al-Qaeda-inspired actors, to varying degrees and in varying combinations, can be genealogically traced through the ideas of the following ideologues: Abd al-Wahhab, Abu al-A'la al-Mawdudi, Sayyid Qutb, Ayman al-Zawahiri, Osama bin Laden, Abu Muhammad 'Asim Al-Maqdisi, 'Abdul-Qadir Ibn 'Abdul-'Aziz, and Anwar al-Awlaki.[87] However, these ideologues are not religious figures in any formal sense: they are not recognized as religious scholars who have received formal training in the Islamic jurisprudential tradition nor do these ideologues possess any formal accredited knowledge of this same jurisprudential tradition. Instead, these ideologues are indicative of what, according to Abou El Fadl, "has become a well-known phenomenon in contemporary Islam—that of self-declared experts who claim to take on the job of reforming Islamic thought without being minimally qualified to do so."[88] As El Fadl goes on to observe:

> Typically these magic-wand reformers are by profession engineers, medical doctors, or even social scientists who might be competent as sociologists or political scientists, but their knowledge and command of the Islamic intellectual tradition or its texts is minimal at best. Despite their poor knowledge of Islam, or perhaps because of their lack of familiarity with the Islamic intellectual tradition, these magic-wand reformers write books containing sweeping and unsubstantiated generalizations about what Islam is and what it ought to be. Although invariably lacking any systemic training in Islamic jurisprudence and its methodologies, often such writers designate themselves as *muftis* and call for what they describe as widespread personalized *ijtihad*, which often amounts to nothing more than a call for egotistical self-idolatry.[89]

As Abou El Fadl identifies, the professions of the vast majority of the Islamitic ideologues in general, and the professions of the Islamitic ideologues of the al-Qaeda or al-Qaeda-inspired type in particular, are secular by training, e.g. Sayyid Qutb (Teacher), Ayman al-Zawahiri (Physician), 'Abdul-Qadir Ibn 'Abdul-'Aziz (Physician), and Anwar al-Awlaki (Civil Engineer). Therefore, in effect, these ideologues are not products of what Louis Althusser has termed a "religious Ideological State Apparatus" but rather products of a secular "educational Ideological State Apparatus."[90] As such, these ideologues and their adherents cannot be understood to be religious actors when, in actuality, they are secular actors regardless of their own prognostications and claims to religious authority. Nonetheless, through maintaining explicit or implicit linkages between these ideologues and the religion of Islam, as dominant typologies currently maintain irrespective of intent, a degree of religiosity is conferred upon these figures. Consequently, for those who are ignorant of the religion of Islam, these ideologues are afforded a degree of religious authority which obfuscates the secular orientation and secular objectives of these figures and the actors and/or groups they inform. Furthermore, perhaps most importantly, on an epistemological register, many, if not all, of these ideologues rely upon a philological method of knowledge production. As such, these figures are indebted to the secular Western Enlightenment tradition rather than the

Islamic jurisprudential tradition for the knowledge they produce and disseminate in various written and recorded forms.

The third dimension which exemplifies the political and secular orientation of the actors and groups of the Islamitic type is their strategic and tactical organization. Although Islamitic actors and groups are highly variegated and have political agendas that are equally diverse, the strategic and tactical organization of Islamitic formations can be conceptualized as two distinctive movements: those engaged in, what Antonio Gramsci codifies as a "War of Position" and those engaged in a "War of Manoeuvre."[91] However, before continuing, it is important to establish some of the key characteristics of Islamitic actors and groups so that the distinctiveness of the two movements can be further explicated.

The vast majority of Islamitic actors and groups renounce violence, have national(ist) agendas, and operate within the constitutional mechanisms of the state. As Mohammed Ayoob states:

> The extremist transnational organizations that purport to act politically on behalf of Islam, such as al-Qaeda, are fringe groups, which, while they capture the West's imagination by their dramatic acts of terror, are marginal to the large majority of [Islamitic] movements and irrelevant to the day-to-day political struggles within Muslim countries. Most mainstream [Islamitic] movements operate peacefully within national boundaries and attempt to influence and transform their societies and polities largely through constitutional means, even when the constitutional and political cards are stacked against them.[92]

Given the constitutional national agenda of most Islamitic formations and the marginality of Islamitic formations that pursue a violent transnational and/or domestic agenda, one can begin to establish a divergence between the Islamitic formations engaged in a war of position versus a war of maneuver.

Islamitic formations engaged in a war of position generally have a national agenda that is organized around three distinct, yet at times entangled, geopolitical strategies. These geopolitical strategies can be characterized as *Islamitic nationalist* (e.g. Muslim Brotherhood, Islamic Revival Party of Tajikistan (IRPT), Islamic Party of Uzbekistan (IPU) and Al Shabaab in Somalia), *Islamitic secessionist* (e.g. Moro Islamic Liberation Front, Free Aceh Movement (GAM), and Boko Haram), or *Islamitic irredentist* (e.g. Hezbollah, Hamas, and the Kashmiri Harkat-ul-Ansar/ Harkat-ul-Mujahideen (HUA/HUM)). To achieve their geopolitical objectives, in most instances, these Islamitic formations have, as Richard Jackson suggests, developed a multitude of tactics that engage both the state (political parties, militant wings) and civil society (social services and communications, including newspapers, newsletters, magazines, websites, radio and television, etc.) in an effort to challenge the hegemony of the state and build support for their own specific national territorial objectives, which include achieving constitutional political power.[93] Furthermore, a defining characteristic of Islamitic formations engaged in a war of position is that their strategic and tactical organization is organically linked to a single national territory and the political conditions therein, including various forms of state repression and/or occupation. However, in order for these Islamitic formations to successfully execute their strategies and tactics requires an effective organizational structure.

Islamitic formations engaged in a war of position require a sophisticated institutional and organizational structure, e.g. Muslim Brotherhood, Hezbollah, and Hamas, if they are to productively subvert the hegemony of the state and realize their own ascendancy to political power. Therefore, many of these Islamitic formations are formally, centrally, and hierarchically organized with not only clearly defined divisions of labor but highly coordinated activities that fulfill particular functions, such as administrative, technical, and extra-institutional social networking. For example, the Muslim Brotherhood in Egypt developed a centralized leadership model that was comprised of three components: the General Guide, the Consultative Assembly, and the Guidance Council. These three components of the leadership were situated in the headquarters of the Muslim Brotherhood located in Cairo. According to Richard Mitchell, "the leading figure at the headquarters was the secretary-general, and both his secretariat and that of the General Guide were defined as 'the officials of the general headquarters.'"[94] The Guidance Council was responsible for overseeing and administering both the "technical operation" and the "field apparatus" of the Muslim Brotherhood.[95]

The technical operation branch of the Muslim Brotherhood consisted of two units called committees and sections. The committees unit consisted of six constituent administrative parts: financial, policy, legal, statistics, services, and legal opinions. The *sections* unit was responsible for indoctrination and consisted of ten constituent parts: propagation of the message, labor, peasant, family, students, liaison with the Islamic world, bodily training, professions, press and translation, and Muslim sisters.[96]

The technical operation branch was primarily responsible for the administrative and propagative components of the Muslim Brotherhood, while the field apparatus branch was primarily responsible for the on-the-ground action and affairs of the Muslim Brotherhood throughout the Egyptian nation-state.

The field apparatus branch consisted of four hierarchical units—Administrative Office, District, Branch, and Family (listed in descending order)—that were administered by their own councils with a representative from the Guidance Council. The two largest units (Administrative and District) were divided to coincide with the official provincial units and its related sub-divisions. For, as Mitchell describes, "to follow the governmental divisions on these two levels had the obvious value of benefiting from the communication lanes between and among the various divisions and sub-divisions already in official use."[97] The other two smaller sub-units were then situated and organized within the geography of the higher divisions. The result of the overall structure of the Muslim Brotherhood was the development of a highly integrated and sophisticated organization whose tactical penetration of civil society vis-à-vis their technical and field branches and concomitant activities enabled, and continues to enable, them to mobilize support as a viable alternative to the hegemony of the Egyptian state. Conversely, Islamitic formations engaged in a war of maneuver (the focus of this book) possess different strategic, tactical, and organizational characteristics.

Islamitic formations engaged in a war of maneuver manifest in two different forms: Transnational Islamitic Extremism and Domestic Islamitic Extremism. The geopolitical objectives of Islamitic formations engaged in a war of maneuver are to change the foreign policies and practices of governments vis-à-vis specific conflict zones, such as Afghanistan and Iraq. To achieve their respective geopolitical objectives, the tactics these formations utilize can be both violent and non-violent by design and involve both the targeting and engagement of state entities and civil society in order to persuade various governments to change policies and practices in particular areas of the world. Similar to other political entities, the mode of engagement is predicated on the geographical location and place-specific context of the group, the resources available to the group, their level of organization, and their degree of sophistication. Although the use of physical violence of these Islamitic formations can represent an important dimension of their mode of engagement with a respective government, the tactical repertoire of these types of formations can be much more complex than the sole use of violence as the method to facilitate change. For instance, as demonstrated by Transnational Islamitic Extremist formations like al-Qaeda, these formations utilize propaganda and media campaigns; release communiqués; actively engage in indoctrination, recruitment, and training; participate in fundraising drives; and participate in financial and political network building as tactics to achieve their geopolitical objectives.

The salient feature and defining characteristic of these Islamitic formations is that they are organically linked to the foreign policies and practices of various governments in a variety of regions located around the world, such as the USA, the UK, Spain, Russia, Canada, and so on. Arguably, without this linkage, it is doubtful that these types of Islamitic formations would emerge or even exist. Indeed, the necessity of this linkage is quite evident in both Transnational Islamitic Extremism (e.g. al-Qaeda[98]) and Domestic Islamitic Extremism (e.g. the Toronto 18 and the group involved in the London transit bombings).

The organic linkage between Islamitic formations engaged in a war of maneuver and the foreign policies of various governments is clearly demonstrated in a statement made by one of the adult members of the Toronto 18. On 4 March 2011, the final adult convicted of terrorism-related crimes (who, incidentally, is an urban, middle-upper class professional computer scientist) asked for permission to address the court before receiving his sentence. In this address, which one must assume is sincere as the judge had already determined the length of this individual's rehabilitation in a penal environment, the accused outlined the motivations for his actions:

> The third topic I'd like to address is—is my political motivations for all of this and how they've been portrayed—portrayed by the media and by the Crown. They've always said that—that, you know, whoever commits this kind of crime and the Muslims that are upset about what's happening in the world, they use the phrase, "Perceived Injustice" by the west, the Muslims by the west. The word "Perceived" specifically that troubles me. I have mentioned in my psychiatrist report, page 17, I became very ardent, animated when talking about this topic, and I will quote from the report.

> "The US puts pro-US people in power and in this regard, he (being me) named the Saudi Arabian royal family and President Mubarak of Egypt. He went on to say that once a US puppet like Saddam Hussein falls then they take him out using the pretext of mass weapons. George Bush shakes hands with these dirty devils. [The accused] was quite worked up and animated

during his discussion. Mr. Mubarak now, as the world has seen is officially a criminal. His papers are before the ICC, the International Criminal Board. I will quote the Globe and Mail, 'Monday the 24th, quoting Ms. Hillary Clinton saying, 'I consider President Mubarak and Mrs. Mubarak to be friends of the family.

[…] Well this is not perceived, this is true, this is western media writing this. Does it take a revolt to bring out the truth? Four hundred and fifty million people have to get up. I am not mad. I am not crazy and this is not perceived. The Globe and Mail, same article, Monday, 24th,

"Mr. Mubarak is getting dumped. Not since the Shah of Iran was dumped in 1979 has Washington abandoned an ally so quickly."

There's an old Arabic saying, if you want to know who you are you look at your friends. The revolt in Egypt, Yemen, Algeria, Jordan, Cairo, Bahrain, and Tunisia against brutal repressive autocratic regimes were financed and given military aide to exercise their brutality by their western allies has brought out this piece of dirt—you know, has brought out this piece of dirty laundry and it does things—as a demonstrator downtown once said, "We come to the west to escape the tyrannical system that are backed up by the west." To call this perceived just doesn't trouble me, it troubles normal western citizens now. […] So I would encourage everyone to refrain from using the world, "perceived."[99]

Not only does this portion of the address demonstrate the organic linkage between these types of Islamitic formations and the foreign policies and practices of various Western governments, but it lays bare the political rather than religious motivations for the activities for which this individual stood accused. Although Islamitic formations engaged in a war of maneuver are similar to those engaged in a war of position with respect to being political entities, those engaged in a war of maneuver have no desire to achieve constitutional political power or to exercise hegemony over a particular areal unit. As a result of the differing political objectives of these formations, the organizational structure of these Islamitic groups assumes a different form.

The organizational structure of the majority of these formations is generally fluid, vaguely defined, and decentralized. This organizational structure is a result of the small size of these formations, the non-permissive security environment in which they operate, and the reactive and retaliatory character of their geopolitical objectives. Although some Islamitic formations with either the support of state resources or provision of safe haven are able to develop a more rigid and bureaucratic organization, this situation is certainly the exception and not the rule. For instance, contrary to its representation in dominant discourse, even the much fabled "al-Qaeda" was neither as sophisticated nor influential as it is made to appear. As Jason Burke states:

> even when at its most organized in late 2001, it is important to avoid seeing 'al Qaeda' as a coherent and structured terrorist organization with cells everywhere, or to imagine it had subsumed all other groups within its networks. This would be to profoundly misconceive its nature and the nature of modern Islamic militancy. For example, bin Laden's group was only one of very many radical Islamic outfits operating in and from Afghanistan at the time. It had no monopoly on militant Islamic activism.[100]

Indeed, following the US-led invasion of Afghanistan, the organizational structure al-Qaeda, such as it existed, was systematically dismantled and was transformed from a material Islamitic formation to a symbolic Islamitic formation that served as a source of inspiration for other autonomous Islamitic formations operating in various jurisdictions and under differing socio-political contexts. The majority of these autonomous Islamitic formations, e.g. the Toronto 18, are small in membership, are unsophisticated and disorganized, and have very few financial resources at their disposal, and their political engagement with the state or broader civil society through constitutional communicative means is virtually non-existent. The characteristics of these Islamitic formations render them more susceptible to dissolution before an actual violent act has been committed; however, even those that carry out an actual violent act tend to immediately dissolve as the weak infrastructure of these formations precludes their sustainability over the long term. Therefore, these Islamitic formations tend to sporadically appear and then quickly disappear with varying degrees of effect.

Another important characteristic of Islamitic formations that engage in a war of maneuver is that these formations are not ideologically, politically, or operationally static formations. These formations are influenced by and respond to both external and internal moments that can cause these formations to shift their strategy and tactics. In effect, the external and internal moments co-determine the strategic and tactical orientation of these formations. As a result, these formations are inherently dynamic and can change over space and time. Furthermore, Islamitic formations engaged in a war of maneuver are not comprised of homogeneous actors that operate in concert or agree on specific strategies or tactics. Rather, these formations are comprised of heterogeneous actors whose power struggles and other forms of conflict can change the organizational structure or composition of the formation in question. This is evidenced by the factionalism customary of many political groups. For example, in the case of the Toronto 18, in March 2006, the group splintered into two factions: the Mississauga Group and the Scarborough Group. This splintering resulted from tactical differences between the two principal figures of the group. The leader of the Mississauga Group thought that the leader of the Scarborough Group was too inactive and was more of a polemicist engaged in self-aggrandizement rather than an action-oriented figure with concrete plans in place. As a result, the two groups diverged and oriented themselves on different operational trajectories. The dynamism of Islamitic formations is important to recognize as these groups cannot be apprehended as ahistorical formations that are unchanging and insensitive to the spatial and socio-political context in which and through which they operate.

As one assembles the socio-structural, intellectual, and organizational dimensions discussed above, a three-dimensional formation is brought into view that exposes the necessity of a discursive and conceptual break from dominant formal, practical, and popular discourse on "Islamic" or "Islamist" terrorism: a political formation that is a product of a modern urban and secular power/knowledge nexus that emerges from and is a reaction to specific socio-political contexts and conjunctures. Through enacting a discursive and conceptual shift that departs from dominant discourse, one can avoid the conceptual inaccuracies and confusion that perpetuate the mythologies that have been constructed regarding the Islamitic extremism of the al-Qaeda-inspired type. Therefore, the adoption of the Islamitic term and concept serves as a strategy to distance oneself from a dominant discourse that demonizes and vilifies entire communities and informs policies and practices that discipline the bodies of the innocent in very real and embodied ways. Without a shift, dominant opinion and the terrorism experts[101] that inform these opinions will continue to be haunted by Orientalist apparitions of their own design in phantasmagoric proportions.

In this chapter, I have attempted to illustrate both the conceptual deficiencies and ideological violence embedded within the dominant constructions and representations of the contemporary incarnation of extremism of the al-Qaeda-inspired type. In response to these deficiencies and their related violence, I have also attempted to facilitate a departure from these dominant constructions in order to not only help provide greater conceptual clarity for this phenomenon but help to eliminate the ideological violence that is consciously or unconsciously directed at particular community groups. In Chap. 2, I attempt to reveal the constellation of moments that have made the emergence of dominant discourses on Islamitic extremism possible.

Notes

1. See Rose (2004), *Guantanamo: The War on Human Rights*; and Margulies (2006), *Guantanamo and the Abuse of Presidential Power.*
2. See Paglen (2010), *Black Spots on the Map.*
3. See Sidaway, James. (2010), "'One Island, One Team, One Mission': Geopolitics, Sovereignty, 'Race' and Rendition." *Geopolitics*, 15: 667–683.
4. See Grey (2006), *Ghost Plane: The True Story of the CIA Torture Program*; and Paglen & Thompson (2006), *Torture Taxi: On the Trail of the CIA's Rendition Flights.*
5. See Gray and Wyly (2007), "The Terror City Hypothesis" in *Violent Geographies.*
6. As of January 2008, new documentation requirements for all Canadians traveling to the USA via land or air were introduced: Canadians are now required to produce a valid passport for entry to the USA. Furthermore, border officials are using enhanced screening methods that can include the seizure and review of computer equipment and the use of x-rays to search automobiles. For popular commentary on this issue, see, for example, Clark, Campbell. (2009, December 14). "Canadians don't forfeit right to privacy at border, Obama official says." *The Globe and Mail*, A5.
7. In a North American context, some of the most visible and experiential examples of the incremental increase in security are demonstrated through the passenger screening process in major airports throughout Canada and the USA. Although in the immediate aftermath of 11 September 2001 passenger screening at airports became much more rigorous, the intensification of the screening process has continued, following a distinctive chronology of events. For instance, in December 2001, a British national attempted to detonate a pair of his shoes which contained plastic explosives aboard American Airlines Flight 63. This resulted in the security requirement that all airline passengers in the USA be

required to remove their shoes for screening. Following the arrests of 24 individuals suspected of planning to detonate liquid explosives aboard various flights en route from the UK to various destinations in the USA in Canada in August 2006, the ability of passengers to carry liquids and gels onto an aircraft has been severely restricted. And, finally, following the attempted detonation of plastic explosives concealed in the underwear of a Nigerian national aboard Northwest Airlines Flight 253 en route from Amsterdam to Detroit in December 2009 ultimately resulted in the installation and use of full-body scanners in a variety of airports throughout the USA and Canada and/or the use of invasive physical body search procedures. For popular coverage of the December 2009 event and the ensuing aviation security protocols, see, for example, Koring, Paul. (2010, January 8). "'We are at War.'" *The Globe and Mail*, A1; Mclean, Jesse. (2009, December 29). "Rules tighten on air travel." *Toronto Star*, A1; and Ryall, Rebecca. (2009, December 29). "Security Under Scrutiny." *National Post*, A1, A2.
8. Canetti, *Crowds and Power*, 15.
9. As Hillyard outlines in his text *Suspect Community*, a suspect community refers to particular groups perceived by the state to be a problem population and, therefore, require discipline, regulation, and control (1993, 3). Although Hillyard's argument focuses on the experiences of the Irish population under the British Prevention of Terrorism Act, the same relations of power are evident in the treatment of people believed to be members of the "Muslim" population in North America, Europe, and beyond.
10. Mathur, "Surviving the dragnet: 'special interest' detainees in the US after 9/11," 32.
11. For a discussion of the legal justification for the use of torture on detainees in the war on terror, see Greenberg, Karen & Dratel, Joshua. (2005). *The Torture Papers: The Road to Abu Ghraib*. Cambridge University Press: New York. For a discussion of not only the use of torture and its political and social implications but the torturing of children in the war on terror, see Giroux, Henry. (2010). *Hearts of Darkness: Torturing Children in the War on Terror*. Paradigm Publishers: London.
12. Cowell, Allan & Van Natta, Don. "Britain Says Man Killed by Police Had No Tie to Bombings," http://www.nytimes.com/2005/07/24/international/24london.html.
13. The following is a description by Rizwaan Sabir of the initial charges brought against him (personal communication, 10 February 2011): "I was arrested under Section 41 of the Terrorism Act 2000 which authorises the police to arrest any individual that is suspected of being involved in the 'commission, preparation or instigation of an act of terrorism' in

the UK. This power is solely used as an arrest power. In other words, anybody that is arrested is arrested under S. 41. In relation to actual charges that the police wanted to bring against me were under Section 57 and Section 58 of the Terrorism Act 2000. Section 57: Under section 57, it is an offence to be in possession of an 'article' that is reasonably believed to be useful to somebody involved in the 'commission, preparation or instigation of an act of terrorism'. An 'article' is anything therefore intent needs to be proven. For example, a map of London can be used for tourism purposes, but in the context of a terrorism investigation, it can be used to plot the route that an assassin would take, or to locate potential vulnerable or high-profile targets. In my case, I had an edited version of an al-Qaeda manual which is reasonable for a researcher to possess, but suspect for an individual that is believed by the State to be involved in planning terrorism. Section 58: Under Section 58, it is an offence to make a 'collection of information' that can be of use to someone that is involved in the 'commission, preparation or instigation of an act of terrorism'. Again, the information can be innocuous, but it's the intent that needs to be proven. So a range of information documenting the best type of detonators to blow concrete is not criminal, especially if you are in the demolition trade, but for somebody who is 'suspected' of being involved in terrorism, it's becomes suspicious and therefore can be used against them. Again, it all depends on the suspicion and whether the police can 'prove beyond reasonable doubt' that you were using it for nefarious purposes. Another example—The contact details and travel arrangements of the PM is innocent for a journalist to possess if they are shadowing him on a foreign trip, but if that journalist is suspected of being a terrorist, he's made a 'collection of information' which gives rise to suspicion that it's for a purpose related to terrorism. However, he has to have done something to generate suspicion. Unfortunately, the state of the UK at present means that every Muslim who doesn't agree with the State is of 'reasonable suspicion.'"

14. Giroux, *Hearts of Darkness*, 64.
15. Ibid., 64.
16. Schmid & Jongman, *Political Terrorism*, 40.
17. Crozier and Smith quoted in Schmid & Jongman, *Political Terrorism*, 45.
18. See, for example, Horgan, John. (2005). *The Psychology of Terrorism*. New York: Routledge. Silke, Andrew. (Ed.). (2003). *Terrorists, victims and society: Psychological perspectives on terrorism and its consequences*. Chichester, UK: Wiley; and Post, Jerrold M. (2007). *The Mind of the Terrorist: The Psychology of Terrorism from the IRA to Al-Qaeda*. New York: Palgrave Macmillan.
19. Waxman, "Terrorism: Why Categories Matter," 19.

20. Zulaika and Douglass, *terror and taboo*, 100.
21. Ibid., 177.
22. For the complete newspaper article in which these comments appeared, see Freeman, Alan. (2006, June 9). "U.S. politician blasts 'South Toronto' as a hotbed of Islamic extremism." *Toronto Star*, A1, A10.
23. Gottschalk & Greenberg, *Islamophobia: Making Muslims the Enemy*, 7, 65–75. For an analysis of the relationship between political cartoons and Islamophobia, see the text referenced in this citation.
24. Der Derian, "Imaging terror: logos, pathos and ethos," 27.
25. Ibid, 27.
26. George W. Bush quoted in Der Derian, "Imaging terror: logos, pathos and ethos," 26.
27. The following newspapers were used to analyze the popular constructions of this incarnation of the extremist phenomenon: *Toronto Star*, *Globe and Mail*, and the *National Post*. These newspapers were selected not only because they collectively represent the newspapers of record in the GTA and beyond but because they reflect, to varying degrees, both conservative and liberal opinion.
28. See, for example, Kay, "Terror and Tolerance," A17.
29. See, for example, Walkom, "The incredible shrinking terror case," AA8.
30. See, for example, Wente, "Generation jihad: angry, young, born-again believers," http://www.theglobeandmail.com/globe-debate/generation-jihad-angry-young-born-again-believers/article1100587/.
31. See, for example, Teotonio & Leeder, "'Jihadist generation': In search of roots," A1, A12, A13.
32. See, for example, Blatchford, "A Judgment Drenched in Common Sense," A7.
33. Gwyn, "How do you fight a moral sickness?" A21.
34. Jamal, T. 2006. "I'm the one who defines myself as a Muslim." *Globe and Mail*. 8 Jun.: A20.
35. Gottschalk & Greenburg, *Islamophobia: Making Muslims the Enemy*, 69.
36. Bakht, *Belonging and Banishment: Being Muslim in Canada*, v.
37. Eid, *Being Arab*, 153.
38. Peach, "Islam, Ethnicity and South Asian Religions in the London 2001 Census," 368.
39. Jamal, "I'm the one who defines myself as a Muslim," A20.
40. Blatchford, "Ignoring the biggest elephant in the room," A1.
41. For example, see *Globe and Mail*, 5 June 2006, A6; *Toronto Star*, 7 June 2006, A1; *National Post*, 7 June 2006, A1; *Toronto Star*, 6 June 2006, A8.
42. Eid, *Being Arab*, 51.
43. A portion of the section above describing and analyzing the corporate media coverage of the "Toronto 18" originally appeared in Kowalski,

Jeremy. (2013). "'Framing' the Toronto 18: Government Experts, Corporate Media, and the Orientalizing of the Other." In Jenna Hennebry & Bessma Momani. (Eds.). *Targeted Transnationals: The State, the Media, and Arab Canadians.* Vancouver: UBC Press.
44. Peach, "Islam, ethnicity and South Asian religions in the London 2001 census," 353–354.
45. Ibid., 354.
46. Ibid., 354.
47. Al-Azmeh, "The Articulation of Orientalism," 97.
48. Turner, *Orientalism, Postmodernism & Globalism*, 45.
49. Gramsci, *Prison Notebooks*, 323–333.
50. Turner, *Orientalism, Postmodernism & Globalism*, 37.
51. Said, *Orientalism*, 2.
52. Said, *Orientalism*, 3.
53. The geographical referent of the term "Orient" is historically and geographically contingent and changes depending upon the time period one is analyzing and from where the Orientalist discourse is emanating.
54. Lockman, *Contending Visions of the Middle East: The History and Politics of Orientalism*, 110.
55. The geographical construction "Southwest Asia" is used to refer to the region rather than the Middle East because the geographical region codified as the Middle East is an imperial construction that is closely associated with the genealogy of Orientalist discourse.
56. Lockman, *Contending Visions of the Middle East: The History and Politics of Orientalism*, 111.
57. Ibid., 141. For an elaborate discussion of Orientalism in the USA during the Cold War period and its influence on US foreign policy in the Middle East, see Chapter 4 in the text cited above.
58. Barnes & Farish, "Between Regions: Science, Militarism, and American Geography from World War to Cold War," 807.
59. See, Gramsci, *Prison Notebooks*, 3–14, for a more detailed discussion of the roles of intellectuals in civil society.
60. Al-Azmeh, *Islams and Modernities*, 167.
61. See, for example, Little, Douglas. (2002). *American Orientalism*. Chapel Hill and London: University of North Carolina Press., for an informed and detailed analysis of American foreign policy regarding the Middle East (Southwest Asia) from 1945 onward.
62. See, for example, Said, Edward. (1997). *Covering Islam*. New York: Vintage Book., for an illuminating analysis of how Western media and related experts construct, (re-)produce, and propagate Orientalist stereotypes of Islam.
63. Pruett, "Islam" and "Orientalism," 43.

64. Following the events of 11 September 2001, several prominent scholars who study the subject of terrorism have provided credence to Orientalist stereotypes of Islam by equating the religion of Islam with violence through arguing that acts of terrorism committed by people who self-identify as Muslim are a result of or are motivated by religion. See, for example, Israeli, Raphael. (2003). *Islamikaze: Manifestations of Islamic Martyrology*. London: Frank Cass; Juergensmeyer, Mark. (2001). "Terror in the Name of God." *Current History*, 357–361; Laqueur, Walter. (2004). *No End to War: Terrorism in the Twenty-First Century*. New York: continuum; Ruthven, Malise. (2002). *A Fury for God*. London: Granta Books; Stern, Jessica. (2003). *Terror in the Name of God*. New York: Harper Collins Publishers. The works of several of these authors are not insignificant with respect to their influence in the academy and beyond as various works of these authors are some of "the most commonly cited and authoritative 'religious' terrorism texts" as noted by Richard Jackson in, "Constructing Enemies: 'Islamic Terrorism' in Political and Academic Discourse," 398.
65. Jackson, "Constructing Enemies: 'Islamic Terrorism' in Political and Academic Discourse," 401.
66. Al-Azmeh, "The Articulation of Orientalism," 95.
67. Boroumand & Boroumand, "Terror, Islam, Democracy," 9.
68. Although I contend that the use of the term "Islamist" is problematic, this contention should not be confused with an absolute abrogation of some of the important research and analysis that has been conducted using the term Islamist as a particular analytical category. Some of this work has made significant contributions to developing a more robust understanding of this phenomenon not only through identifying the heterogeneity of the political movements operating in Southwest Asia, North Africa, and beyond but through elucidating both the complex and differing ideological orientation of these various movements and the confluence of conditions that make the emergence and sustainability of these movements and related subjectivities probable. See Ayubi, Nazih. (1991). *Political Islam*. Routledge: London and New York; Gerges, Fawaz. (1999). *America and Political Islam*. Cambridge University Press: United Kingdom; Ismail, Salwa. (2006). *Rethinking Islamist Politics*. I.B. Tauris: New York; and Ayoob, Mohammed. (2008). *The Many Faces of Political Islam*. The University of Michigan Press: Ann Arbor.
69. Tibi, "Post-Bipolar Order in Crisis: The Challenge of Politicised Islam," 847.
70. Ibid., 847.
71. Taylor & Jasparo, "Editorials and Geopolitical Explanations for 11 September," 220.

72. Bartolucci, "Analysing elite discourse on terrorism and its implications: the case of Morocco," 126.
73. According to Salwa Ismail, a significant proportion of contemporary analysis of Islamism counter-poses Western modernity and Islam, thereby reinforcing and reproducing the West/Islam dichotomy (1–4). See, for example, Shepard, William. (1987). "Islam and Ideology: Towards a Typology." *Journal of Middle East Studies*, 19: 307–336; and Dekmejian, R. Hrair. "Islamic Revival: Catalysts, Categories, and Consequences," in Hunter, Shireen. (Ed.). (1988). *The Politics of Islamic Revivalism*. Indiana University Press: Bloomington & Indianapolis, for a categorical analysis of Islamism that evaluates actor types using performance indicators prescribed through an understanding of a Western prime modernity.
74. Shklovsky, "Art as Technique," 268. As argued by the Russian Formalist Victor Shklovsky, the technique of defamiliarization is to cast anew that which is familiar and to unsettle that which has become habitualized. In the context of this argument, the technique of defamiliarization is deployed so that the "common sense" assumptions and associations which devour the contemporary manifestation of terrorism of the al-Qaeda type can be unsettled and fundamentally revised.
75. Shanahan, "Betraying a certain corruption of mind: how (and how not) to define 'terrorism'," 177.
76. Alnasseri, recorded in private conversation, 9 May 2011.
77. I use the term "unstable" to describe Alnasseri's treatment of his neologism "Islamitic" because as a new analytical tool it has yet to acquire institutional acceptance and support.
78. See, for example, Gunning, Jeroen & Jackson, Richard. (2011). "What's so 'religious' about 'religious terrorism'? *Critical Studies on Terrorism*, 4 (3): 369–388, for a deconstruction of the origins, assumptions, and arguments associated with the concept of "religious terrorism." See, also, the chapters "The Roots of Liberal Rage" and "The Myth of Radicalization" in Kundnani, Arun. (2014). *The Muslims are Coming: Islamophobia, Extremism, and the Domestic War on Terror*. London: Verso., for an analysis of the problematics associated with reducing particular forms of extremism to a religious/cultural moment.
79. In the context of this argument, I focus on the actors involved in Islamitic extremism.
80. Blair et al., "Poverty and Support for Militant Politics: Evidence from Pakistan," 9.
81. Ibid., 9.
82. Blair et al., "Poverty and Support for Militant Politics: Evidence from Pakistan," 22.

83. Discussion of jihad and motivations of the group recorded through a wiretap intercept on 03/03/06, Tab 37, between various members and associates of the group. Author's own notes.
84. Benmelech & Berrebi, "Human Capital and the Productivity of Suicide Bombers," 224.
85. Miniter, *Mastermind: The Many Faces of the 9/11 Architect, Khalid Shaikh Mohammed*, 126.
86. Teotonio, http://www3.thestar.com/static/toronto18/index.html. Last accessed on 16 June 2011.
87. For an excellent analysis of the influence of Abd al-Wahhab, Abu al-A'la al-Mawdudi, and Sayyid Qutb on contemporary Islamitic movements, including those of the al-Qaeda type, see chapters 3 and 4 in Abou El Fadl, Khaled. (2005). *The Great Theft: Wrestling Islam for the Extremists*. New York: HarperOne. Moreover, for a comprehensive matrix and subsequent analysis of the most cited ideologues and concomitant texts of "militant" groups, see William McCants et al. (2006). *Militant Ideology Atlas*. Counter Terrorism Centre, US West Point Military Academy: New York. In the case of the Toronto 18, various documents/recordings authored by Abu Muhammad 'Asim Al-Maqdisi, 'Abdul-Qadir Ibn 'Abdul-'Aziz, and Anwar al-Awlaki were seized and ultimately presented as evidence against the accused throughout the various trials.
88. About El Fadl, *The Great Theft: Wrestling Islam from the Extremists*, 108.
89. About El Fadl, *The Great Theft: Wrestling Islam from the Extremists*, 108.
90. Althusser, *On Ideology*, 17.
91. Gramsci, *Prison Notebooks*, 238–239.
92. Ayoob, *The Many Faces of Political Islam*, 17. For example, Ayoob cites the following contemporary Islamitic political formations that operate constitutionally: Muslim Brotherhood (Egypt), Jamaat-i-Islami and Jamiat-ul-Ulema-i-Islam (Pakistan), Nahdlatul Ulama (Indonesia), and the Parti Islam se-Malaysia (Malaysia) (17). This statement is brought into force when one considers the political, social, and economic reforms that have been transpiring across Southwest Asia and North Africa, which has been popularly called the "Arab Spring." Contrary to the fears of Western countries, which have resulted in the active prevention of political, social, and economic reform in these regions for the last half century, the reforms are being pursued through peaceful and democratic principles. Moreover, the reforms were initiated by secular groups and not "religious" extremists active in these regions.
93. Jackson, "Constructing Enemies: 'Islamic Terrorism' in Political and Academic Discourse," 415.
94. Mitchell, *The Society of the Muslim Brothers*, 169.
95. Ibid., 164.

96. Ibid., 170.
97. Mitchell, *The Society of Muslim Brothers*, 176.
98. See, for example, the following addresses by Osama bin Laden: "To the Americans," "To the Allies of America," and "To the Peoples of Europe," in Lawrence, Bruce. (Ed.). (2005). *Messages to the World: The Statements of Osama bin Laden*. Verso: London. In these addresses, Osama bin Laden clearly articulates the political motivations for his operations and how these operations are explicitly linked to the foreign policy of Western governments in various parts of the world.
99. R v SA. "Comments to the Court Before Sentencing." Court File No. CR-O7–2025. Although this individual cannot be taken as emblematic of all Islamitic Domestic Extremist actors and/or groups, this actor's candid remarks should reveal the problematic assumptions in dominant discourse that seek to link these actors and/or groups not to concrete political motivations but to religious motivations that transcend material political conditions.
100. Burke, *Al Qaeda: The True Story of Radical Islam*, 6.
101. For an analysis of the history of the discourse of terrorism and terrorism expertise, see Stampnitzky, Lisa. (2013). *Disciplining Terror: How Experts Invented "Terrorism."* Cambridge: Cambridge University Press.

CHAPTER 2

Displacement and Condensation: The Internalization of the *Clash* and the Construction of the *Homo Terrorismus*

As Yi Fu Tuan states in his phenomenological study of fear, "Many people in the modern and affluent Western world are haunted by fear."[1] Although this fear manifests in a multitude of different forms and at different scales, a sacerdotal fear emerges within specific temporal and spatial conjunctures that diffuses through and transfixes the national imagination.[2] However, this sacerdotal fear is not permanent and is not linked to "invariant segments of tangible reality"[3] that are atemporal in their expression. Rather, sacerdotal fear changes over time and space and is contingent upon political moments both external and internal to a given nation-state. For instance, during World War II the sacerdotal fear for many Western nation-states was Fascism/Nazism. Subsequent to World War II, the sacerdotal fear was characterized by Communism. The effect of this fear is that particular types of political/social/cultural differences become objects of abjection because of the perceived threat these differences pose to the identity, system, and order of the national body. Consequently, particular social groupings both external and internal to the nation-state that are associated with these differences become an abject Other who is the subject of not only national contempt and derision but political and social exclusion, division, and violence.

In the contemporary North American and Western European context, the sacerdotal fear and its attendant abject Other is characterized by the threat of Islam in general and the threat of Transnational/Domestic Islamitic Extremism in particular. This fear and abjection finds its most demonstrable expression in the resurgent ethnocentric and xenophobic

© The Author(s) 2016
J. Kowalski, *Domestic Extremism and the Case of the Toronto 18*,
DOI 10.1057/978-1-349-94960-1_2

right-wing nationalism that has been gaining momentum and increasing populist support across Western Europe since 11 September 2001. In countries as diverse as Austria, Belgium, Denmark, Finland, France, Germany, Netherlands, Norway, Sweden, Switzerland, and the UK, political, elite, and popular discourse vis-à-vis immigration, multiculturalism, and security has, to varying degrees, become Islamophobic in tone, quality, and substance. The effects of this can be seen in the banning of the building of minarets on mosques in Switzerland (November 2009); the banning of the niqab in public spaces in Belgium and France (April 2011); and the imbrications of far-right anti-immigration political party rhetoric (e.g. Austrian Party for Freedom (FPO), the Swiss People's Party (SVP), the Dutch Party for Freedom (PVV), the British National Party (BNP), and the French National Front (FN)) in the political mainstream as evidenced by the declarations of German Chancellor Merkel (October 2010), British Prime Minister Cameron (February 2011), and French President Sarkozy (February 2011) about the failure of multiculturalism with respect to their Muslim populations. Perhaps the most abhorrent effect of this anti-Muslim posturing is found in the actions and words of Anders Behring Breivik, the right-wing extremist who on 22 July 2011 detonated an explosive device in Oslo, Norway, and then proceeded to murder approximately 90 people on nearby Utoya Island using semi-automatic weapons. In a 1500-page manifesto released prior to these violent activities, he outlined the motivations for his actions: "Around year 2000 I realized that the democratic struggle against the Islamisation of Europe, European multiculturalism was lost. ... It would now only take 50–70 years before we, the Europeans are in a minority. As soon as I realized this I decided to explore alternative forms of opposition."[4] Although the fear and abjection of Muslim communities is most pronounced in Western Europe, as alluded to above, this fear and abjection is not the sole preserve of Western Europe. Indeed, anti-Muslim attitudes in elite and popular opinion are also evident in both Canada (my focus) and the USA.

As Haroon Siddiqui observes, "Canada has not been immune from post-9/11 Islamophobia and the politics of fear."[5] In his analysis, some of the examples of anti-Muslim bigotry in the Canadian context are demonstrated through several public policy debates and decisions that have received prominent attention since 11 September 2001. Some of the examples Siddiqui cites include, as he describes: "the highly charged and falsely labeled sharia controversy in Ontario in 2005–06; the Harper government's crude attempts in 2007 at banning niqabi women from voting; the 2007–08 reasonable accommodation debate in Quebec which was anything but; [and] the disbarring of hijabi girls from sundry soccer, tae kwon do, and judo competitions."[6] Certainly other examples of anti-Muslim attitudes include but are not limited to the following:

- The recent protests in Toronto against the Toronto District School Board (TDSB) for providing space to Muslim students to pray, at which time protesters held placards that warned of "creeping jihad" and read "Islam must be reformed or banned" while chanting, "No Islam in our schools," "No Mohammed in our schools," and "No Sharia law in our country"[7]
- The hypocrisy of the Canadian government in allowing the Dutch politician Geert Wilders to enter Canada in May 2011 and promulgate his anti-Muslim vitriol—which is encapsulated in the following quotation: "Our Western culture is far superior to Islamic culture. And only once we are convinced of this will we be able to defend our civilization"[8]—while the Canadian government banned British parliamentarian George Galloway from speaking in Canada because of his sympathies for the Palestinian people and criticism of the war in Afghanistan
- The canceling of an address by the President of the Canadian Islamic Congress (CIC), Imam Zijad Delic, at the Canadian National Defence Headquarters in Ottawa in October 2010 by the Canadian government after claims that the CIC espouses an extremist ideology
- The targeting of mosques in cities, such as Montreal, Kitchener-Waterloo, Toronto, and Port Coquitlam, British Columbia, by vandals expressing anti-Muslim prejudices.

Cumulatively, these examples, which are by no means exhaustive, illuminate the contours of an anti-Muslim ideology that is not only shaping state policy but is influencing and animating the divisive behavior and attitudes of various segments of Canadian society. However, an anti-Muslim ideology or "anti-Muslimism,"[9] as Halliday refers to it, and the fear and abjection it engenders does not emerge in a temporal and spatial vacuum.

According to Halliday, "unless we argue for the existence of transhistorical ideological formations, Jungian archetypes or Blochian *mentalites* which determine our behavior, the appeal to history is unilluminating. While […] history certainly provides a reserve of ideological themes upon which to draw, the question of why and how a certain rhetoric emerged when it did still has to be asked."[10] As Halliday goes on to state, "this search for contingent causes suggests that even in the present historical period there may be no single reason for the re-emergence of anti-Muslimism. The rhetoric of one country may well influence another, [...] but while there may be elements of common determination, it may also be the case that in each particular instance rhetoric originates from different causes and serves different purposes."[11] In effect, the emergence of an anti-Muslim ideology in particular national spaces and/or regions is geographically sensitive and not universal in its expression. Similarly, the conditions that make the emergence of an anti-Muslim ideological formation possible are equally as varied. Therefore, if one is to develop an understanding of the causes of anti-Muslimism and Islamophobia, one needs to consider the context in which it is gestated.

What caused the emergence of anti-Muslimism in Canada and/or Toronto? What are the socio-ideological effects of this anti-Muslimism? What behaviors and/or activities does anti-Muslimism make possible? In an effort to answer these questions, this chapter argues that the following external and internal moments: the end of the Cold War, immigration trends in the 1990s, the tragic spectacle of 11 September 2001, and the ensuing War in Afghanistan resulted in the construction of a *homo terrorismus*, an internal enemy against which Canadian "society must be defended."[12] Furthermore, this chapter argues that as a consequence of this construction, the conditions for the emergence of subversive ideological and discursive formations were made possible.

THE POST-COLD WAR POLITICAL LANDSCAPE

Following the collapse of the Berlin Wall in November 1989 and the formal dissolution of the Soviet Union in December 1991, the ideologically bifurcated world system of Capitalism/Communism that actively shaped the global geopolitical order since the end of World War II came to a conclusion. With the absence of the communist threat to both orient and justify the geopolitical and geostrategic policy preoccupations and related maneuverings of the USA and by extension its allies, the governments of many Western countries were confronted with a Gramscian "crisis of authority"[13]—a crisis that was precipitated by the perceived political, economic, and social instability that would arise as a result of a rupture in the ideological commitments of the state to security.

If the primary obligation of governments is to secure and defend their respective nations against real or imagined threats, the demise of the Cold War and the internationalization of the state invariably called into question its legitimacy vis-à-vis the enormous public resources, sacrifices, and consent commanded, indeed demanded, by the state to fulfill its principal obligation. Consequently, in the context of the USA, rather than seizing the opportunity to ideologically reorient itself away from a political, economic, and social order that was predicated on the threat of war and the accompanying national security imperative, the USA sought to reassert its authority and legitimacy through redefining its conflict paradigm. The necessity was "[...] to ensure that the domestic population remains largely inert, limited in the capacity to develop independent modes of thought and press effectively for alternative policies—even alternative institutional arrangements—that might well be seen as preferable if the framework of ideology were to be challenged."[14] To achieve this redefinition, elements of the US government, i.e. the State Department and Department of Defense, relied upon its elite ideological state apparatuses and its approved "ideology managers"[15] for assistance and received the help of state intellectuals, Francis Fukuyama and Samuel Huntington.

Both Fukuyama and Huntington introduced two paradigms for interpreting the sources of conflict in the post-Cold War era: the *end of history* (Fukuyama) and the *clash of civilizations* (Huntington). As Shireen Hunter observes, "the ideologization of international politics and the paradigmatic methodology of studying it bear most responsibility for advancing two paradigmatic theories—the end of history and the clash of civilizations—to replace the East-West conflict as the principal determinant of the character of international relations in the post-Soviet era."[16] For Fukuyama, the end of the Cold War solidified the ideological triumphalism of liberal democracy and the defeat of authoritarian and totalitarian ideologies and related modes of governance. The significance of this, as he outlines, is that "liberal democracy may constitute the 'end point of mankind's ideological evolution' and the 'final form of human government,' and as such 'constituted the end of history.'"[17] In effect, according to Fukuyama, the war of competing ideas and the struggle for the supremacy of those ideas that shaped the arc of human history had been eliminated as the superiority of Western liberal democratic principles had reached its universalist ascendancy. Therefore, whereas past conflicts were precipitated by ideological antagonisms and cleavages, future conflicts, to varying degrees, would emerge from other nation-states and/or internal minority groups struggling to adapt and conform to these principles of governance. For example, one minority group of particular concern for Fukuyama is the Muslim minority living in liberal democratic societies. As Fukuyama states, "the bigger problem for the future of liberal democracies will be the one internal to democratic societies, particular on the part of countries like France or Holland that have large Muslim minorities."[18] Fukuyama goes on to argue that "Europe by and large has been less successful in integrating culturally distinct minorities than the United States, and growing violence on the part of second- and third-generation European Muslims points to a far darker side of identity politics than the demands made by, for example, Quebec or Scottish nationalists."[19] Indeed, as he explains, this violence and the dark side of identity politics that it reveals are a result of the tensions generated by the convergence of "traditional cultural identities" and a modernization process characterized by a "pluralistic democratic order."[20] Although both Fukuyama's *end of history* and Huntington's *clash* paradigms are connected vis-à-vis the crisis of authority precipitated by the end of the Cold War and both perpetuate ideas of internal unpredictability, instability, and disorder, Huntington's paradigm resonated with the political elite and Cold War mandarins in the USA as this paradigm more closely supported not only the external geostrategic interests but also those of an internal nature for the USA. As a result, rather than the end of the Cold War signifying "the end of history," the end of the Cold War witnessed the continuation of history—a continuation of history that is encapsulated by the much more bellicose and pugnacious *clash of civilizations* paradigm.

In an article published for *The Atlantic* in September 1990 entitled "The Roots of Muslim Rage," Bernard Lewis, after describing the origins of Muslim resentment and hostility toward the West in general and the USA in particular, opined: "It should by now be clear that we are facing a mood and a movement far transcending the level of issues and policies and the governments that pursue them. This is no less than a clash of civilizations—the perhaps irrational but surely historic reaction of an ancient rival against our Judeo-Christian heritage, our secular present, and the worldwide expansion of both."[21] Subsequent to the publication of this article and the West/Islam dichotomy it portended, Huntington advanced Lewis' dichotomous and divisive worldview in an article entitled "The Clash of Civilizations?" which was published in 1993 in the journal *Foreign Affairs*. Shortly thereafter, Huntington elaborated or, as Edward Said remarked in a lecture delivered at the University of Massachusetts at

Amherst in 1996, "some would say bloated,"[22] his argument into a book entitled, *The Clash of Civilizations and the Remaking of World Order*. Although Huntington's argument has been widely criticized,[23] Richard Bonney states that "Whatever the strengths or weaknesses of Huntington's analysis, it has been claimed that no thesis has had a comparable influence on Western, especially American, strategic thinking since the end of the Cold War."[24] One partial explanation for the currency afforded to Huntington's ideas can be found in his long history as a well-established and high-ranking figure of intellectual statecraft. As Julie-Anne Davies explains:

> [...] Huntington is deeply, intricately and inextricably interlinked to a complex array of political actors and organizations. Huntington has been a US establishment figure since the days of the Kennedy administration and served on the US National Security Council. He was an advisor to Lyndon Johnson and, in 1968, defended the heavy bombardment of South Vietnam to drive the peasants out of the countryside and into the cities. More recently, his department, and position at Harvard has received funding from right-wing organizations linked to, among others, the Neoconservative Project for a New American Century (PNAC).[25]

Certainly, the influence of Huntington as an "establishment figure" and his *clash* thesis became readily apparent following the events of 11 September 2001 (a point that is returned to below). However, why did Huntington's thesis become so influential and appealing? And, what are the consequences of his argument? The answer to both of these questions lies precisely in the nascent antagonisms and the existential threats his paradigm constructs.

According to Huntington, conflict in the post-Cold War era would result not from ideological, political, or economic difference but from something much more elemental to various societies: culture. As he states,

> In the post-Cold War world, the most important distinctions among peoples are not ideological, political, or economic. They are cultural. Peoples and nations are attempting to answer the most basic question humans can face: Who are we? And they are answering that question in the traditional way human beings have answered it, by reference to the things that mean most to them. People define themselves in terms of ancestry, religion, language, history, values, customs, and institutions. They identify with cultural groups: tribes, ethnic groups, religious communities, nations, and, at the

broadest level, civilizations. People use politics not just to advance their interests but also to define their identity. We know who we are only when we know who we are not and often only when we know whom we are against.[26]

Furthermore, for Huntington, it is obvious that cultural/civilizational divisions will emerge as the primary source of conflict as the contempt for otherness is endemic and natural to the human condition:

> It is human to hate. For self-definition and motivation people need enemies: competitors in business, rivals in achievement, opponents in politics. They distrust and see as threats those who are different and have the capability to harm them. The resolution of one conflict and the disappearance of one enemy generate personal, social and political forces that give rise to new ones. "The 'us' versus 'them' tendency is," as Ali Mazrui said, "in the political arena, almost universal." In the contemporary world the "them" is more and more likely to be people from a different civilization.[27]

Therefore, in adhering to this logic, Huntington conceptualizes other cultures/civilizations in the following hierarchy of spatial scales: "In a world where culture counts, the platoons are tribes and ethnic groups, the regiments are nations, and the armies are civilizations."[28] The significance of this is that in conceptualizing other cultures/civilizations in spatio-militaristic terms, Huntington reinforces the impression that all intercultural encounters and interactions will result in rivalry, confrontation, and/or violent conflict. Consequently, he renders the eight monolithic cultural/civilizational entities he identifies—Western, Latin American, African, Islamic, Sinic, Hindu, Orthodox, and Japanese—as inherently incommensurate and incompatible, which, for him, makes conflict between some of these civilizations in the post-Cold War period highly probable. Although Huntington believes that a global intercivilizational war is improbable, he argues that the most likely source of intercivilizational conflict will emerge between Muslims and non-Muslims.[29] As a result of this conviction, he devotes a considerable amount of effort constructing a West/Islam dichotomy in his text.

The contemporary West/Islam dichotomy that Huntington constructs is predicated on his assertion that the historical encounter between Islam and Christianity (the West) has been defined by opposing interests and conflict. As he states, "Some Westerners, including Bill Clinton, have argued that the West does not have problems with Islam, but only with violent Islamist extremists. Fourteen hundred years of history demonstrate otherwise."[30]

In effect, in reference to the historical relationship between Islam and Christianity (the West), he declares that "each has been the other's Other."[31] For Huntington, this perceived historical reality will continue to define and characterize any and all future West/Islam intercivilizational interactions and/or encounters. In fact, as Huntington goes on to argue, the animosities between the West and Islam will only intensify because of five factors that are exacerbating the tensions between the Western and the Islamic civilization:

> First, Muslim population growth has generated large numbers of unemployed and disaffected young people who become recruits to Islamist causes, exert pressure on neighboring societies, and migrate to the West. Second, the Islamic Resurgence has given Muslims renewed confidence in the distinctive character and worth of their civilization and values compared with that of the West. Third, the West's simultaneous efforts to universalize its values and institutions, to maintain its military and economic superiority, and to intervene in conflicts in the Muslim world generate intense resentment among Muslims. Fourth, the collapse of communism removed a common enemy of the West and Islam and left each the major perceived threat to the other. Fifth, the increasing contact between and intermingling of Muslims and Westerners stimulate in each a sense of their own identity and how it differs from that of the other.[32]

As a result of these factors among others, Huntington arrives at the conclusion that "the underlying problem for the West is not Islamic fundamentalism. It is Islam, a different civilization whose people are convinced of the superiority of their culture and are obsessed with the inferiority of their power."[33] And it is precisely because of this superiority-inferiority complex, operating in conjunction with the factors outlined above, that makes the Islamic civilization's proclivity for violence against others, especially Western civilization, possible. For, as Huntington declares, "Islam's borders *are* bloody, and so are its innards."[34] Therefore, in light of the ostensible cultural pathologies of the Islamic civilization, which invariably manifest in and through violence, violent conflagrations between the West and the entirety of Islam are inevitable.

The appeal of Huntington's construction of Islam as a threat to, and by extension enemy of, the USA and more broadly Western civilization to the high priests of Western geopolitical policy and opinion is succinctly summarized by Edward Said: Huntington essentially provides a manual for "maintaining a wartime status in the mind of Americans and others" which directly benefits "Pentagon planners and defense industry executives who may have temporarily lost their occupations after the end of the cold war but have now discovered a new vocation for themselves."[35] However, as Mohammad Nafissi argues, "though China and the so-called 'Sinic civilization' may pose the greatest challenge to Western hegemony in the longer term, the clash thesis 'would not have achieved its tremendous resonance without the spectre of a perceived Islamic threat.'"[36] Although it is apparent, as Said suggests above, as to why constructing a threat and enemy is appealing to particular state apparatuses/actors and their concomitant industrial beneficiaries, what is not immediately apparent is the appeal of specifically constructing Islam as the salient threat to the USA and Western civilization. So, why is constructing Islam as the primary threat and enemy so appealing? To answer this question, one must first establish an understanding of Samuel Huntington's role as a state intellectual.

As a state intellectual, Samuel Huntington, arguably, reveals his role in a statement he made in 1981: "you may have to sell [intervention or other military action] in such a way as to create the misimpression that it is the Soviet Union that you are fighting."[37] However, the antecedents of this statement can be traced back to two of his earlier works: *Political Order in Changing Societies* (1968) and the co-authored *Crisis of Democracy* (1975). In both of these texts, Huntington advances a similar argument: that expanding political consciousness and uncontrolled political participation creates conditions of domestic instability and disorder; therefore, the threat to advanced Western democracies, like the USA, is democracy itself. As such, political participation needs to be limited so that democracy can function properly.[38] To achieve this objective requires that the domestic population be lulled into quietude and passivity, which can be most readily achieved through the inculcation of fear and threat in the body politic. Hence, the importance of creating misimpressions as outlined by Huntington in his statement quoted above. In effect, as Huntington discloses both in his earlier writings and in the statement above, the role of the state intellectual, including his own, is to perpetuate state power and unquestioned governability. Indeed, 15 years after making his original statement, Huntington's post-Cold War *clash* thesis appears to be repeating this role through creating the misimpression that it is Islam that the USA and the Western world are fighting. However, to successfully create this misimpression, which requires that it ultimately resonate with the mass populace, the construction of Islam, like that of the Soviet Union, as the enemy Other must be credible, justifiable, and convincing. And therein is the appeal of specifically constructing Islam as the enemy Other: Huntington and his supporters can adroitly build upon familiar historical and geopolitical narratives that the body politic has already synthesized and, in many regards, accepted as a form of Gramscian "common sense."

The historical narrative that Huntington builds upon is the seemingly irrepressible and perpetual divergences that have punctuated West (Christian)/Islam relations ever since these abstracted entities first made contact. As Shireen Hunter observes,

> for more than a thousand years, Islam was the main enemy, the hostile "other," of the West. This well established cultural memory makes it no surprise that any challenge from the Muslim world conjures up barely forgotten images of enemies at the gate and reawakens fears of a repetition. With its burden of history, Islam is the ideal candidate for the new enemy figure that will fill the gap created by the fall of Communism.[39]

However, whether or not this well-established cultural memory is accurate is immaterial, as its durability is sustained by a complex interplay of formal, practical, and popular discourses that validate particular Orientalized geographical imaginings and enemy Others.[40] As a result of this "well-established cultural memory" and the "burden of history," Huntington's construction of Islam in the post-Cold War period as the enemy Other is relieved of the necessity of providing any robust burden of proof as the myopic historical narrative of divergences he revitalizes has become so naturalized as to be tacitly accepted as a commonsensical truism for explaining present and future West/Islam encounters.

The geopolitical narrative that Huntington builds upon is the supposed threat of "international terrorism"[41] that became a centerpiece of Ronald Reagan foreign policy doctrine in the 1980s. During this period, as Noam Chomsky explains, "the United States sought to concoct an enemy weak enough to be attacked with impunity but sufficiently threatening to mobilize the general population in support of the Reaganite expansion of state power at home and violence abroad."[42] However, the conundrum that the Reagan administration was forced to confront was how to frighten the domestic population into acquiescing to the policy prescriptions of the state while avoiding direct conflagrations with the Soviet Union. The solution to this problematic was found in devising a new formula for identifying and detecting threat: the targeting of Kremlin-supported international terrorist groups.[43]

To inaugurate the threat of international terrorism to the USA and Western civilization as a whole, Ronald Reagan characterized these groups using the following terms: "the evil scourge of terrorism," which is "a plague spread by 'the depraved opponents of civilization itself'" and is the embodiment of "'a return to barbarism in the modern age.'"[44] Although the evil, depraved, and barbaric groups to which Reagan referred encompassed a variety of entities that shared a similar "revolutionary ethos,"[45] e.g. German Red Army Faction, Italian Red Brigades, ETA, Provisional IRA, Shining Path, Hezbollah, and the PLO, as the 1980s progressed, the connotative quality of those associated with the international terrorism codification began to assume a much stronger denotative correlate in authorized formal, practical, and popular narratives on the phenomenon of international terrorism: religious groups operating in the Southwest Asian and/or the Mediterranean region. For instance, "by 1985, terrorism in the Middle East/Mediterranean region was selected as the top story of the year in an Associated Press poll of editors and broadcasters, and concern reached fever pitch in subsequent months."[46] This shift in the correlation of international terrorism from Kremlin-supported entities to religiously motivated groups based in Southwest Asia and/or the Mediterranean region was precipitated by a change in the geopolitical conditions that made the focus on Kremlin-supported entities possible. As David Rapoport explains, the revolutionary incarnation of international terrorism began receding in the 1980s as these respective entities were systematically eradicated in their various spaces of operation. For example, the Israeli invasion of Lebanon in June 1982 eliminated PLO training facilities. Furthermore, as a result of enhanced counter-terrorism cooperation throughout the 1980s, these same entities began to dissolve or were rendered impotent as leaders were incarcerated and/or their various bases of support were eroded due to a lack of leadership, financial support, and so on. Consequently, with the entities that espoused a revolutionary ethos in decline, religious groups, purportedly inspired by the 1979 Islamic Revolution and the defeat of Russia in Afghanistan a decade later, were identified as the nascent threat to a Western-centric geopolitical order.[47] However, unlike revolutionary entities that had defined political objectives, these new religious groups were represented as signifying a departure from the norm. Although, as Mark Juergensmeyer states, this "new terrorism emerged in the 1980s from more traditional forms of political conflict in the Middle East," variants of "strident Muslim terrorism began to appear that were unrelated to the Palestinian or any other definable political cause."[48] In effect, these new Muslim groups were considered more dangerous and terrifying than previous entities as their very existence appeared bereft of any material strategic goals. Rather, these Muslim groups seemed to be motivated by a messianic vision of an eternal eschatological struggle between the righteous and the damned. As such, these spiritually fortified groups existed outside the order of Western enlightenment rationality and reason and sought to reorder the world with bombs of divine fervor. In short, "Muslim terrorism," as Juergensmeyer refers to it, became the embodiment of "the anti-order of the new world order of the twenty-first century."[49] However, the change in the geopolitical conditions that made the definitive shift in focus from Kremlin-supported international terrorism to religious (Islamic) terrorism possible was catalyzed by the collapse of the Berlin Wall and the end of the Cold War.

Following the end of the Cold War, the historical and geopolitical narratives, as discussed above, that helped to establish the preconditions for Huntington to plausibly construct Islam as the enemy Other were further reinforced by the first Gulf War in 1991. For instance, Huntington argued that the first Gulf War represented the culmination of conflict between Arabs/Muslims and the West. According to him, this culmination point was evidenced by the universal support of Iraq by Islamic fundamentalist movements rather than the Western-supported countries of Kuwait and Saudi Arabia.[50] Certainly, the confluence of these long-running narratives and this particular moment would have enabled Huntington's introduction of his *clash* paradigm to be widely accepted by the body politic as a commonsensical explanation of future threat and conflict as this particular construction of Islam had achieved legitimacy not only by virtue of its established position in dominant discourse but also through contemporaneous conflicts that appeared to confirm a violent West/Islam confrontation and divide. If there was any question as to the legitimacy of Huntington's *clash* paradigm after its initial introduction, by the time Huntington released the book-length version in 1996, the violent West/Islam dichotomy that he envisioned would have become almost axiomatic as a result of the bombing of the World Trade Center in 1993 by transnational Islamitic extremist actors.

The transition from the Cold War to the post-Cold War period and the simultaneous construction of Islam as the enemy Other vis-à-vis the state and its various security and ideological apparatuses (of which Huntington was a prominent and notable figure) represents a significant and enduring geopolitical transmogrification that continues to haunt elements of

Western society to the present. This geopolitical transmogrification is accurately captured and elucidated by Sabah Alnasseri in the following observation:

> the prompt reactivation of Orientalist stereotypes and the construction of Islam/Islamism as a global enemy image at the end of the 1980s owe themselves to a bipolar structured world, whose negative pole (Communism) was itself over-determined in an Orientalist sense: Communism as an Asiatic, that is, Oriental despotism, which is always associated with China and Russia, and their 'vassal.' With the disappearance of Communism, its displaced essence re-emerged to the surface: a return of the ever threatening Oriental species in the form of overt or latent terrorists: Osama bin Laden/ Saddam Hussein and the Muslim migrant sleeper cell.[51]

As this observation explicates, the transition from the Cold War to the post-Cold War period, marked by the dissolution of Communism, and the immediacy of constructing Islam as the enemy Other, reveals, in effect, an Althusserian process of *displacement* and *condensation*,[52] whereby the metonymic fearful geopolitical imaginings of Communism are recondensed and are returned to their metaphoric origin: the fearful geopolitical imaginings of Islam/Islamism. The significance of this geopolitical transmogrification, the articulation of which is most clearly expressed by Huntington in his blueprint for a clash of civilizations, is that the relationship between global space and power was represented and reinscribed in such a way so that threats characterized by ideological/political impermanence (Communism) were replaced with threats characterized by cultural permanence (Islam/Islamism).

The implications of situating threat, in this case Islam/Islamism, within a framework of cultural permanence are threefold. First, geographic regions and/or nation spaces perceived to be primary (Southwest Asia, South Asia, and North Africa) or secondary primogenitors of Islam/ Islamism (Central Asia, Southeast Asia) become objects of a Western securitized gaze and concomitant geographical imaginary that gives a fixity to these regions and/or spaces as sources of an unalterable, unpredictable, unstable, and dangerous Otherness that Western civilization must be guarded against with eternal vigilance. Second, the collective body of minority groups from these spaces becomes a site of inscription of an imposed identity and subjectivity that is composed of the negative projections that emanate from this particular geographical imaginary. As a result, not only is the identity and subjectivity of these minority groups always determined from without rather than from within, but these minority groups are effectively forced to occupy a proscribed geopolitical subject position that is inextricably linked with or sympathetic to this threatening outside. Therefore, these minority groups become internally externalized as an enemy Other—a fifth column—because of their perceived rootedness in, and allegiance to, another place. Third, and most notably, the characterization of threat as being culturally fixed produces an eternal enemy Other: as long as Islam as a cultural system exists, the threat inherent to that cultural system will persist. Indeed, a concretized symptom of the process of condensation referred to above and its related implications is revealed by and made manifest in works like Huntington's *clash of civilizations*.

Although Huntington's *clash* paradigm is a symptom of this process of condensation and not its cause, the enduring consequences of his work are no less significant. Firstly, the clash that Huntington envisages reifies, revitalizes, and reinforces a West/Islam, Dominant/Other, We/They, and Us/Them dichotomous worldview that is predicated on an ontological distinction that not only reconstitutes and reasserts primordialist and essentialist identities and subjectivities but actually produces the enemy Other he discusses. Secondly, Huntington's clash paradigm provides the foundation for an obsessive, exclusionary, and violent identity politics that has become a meta-narrative in dominant discourse vis-à-vis Western external and internal encounters with Islam.[53] Lastly, following the events of 11 September 2001, the hermetically sealed identities and subjectivities Huntington constructs are used, at least conceptually, to frame, inform, and animate the West/Islam antagonisms that make particular forms of political mobilization probable, including Domestic Islamitic Extremism. The evidence of this is revealed in Canada in the case of the Toronto 18. As one of the adult actors explained during his testimony, prior to the events of 11 September 2001 discussions of a clash of civilizations occurred among many adult community members. However, following the events of 11 September 2001, he added that everybody engaged in clash of civilizations discussions.[54] In effect, Huntington's *clash* paradigm establishes a normative oppositional hermeneutic through which West/Islam conflict can be conceptualized, legitimated, and subsequently actualized. Although the enduring destructive capacity of Huntington's *clash of civilizations* did not immediately register following its introduction at the beginning of the post-Cold War period, the ideologically, politically, culturally, and socially poisonous mimetic qualities of his paradigm are becoming apparent in the post-11 September 2001 period as subtly evidenced by the comments made by one of the actors involved in the Toronto 18.

The significance of the post-Cold War moment and the crisis of authority it engendered is that it facilitated and helped to concretize Islam as the predominant and superlative threat to Western security and stability. Although Huntington's clash paradigm did not in itself cause Islam to be constructed as the enemy Other, his paradigm was a symptom of historical, political, and geographical processes and forces that he synthesized and used as a prescription for geopolitical actions to maintain political order both domestically and internationally. The divisive, exclusionary, and atavistic identities and subjectivities that he reconstitutes became conceptually foundational to the materialization of conflict between particular states and specific actors and/or groups.

Immigration Trends from Muslim Majority Countries

In order to properly assess the emergence of anti-Muslimism in Canada and Toronto, to determine its socio-ideological effects, and understand the potential social and political ramifications of this form of discrimination, it is necessary to discuss the presence of Muslim communities in the Canadian landscape. The most prominent display of Canada's diverse multicultural mosaic can be found in Canada's three so-called gateway cities: Toronto, Vancouver, and Montreal.[55] Although all of the gateway cities with relatively large Muslim populations would be fascinating to study as important communities within the urban fabric of these cities, for the purpose of my argument I focus on the Toronto Census Metropolitan Area (CMA). In the Toronto CMA, there are "more than 2 million immigrants drawn from every region of the world."[56] Moreover, approximately 44 % of the Toronto CMA's population is comprised of foreign-born residents.[57] In fact, the city of Toronto proudly advertises itself as one of the most diverse cities in the world. Although many immigrant communities have a defined presence in the physical and cultural landscape of Toronto's CMA, one community which has established a strong presence in the region since the 1990s is the highly variegated Muslim community of communities.[58]

According to Statistics Canada, the 2001 census revealed that 256,181 people self-identified as Muslim in the Toronto CMA, representing approximately 50 % of the 579,600 people who self-identified as Muslim across

Canada at that time. Of the 256,181 people who self-identified as Muslim, 56,360 categorized themselves as Canadian born and 199,821 as foreign born. Of the foreign-born Muslim population, 44, 273 immigrated to the Toronto CMA during the 1991–1995 period and a further 84,002 during the 1996–2001 period. Furthermore, the primary source regions of these foreign-born immigrants were South and West Asia, respectively.[59]

The vast majority of Canadians who self-identify as being of either South or West Asian origin live in the Toronto CMA. According to the information obtained in the 2001 census, over 500,000 people of South Asian origin and 90,000 people of West Asian origin reside in Toronto (combined, these two groups represented approximately 13 % of the total population of Toronto at the time of the census). Although Canadians of South and West Asian origin are religiously diverse (Sikh, Hindu, Muslim, Christian, Christian Orthodox, Protestant, and Catholic), 22 % of the South Asian population and 53 % of the West Asian population self-identified as being members of the Muslim faith group.[60] Furthermore, Canadians of both South and West Asian origin are relatively young when compared to the overall population. For instance, 40 % of the South Asian population and 41 % of the West Asian population were under the age of twenty-five in 2001, whereas 32 % of the overall Canadian population fell into this demographic category. In addition, Canadians of South and West Asian origins are considerably more likely than the rest of the Canadian population to have earned a university degree. For example, at the time of the 2001 census, 25 % of the South Asian population and 29 % of the West Asian population aged fifteen or older possessed either a BA or post-graduate degree, whereas 15 % of the overall Canadian adult population had achieved the same level of post-secondary education. However, despite the high level of educational achievement of the Canadian South and West Asian populations, these groups have lower incomes on average than the overall population. Moreover, these same populations are more likely to have an income that falls below Statistics Canada's low-income threshold than the overall population. For instance, approximately 23 % of the South Asian population and 40 % of the West Asian population earn incomes below the low-income threshold compared to 16 % of the overall Canadian population. Although Canadians of South and West Asian origin have experienced difficulty accessing the higher-wage sectors of the economy and, according to an Ethnic Diversity Study conducted in 2002, 35 % of South Asians and 27 % of West Asians reported experiencing discrimination or unfair treatment based on their ethnicity, race, religion, language, or accent, the vast majority of the South Asian (88 %) and West Asian (86 %) population reported feeling a strong sense of belonging in Canada.[61] Although this statistical data certainly denotes that there is a defined and growing South and West Asian, and by extension Muslim, presence in the Toronto CMA, one of the most salient and identifiable features of the Muslim presence in this area is revealed through the appearance and growing prevalence of mosques and/or masjids in the urban landscape.

Currently, there are approximately 122 mosques and/or masjids operating in the Toronto CMA. These 122 mosques and/or masjids appear in the following areas:

- (55) City of Toronto, including Etobicoke: East York, North York, and Gerrard Street
- (10) Durham Region: Ajax, Pickering, Oshawa, Whitby
- (6) Halton Region: Burlington, Oakville, Halton Hills, and Milton
- (15) York Region: Vaughan, Richmond Hill, Markham, and Newmarket
- (35) Peel Region: Brampton, Mississauga, and Caledon
- (30) Scarborough: includes Lawrence Avenue East[62]

These mosques and/or masjids serve a variety of Islamic denominations, which is indicative of the heterogeneity of the Muslim communities in the Toronto CMA: Shia, (including Jafari, Ismaili, and Bohra Ismaili), Sunni including Traditional (Shafi'i, Hanafi, Maliki, Hanbali) and Salafi (Wahhabi), non-denominational Muslims, and the Ahmadiyya Movement in Islam.[63] In addition to mosques and/or masjids serving as markers of the Muslim presence in the Toronto CMA, there are a multiplicity of ethnic restaurants, markets, and Islamic schools that have emerged that not only support the needs of various Muslim communities but have become a part of the urban fabric of the Toronto CMA and the everyday geographies of many of its inhabitants. Although the growing presence of Muslim diasporic communities is certainly most apparent and felt in the physical landscape of the Toronto CMA, the growing presence of these communities throughout the 1990s also finds expression in the popular imagination vis-à-vis popular and practical discourse as embodied by the corporate media and some state apparatuses.

It is clear that the presence of the subject of Islam in Canadian popular and practical discourse following the events of 11 September 2001 was, and remains, quite ubiquitous. However, prior to these events, as Muslim communities grew and their presence became more defined, the subject of Islam began to emerge in popular and practical discourse with greater frequency. For instance, in the *Toronto Star*, approximately 940 articles and/or opinion pieces and/or letters to the editor appeared between January 1990 and August 2001 regarding the subject of Islam in Toronto.[64] Is this discourse different than that which appeared after the events of 11 September 2001? More specifically, do the events of 11 September 2001 signal a discursive shift regarding the apprehension of Islam or a continuation and intensification of an established discourse?

Throughout the 1990s various acts of Islamitic extremism captured the attention of the North American popular imagination: the 1993 World Trade Center bombing; the 1995 bombing of the Alfred P. Murrah Federal Building in Oklahoma City, which was initially suspected of being perpetrated by an Islamitic extremist group[65]; the 1996 Khobar Towers bombing in Saudi Arabia; the 1998 US Embassy bombings in Tanzania and Kenya; the 1999 arrest of Ahmed Ressam (the "millennium bomber") for entering the USA from Canada with explosives destined for Los Angeles International Airport; and the 2000 bombing of the USS Cole in Yemen. The significance of these events is that the popular perception of the internal Muslim presence—informed by ideological apparatuses like the *Toronto Star*—is shaped and is ultimately determined by, in large measure, an experience of Islam that is almost always, at least discursively, mediated by violent externalities. In the context of Toronto, this experiential mediation is most notable when one takes account of the succession of articles and/or letters to the editor that appear throughout this period condemning the popular representations of Islam and/or Muslims. For example, in June 1990 a letter to the editor appeared entitled, "Don't Link Terrorists with Muslim Beliefs."[66] This same theme appeared in a letter to the editor in March 1992: "in this supposedly multicultural society, Islam is treated like a foreign faith, a faith of radicals and terrorists. Any chance to disparage Islam is leapt upon, while the positive contributions Muslims make are consistently ignored."[67] In another letter written in August 1992, the author asks, "Think about it: does it make sense that the entirety of Islam today can be reduced to a struggle between 'good' secularists and 'bad' fundamentalists?"[68] Similarly, this thematic current appeared in December 1993 in a letter entitled, "Pious Muslims are not violent or dangerous."[69] In January 1997 an analogue of this theme appeared in a letter entitled, "Muslim Fundamentalists not the same as terrorists."[70] In addition to the condemnation of the equation of Islam with violence, in the mid-1990s, many articles and/or letters to the editor began to appear that directly criticized the media for propagating and promulgating stereotypical representations of Islam. For example, in an article published in October 1996 entitled, "Muslims misunderstood, conference told stereotyped as terrorists, scholar says," one individual was quoted as stating: "People make a weapon of their pens. They write and say Muslims are terrorists and you see this everyday."[71] In May 1997, a letter appeared entitled, "Media make life difficult for Muslims."[72] In September 1998, an article described the conclusions of a study conducted by the Canadian Islamic Congress (CIC): "The Canadian media routinely discriminate against Muslims by identifying them with violence abroad, a six month study concludes."[73] According to this study, the *Toronto Star* was identified as the most prejudicial newspaper with respect to its reportage of issues related to Islam/Muslims.[74] Similarly, the experiential mediation of the internal Muslim presence through violent externalities as explicated by the *Toronto Star* also finds expression in practical discourse.

Shortly after the formal dissolution of the Soviet Union, a Strategic Analyst in the Analysis and Production Branch of the Canadian Security Intelligence Service (CSIS) issued a two-part commentary on what this individual entitled, "The Rising Tide of Islamic Fundamentalism." Although this individual acknowledges that the fear of this threat as espoused by Western media, governments, and security organizations is in many regards overstated and unjustified,[75] the threat of Islamic fundamentalism, as this individual suggests, is nonetheless widely publicized in the West: "the concept of a "fundamentalist international" has occasioned widespread attention and an appreciable degree of discomfort and fear in the West. In this post-Cold War era, some would even see it as having replaced communism as a major threat to world peace and security."[76] This threat from Islamic fundamentalism in the post-Cold War era is echoed in another document that appeared approximately two years later as part of the CSIS *commentary* series. This document, which is entitled "Terrorism: Motivations and Causes," written by the prominent state intellectual and terrorologist, Paul Wilkinson, outlines the regional manifestation of different types of terrorism with particular emphasis on the Middle East. As Wilkinson states, "the area of conflict which has generated the most significant and ruthless spillover of terrorist violence since 1968 is, of course, the Middle East."[77] Therefore, as Wilkinson suggests, this region poses and will continue to pose the single most dangerous terrorist threat to the international community and Western democracies. Wilkinson describes the threat in the following terms:

> In almost every Moslem country there are groups of extreme Islamic fundamentalists, inspired and actively encouraged by the Islamic revolutionary régime in Iran, ready to wage *Jihad* against pro-western Arab régimes, with the aim of setting up Islamic republics in their place. [...] However, the Islamic fundamentalist challenge is not directed solely at incumbent régimes in the Moslem world. Frequently they widen their range of targets to include westerners within their country. For example, the GIA in Algeria has deliberately targeted French citizens in Algeria since September 1993, because they allege that France is providing covert support and assistance to the Algerian military régime, and is historically responsible for the situation in Algeria. But, as the GIA's hijack of the Air France Airbus A300 on Christmas Eve 1994 demonstrates, the Islamic terrorist groups are also prepared to take their terrorist war to France itself. There is little doubt that the terrorists fully intended to crash the Airbus over Paris. France is, of course, not the only foreign target of such groups. All these groups are bitterly anti-American and hostile to all the Western countries.
>
> There is a further highly dangerous aspect to the threat of Islamic fundamentalist terrorism against Western targets. The findings of the FBI and the judiciary in America indicate that the group responsible for blowing up the World Trade Centre building in February 1993 was operating as a type of independent or freelance group of Islamic fundamentalists, inspired and encouraged by their spiritual mentor, Sheik Omar Abdel-Rahman, but not directly controlled by a state sponsor or other known major terrorist player. "Amateur" or "freelance" groups of this type pose a particularly difficult problem for the intelligence and police agencies, as they have no known political identity, no identifiable organizational and communications infrastructure and no previous track record. Moreover, as they are able to recruit fanatical members from the expatriate community, including those who have lived and worked in the host country for some time, the possibility exists of many such groups emerging spontaneously in western countries with substantial Moslem minority populations, such as the USA, Canada, France, Britain, Germany and Australia.[78]

Thematically, the threat of Islamic extremism is identified again in three CSIS reports that appeared at the end of the 1990s and at the beginning of the new millennium: "CSIS Report No. 2000/01: Trends in Terrorism," "CSIS Report No. 2000/04: International Terrorism: The Threat to Canada," and the annual public report mandated to be released by CSIS in 2000.[79] In all three of these reports, religious extremism of the Islamic variant is characterized as one of the most salient threats to Canadian national security. For example, as the 1999/2000 public report states: "while state-sponsored terrorism continues to pose a significant threat, one of the prime sources of terrorism today is Islamic extremism, as exemplified by Osama bin Laden." As the same report goes on to state, "terrorism in the years ahead is expected to become more violent, indiscriminate, and unpredictable than in recent years. [...] A hardening attitude and a willingness of certain terrorist organizations to directly support terrorist operations in North American reinforce the belief that Canadians, now more than ever, are potential victims and Canada a potential venue for terrorist attacks."[80] The significance of these successive reports is that *in totem* the presence of Islam in practical discourse exists as an external exigent threat against which the Canadian nation-state must be eternally vigilant.

The intertwined representation of Islam in both popular and practical discourse, as discussed above, mutually reinforces in the Canadian popular imagination an interpretation, understanding, and experience of Islam as threatening, potentially violent, and anti-Western in character. In effect, the representation of Islam in these terms is a continuation of a dominant historical narrative that in both style and substance (in)advertently reaffirms the antagonisms present in Huntington's *clash* paradigm. Therefore, as this analysis illuminates, prior to the events of 11 September 2001, the presence of Islam in Canadian popular and practical discourse was not substantively different than that which appeared after 11 September 2001. Rather, the discourse that emerged after 11 September 2001 was an intensification of, and not a departure from, previously existing constructions of Islam.

The Immediate and Enduring Impact of 11 September 2001

In an address delivered to a joint session of Congress and the American people 9 days after the tragic spectacle of 11 September 2001, President George W. Bush solemnly declared: "Americans have known surprise attacks, but never before on thousands of civilians. All of this was brought upon us in a single day, and night fell on a different world, a world where freedom itself is under attack."[81] However, does the 11 September 2001 moment really signify the emergence of a "different world" as Bush proclaimed? Arguably, the US response to the events of 11 September 2001 and its geopolitical maneuverings provide evidence to the contrary. As William Thornton states:

> Clearly, America is reverting to its Cold War habits, but without the restraint that Soviet competition imposed. This geopolitical recidivism prompts the Bush administration's renewal of aid to Indonesia's military, its antiterrorist accord of 1 August 2002 with the Association of Southeast Asian Nations, and its unabashed support for post-Soviet tyrants such as Turkmenistan's Saparmurat Niyazov, Uzbekistan's Islam Karimov, and Kazakhstan's Nursultan Nazarabyev. In short, Cold War anticommunism has been replaced by anti-terrorism, in what can be described as Cold War II.[82]

In effect, rather than the events of 11 September 2001 serving as a moment of divergence from the United States' previous ideological commitments, it served as a moment of reversion to, and a re-convergence of, its previous ideological commitments.

Prior to the events of 11 September 2001, the geopolitical religion of neoliberal globalism of which the USA was the high priest appeared to have eclipsed Huntington's *clash* paradigm as the defining ethos of international relations in the post-Cold War era. However, the destruction of the World Trade Center on the morning of 11 September 2001 symbolically served as a funeral pyre for this geopolitical religion. In effect, as the Twin Towers fell, the neoliberal globalism that the USA came to worship was instantaneously transmogrified from a geopolitical god into a geopolitical false idol. And in its place, the geopolitical gospel according to Huntington was quickly adopted and instituted as the state scripture for developing and guiding (inter)national security policies and practices.[83] As Mark Bassin explains,

> It is worth noting that this was not so self-evident even a few short years ago, when at the turn of the millennium it seemed that Huntington's grim vision of international relations in the twenty-first century might well fade as a relic of a peculiar sort of anti-euphoria stirred in some observers by the much-unanticipated collapse of the Cold War order. As Edward Said and others have pointed out, however, such expectations were aborted instantaneously, and it would now seem permanently by the attacks of 11 September. Huntington's primordialist view of civilizational essences and of the irrational but indelible antagonisms that set them apart has effectively become a discourse in their own right, which today sets the terms of debate even for those who are resolutely opposed to his message itself.[84]

Certainly, the register of Huntington's *clash* paradigm and the importation of his ideas were most acutely felt in the mainstream US media: "a cursory glance at the US media after September 11 leaves no doubt as to Huntington's triumph. The media framed the whole crisis within the context of Islam, of cultural conflicts, and of Western civilization threatened by the Other."[85] This framing of the crisis was given further impetus by Huntington himself in an interview he gave with the *New York Times*. According to Ervand Abrahamian, in response to the question of whether or not the events of 11 September were the realization of his predictions,

> he modestly replied that bin Laden had hastened the 'clash'; that he was not surprised the hijackers were educated since they were motivated by cultural hatreds; nor was he surprised by the violence since the bloodshed was intrinsically linked to Islam—in Kosovo, Bosnia, Chechnya, Kashmir, and the Caucasus; and that divisions within Islam strengthened rather than weakened his argument since internal competition made the Muslim world even more bellicose against the West.[86]

However, it is important to note that while Huntington's *clash* paradigm was being instrumentalized by the Bush administration to justify and legitimate its war *of* terror, Huntington himself began to recoil from several of the more bellicose positions he maintained in his *clash of civilizations* text. He believed conducting a global war on terrorism was not in the national interest of the USA. As Huntington states, "any global war on terrorism will not really be global at all because only the U.S. has declared such a war, while its allies are more concerned with their own local terrorists. Even the U.S. itself is not interested in fighting terrorism as such (everywhere, all groups globally), but only Muslim terrorists generally and al-Qaeda specifically."[87] Consequently, according to Huntington, the USA and its allies would not only potentially exacerbate and/or escalate tensions and conflict between the West and the Islamic world but would significantly diminish the capacity of the USA to strategically respond to other emergencies in its national interest due to operational overstretch.[88] Nevertheless, Huntington's *clash* paradigm arguably became the primary discursive and operational precept of the USA and the aligned Western states, such as Canada, that supported or continues to support the US-led war. The significance of this is twofold: First, the assimilation of the *clash* paradigm by the USA was a *reversion* to a Cold War geopolitical ethos that divided global space into blocks stylistically dissimilar to the First (friends),

Second (enemies), and Third World (proxy wars) distinctions of the Cold War but similar in substance and effect. Its articulation is best summarized by George W. Bush: "You are either with us or with the terrorists." Second, the instrumentalization of the *clash* paradigm, facilitated by the events of 11 September 2001, signifies a *convergence* of approximately 50 years of policies and practices that actively constructed Islam as an abject Other and existential threat. Although the implications of this geopolitical reversion and convergence were global in scale, the implications for Canada were significant.

According to Neil Smith, the attacks on 11 September 2001 were localized attacks that were transformed into attacks that registered at the national scale. As Smith states, "there was little that was automatically national in the scale of these local attacks. To be sure the targets were on US soil but it was the World Trade Center and the Pentagon that were targeted, not the Statue of Liberty, Disneyworld, or Hollywood, which are arguably much more resonant symbols of American national identity."[89] Nevertheless, as Smith observes, this event was promptly framed in national terms by the corporate media and by various representatives of the US government:

> Within little more than an hour of the first strike, CNN jumped scales, replacing headlines as "WTC attacked" or "Pentagon in Flames" with "America Under Attack." The *New York Times* later led with "U.S. Attacked" and President George W Bush began referring to a "new American Crusade" against terror. "Homeland Security" quickly followed. Perhaps the most astonishing response came from Newt Gingrich, ex history professor and previously leader of the House of Representatives, who on a September 13 television talk show advocated that the US should bomb all "these nations", thus demonstrating "the superiority of western civilization."[90]

Although this event was framed in national terms, the scale of the attack quickly exceeded the limit of the US nation-space and mimetically expanded internationally. In effect, the attack on the USA became an attack on its allies and by extension the idea of advanced Western modernity. Indeed, for many, including neo-conservative policymakers and practitioners and pro-US neoliberal capitalists both within the USA and beyond, this attack represented more broadly an attack on Western civilization as advanced by Huntington.

In the context of Canada, the mimetic transference of the attacks of 11 September 2001 and its framing and interpretation as a collective attack on Western civilization is certainly evident. As Sedef Arat-Koc states, "There has been a campaign to increasingly define Canadian identity along civilizational lines, as part of 'Western civilization' and in a 'clash of civilizations' framework."[91] Although, as Arat-Koc suggests, the success of this campaign to achieve hegemonic status is debatable, the mimesis of this mode of rationality and its transformative and enduring impact on the political and social machinations of the Canadian nation-state is no less real.[92] However, prior to identifying the material consequence of this campaign, it is necessary to explain some of the practical and ideological geopolitical processes and forces that catalyzed the mimetic transference of the events of 11 September 2001 and Huntington's *clash* paradigm to Canada.

Within hours of the attacks on the World Trade Center on 11 September 2001, the US government closed its airspace to all incoming international flights in an effort to begin to secure its nation-space. As a result, Canada agreed to allow flights destined for the USA to land at its various airports. In total, Canadian airports and related communities, such as Gander, Newfoundland, accommodated approximately 33,000 stranded passengers.[93] Similarly, under a directive from David Collenette, the Minister of Transportation, Canadian airspace was systematically closed in stages. On the ground, traffic at the border checkpoints along the 49th parallel were drastically delayed due to the heightened security screening of all border traffic.

Given Canada's significant trade dependence and by extension economic dependence on the USA, the enhanced securitization of the border by the USA was the primary focus and the predominant concern of the Canadian government. This concern was conveyed by John Manley, the Canadian Foreign Minister, in an interview on the Canadian Cable Public Affairs Channel (CPAC) in a retrospective program marking the 10-year anniversary of 11 September 2001. During this interview, Manley described his initial reactions to visually observing for the first time the scale of this devastation on television while at Pearson International Airport after returning to Canada from a G8 Summit in Frankfurt, Germany. As Manley recounted, his largest concern as Foreign Affairs Minister was the Canada/US border and the repercussions of this attack on Canadian economic interests.[94] Although symbolically the threat was, in this context, Transnational Islamitic Extremism, in real political and economic terms, the threat confronting Canada was the US establishment. As Desmond Morton similarly asserts, "Our danger wasn't Islamic fundamentalism but Washington."[95]

The danger Washington posed to Canada was a result of the national security imperative of the US government and its unilateral and isolationist predilections in matters of securing the *homeland*. Although, according to Houchang Hassan-Yari and Abdelkarim Ousman, "given the geographic proximity of Canada to the United States, as well as the defense agreements and military alliances that link the two countries, Canada is almost automatically involved in all anti-terrorist measures taken by the U.S[,]"[96] the credibility of Canada's involvement in and commitment to US anti-terrorist measures in the immediate aftermath of 11 September 2001 was subject to scrutiny. The US corporate media and various political actors speculated that several of the perpetrators had entered the USA via the Canadian nation-space.[97] This speculation and fear was partially fueled by the perceived inadequacies of the Canadian security apparatus because of several prior Islamitic extremist-related instances that (in)directly involved Canada. The first, and most notable instance, was the arrest of Ahmed Ressam, the so-called millennium bomber, at the US border in December 1999. The second was the June 1997 deportation from Canada to the USA of Hani Abdel Rahim al-Sayegh, a Saudi national who allegedly participated in the bombing of the Khobar Towers complex in Saudi Arabia that claimed the lives of nineteen American military personnel. The third was the arrest of Gazi Ibrahim Abu Mezer in August 1997 for plotting to detonate explosives on the New York subway system. Prior to his arrest, Abu Mezer was apprehended on three separate occasions for attempting to enter the USA from Canada. The fourth were the arrests of Ramzi Yousef, Sheik Omar Abdel Rahman, and Biblal Alkaisi in connection with World Trade Center bombing in February 1993. According to Howard Adelman, the significance of these particular arrests is that they mark the beginning of US interest in the security of the Canadian border as these individuals appeared to have utilized forged Canadian immigration documents in an attempt to enter the USA.[98] Therefore, to mitigate the hardening of the Canada-US border and to help minimize the danger Washington posed to Canada in economic terms, it was incumbent upon the Canadian government to assuage the fears of the USA by demonstrating that Canada was not soft on terror and was a willing participant in the war *of* terrorism. As a result of this practical geopolitical reasoning, Canada immediately maneuvered to replicate, integrate, and support the security discourses, policies, and practices of the USA.

In response to the war *of* terrorism, the Canadian government and other allied governments quickly aligned themselves with the USA. In October

2001, Canada launched *Operation Apollo* in Afghanistan as part of the American-led effort to eradicate al-Qaeda and remove the Taliban from power for providing al-Qaeda with provision of safe haven. (Ironically, approximately 15 years earlier, President Ronald Reagan stood on the White House lawn and described these subsequent enemies of civilization as: "the moral equivalents of our founding fathers.")[99] Domestically, the government of Canada initiated a variety of legislative amendments and/or created new legislation to supposedly enhance the anti-terrorism capabilities of various state apparatuses and to demonstrate to Washington Canada's commitment to the national security of both countries. For example, the government of Canada developed two new pieces of legislation, the *Anti-terrorism Act* (the Canadian equivalent of the US PATRIOT Act) and the *Public Safety Act*, and made amendments to, as Hassan-Yari and Ousman identify, the Explosives Act, Export and Import Permits Act, National Energy Board Act, Proceeds of Crime (Money Laundering) and Terrorist Financing Act, the Biological and Toxin Weapons Convention Implementation Act, the Criminal Code, the Official Secrets Act, the Canada Evidence Act, and the Access to Information Act.[100] In addition to those legislative changes, the Canadian government amended several pieces of immigration and refugee legislation in an effort to strengthen the entry and immigration system of Canada, including the Citizenship of Canada Act, the Immigration and Refugee Protection Act, and the Safe Third Country Agreement.[101] Furthermore, the Canadian government implemented the Canada-US Smart Border Declaration, which was designed to increase the security of the border by strengthening the bilateral cooperation of Canada and the USA in border surveillance and enforcement activities. Institutionally, the Canadian government reorganized elements of its security infrastructure to increase its anti-terrorism capabilities and competencies. The two most noticeable institutional changes were the creation of the Ministry of Public Safety and Emergency Preparedness (the Canadian equivalent to the American Department of Homeland Security) and the Canadian Border Services Agency. A less noticeable, but no less significant, institutional change came from refocusing the North American Aerospace Defense Command (NORAD). According to Joseph Inge and Eric Findley, whereas in the past NORAD primarily focused on the Soviet Union and other perceived external threats to North America, NORAD shifted its focus after 11 September 2001 to perceived internal threats, such as that engendered by Transnational Islamic Extremism.[102] As the refocusing of NORAD signifies, a corollary of the legislative and institutional changes that transpired in Canada following the 11 September 2001 attacks was not only the hardening of the Canadian nation-space to appease its economic masters in Washington but the enactment of a scopio-spatial shift where the externalized gaze of security became internalized. The effect of this shift was the systematic erasure of the outside/inside dyad; consequently, the international war *of* terror instantaneously became a domestic war *of* terror.[103] However, as indicated above, operating in conjunction with practical geopolitical processes and forces were important ideological geopolitical processes and forces that catalyzed the mimetic transference of the events of 11 September 2001 and Huntington's *clash* paradigm to Canada as well.

In an interview between the Canadian Broadcasting Corporation (CBC) journalist, Peter Mansbridge, and the Canadian Prime Minister, Stephen Harper, on the tenth year anniversary of the 11 September 2001 attacks, Harper was recorded as stating the following in response to a statement made by Mansbridge regarding Canada's withdrawal from Afghanistan and the attenuation of the threat to Canada from "al-Qaeda" and "domestic Islamicism":

> Yeah, well, we were a target any way. Look, al-Qaeda and people who represent…that's…you know, those types of organizations—it's not a single organization as you know—they hate people like us regardless. It doesn't matter whether we're in Afghanistan or not. You know, we're not being attacked because we were in Afghanistan. We're in Afghanistan because we were attacked on September the 11th.[104]

Separately, as Yves Engler notes, in a speech delivered at the 2011 Conservative convention, Harper is quoted as stating the following:

> "The real defining moments for the country and for the world are those big conflicts where everything is at stake and where you take a side and show that you can contribute to the right side." Asked whether we are in a great conflict or heading towards one Harper responded: "I think we always are."[105]

The significance of these statements is that they reveal two ideological geopolitical processes and forces: First, the rearticulation of Canada as a member of an abstract "West" characterized by particular values and beliefs unique to this part of the world, such as democracy, freedom, human dignity, tolerance, and equality. Second, that Canada is being repositioned as a "warrior nation"[106] that stands allied with the USA, the UK, and other imperial countries in a Manichean struggle to defend the light of Western civilization from the darkness of all Others. The corollary of these ideological geopolitical processes and forces is that Canada is being rescripted as a country where particular racial and religious characteristics become the basis of Canadian national identity and by extension the basis of democracy in the West.[107]

The cumulative effect of these practical and ideological geopolitical processes and forces is that the events of 11 September 2001 not only became a Canadian event but that the civilizational rationality used to frame and interpret this event in the USA became the rationality used to frame and interpret this event in Canada. As a consequence of this mimesis, minority groups identified within the Canadian nation-space as symbolically representative of civilizational Others were converted into what Neil Smith has referred to as a form of "social anthrax."[108] As Arat-Koc explains:

> In Canada—as well as in Australia, the United States, and many European countries—this new, reconfigured notion of the nation (based on a clash of civilizations perspective) in effect jettisoned those of Arab and Muslim background from their place in Western nations and "Western civilization," and made precarious the national belonging and political citizenship of many other Canadians of color.[109]

As a result, specific segments of the Canadian population, most notably Arabs and/or Muslims or those perceived to be Arabs and/or Muslims, were collectively constructed, marginalized, and targeted as suspicious and threatening Others against whom civilized society must be defended.

THE REEMERGENCE OF THE *HOMO ISLAMICUS*

In specific time-space conjunctures, different minority groups have become the object of state violence. However, as Arjun Appadurai explains, "it is difficult to know who might emerge as the targeted minority, the ill-fated stranger. In some cases it seems obvious, in others less so. And that is because minorities are not born but made, historically speaking."[110] Although there are a multitude of techniques through which minorities are made, the production of minorities as targets of state repression is contingent upon the ideological field and political climate within which these minority groups are functioning. As Appadurai goes on to state:

In short, it is through specific choices and strategies, often of state elites and political leaders, that particular groups, who have stayed invisible, are rendered visible as minorities against whom campaigns of calumny can be unleashed, leading to explosions of ethnocide. So, rather than saying that minorities produce violence, we could better say that violence, especially at the national level, requires minorities. And this production of minorities requires unearthing some histories and burying others. This process is what accounts for the complex ways in which global issues and clashes "implode" into nations and localities, often in the form of paroxysmal violence in the name of some majority.[111]

Although examples of the targeting of minorities as the objects of state repression can be found throughout the modern history of the nation-state, e.g. aboriginal populations throughout the Americas and the British Commonwealth, the Irish in the UK, the Jews in Germany, African Americans in the USA, Tamils in Sri Lanka, and the Kurds in Turkey, in the context of Canada, the targeting of minorities is no exception. In fact, the targeting of minorities by the Canadian state is deeply embedded in the political and social history and geography of this country. For instance, during World War I, Canadian citizens of Ukrainian descent were placed in internment/concentration camps;[112] moreover, during World War II, similar policies were pursued by the Canadian government, which resulted in the internment/concentration of Canadian citizens of German, Italian, and Japanese descent.[113] Currently, particular minorities—those identified as Muslim—in Canada have been made vulnerable to the excesses of state securitization, repression, and violence. Cumulatively, the external and internal moments previously discussed provide the ideological and paradigmatic precepts, the national presence, and the perceived threat environment necessary for a particular construction of an abject enemy Other to be reactivated and actualized: the *homo islamicus*.

The *homo islamicus* refers to a distinct sub-species of human being that is unalterably different from its Western counterpart. As Zachary Lockman explains, the *homo islamicus* is "a distinctive 'Islamic man' with a more or less fixed mindset that [is] fundamentally different from, indeed absolutely opposed to, the mind set of Western man.'"[114] As a distinct type of sub-species that is essentially different than Western man and, on a broader scale, the West, the *homo islamicus* must naturally possess beliefs, sensibilities, attitudes, and cultural (including political, social, economic, and religious) predilections that were and are the antithesis of modern Western man and society.[115] As a consequence, the *homo islamicus* is framed using a particular aesthetic in order to emphasize these differences and distinctions. For instance, the present incarnation of the *homo islamicus*, especially following the events of 11 September 2001, relies upon an aesthetic of abjection, menace, and hostility to punctuate the qualities not only of the Islamic man but, more importantly, of this species polar opposite, the Western man. As a result of this aesthetic, representations of angry Arabic men like that found on the cover of the 15 October 2001 issue of *Time* magazine entitled "Facing the Fury" have become representative of the contemporary construction of the *homo islamicus* and the attendant qualities of this sub-species.[116] Moreover, these aestheticized qualities of the *homo islamicus* have become concretized through the process of personification, whereby particular figures become the embodiment of this abject sub-species. For example, one of the most notable figures operating in this capacity is Osama bin Laden as represented on the cover of the 1 October 2001 issue of *Time* magazine entitled "Target: Bin Laden." The significance of this particular aestheticization and personification of the contemporary *homo islamicus* is that this sub-species is imbued with specific qualities, tendencies, and sensibilities that effectively genetically link it with another constructed sub-species: *homo terrorismus* or the terrorist man.[117] Ultimately, the linking of these two sub-species generates a very specific contemporary perception of Islam and Muslims, a perception that seals Islam and Muslims in associative anomie: if the Islamic or Muslim gene (more specifically the Sunni gene) becomes encoded in the DNA of the *homo terrorismus*, making Sunni Muslims, metaphorically speaking, biologically predisposed to violence, then the social construction of representations like the images found on the issues of Time magazine referenced above become natural and, therefore, preclude the necessity of providing the historical, social, and/or geopolitical context through which these representations and the materialities they engender are made possible. In this sense, a (Sunni) Muslim by any other name is still a terrorist with no explanation or evidence required. Indeed, this perception of Islam and Muslims has become deeply naturalized in the Western popular imagination.

Generally, in the popular imagination of Canada, the USA, Western Europe, and other countries typically codified as the "West," the signifier *Islam* in its current usage has come to signify a totalitarian religion that is suffused with inherent primitive, anti-modern, anti-Western, irrational, oppressive, tyrannical, and violent qualities and tendencies.[118] These sentiments are echoed in the following observation: "today, this picture of militant, transnational Islam has become virtually naturalized in the discourse of Islamic terrorism, especially in the wake of 9/11."[119] As a result of this conception of Islam, Muslims in general are cast in a similar light or, at a minimum, are suspected of being sympathetic to these qualities and tendencies. Consequently, both Islam as a faith and Muslims as its adherents have been and are presently perceived in the North American and Western European mainstream as being fundamentally incompatible and incommensurate, as Huntington espouses and reinforces, with the political, cultural, economic, and social systems of Western nation-states. Although, as Aziz Al-Azmeh argues, "the notion of incommensurability and its cognates appears quite absurd, not only because historical units are not analogous to paradigms and apprehension is not analogous to translation,"[120] this understanding of Islam has become a meta-narrative for explaining the encounters between Islam and Western prime modernity. However, this conceptualization of the relationship between the West and Islam and/or Western man and the Islamic man is not a new phenomenon. In the text *Europe and the Mystique of Islam*, Maxime Rodinson outlines the history of this phenomenon:

> The Oriental may always have been characterized as a savage enemy, but during the Middle Ages, he was at least considered on the same level of his European counterpart. And, to the men of the Enlightenment, the ideologues of the French Revolution, the Oriental was, for all his foreignness in appearance and dress is, above all, a man like anyone else. In the nineteenth century, however, he became something quite separate, sealed off in his own specificity, yet worthy of some kind of grudging admiration. This is the origin of the *homo islamicus*, a notion widely accepted even today.[121]

As Zachary Lockman elaborates, this West/East, West/Islam dichotomous worldview gained a considerable amount of mainstream currency in nineteenth-century European thought and was animated by a reflexive belief that Western Europeans were the members of a distinctive and inimitable civilization which was fundamentally different and superior to all other civilizations. This belief was predicated on the assumption that the primary entities through which global space and its inhabitants were organized were not nation-states or empires but civilizations. And each of these civilizations had essential characteristics, values, and codes which actively formed the consciousness and guided the activities of those who were subject to it.[122] Indeed, as demonstrated by Huntington's *clash* paradigm, this powerful system of ideas and the subjects and related differences and divisions these ideas produce are still active today. As a result, popular representations that actively reproduce the West and Islam and/or Western man and the Islamic man as hermetically sealed entities and subjects with unchanging specificities and essentialisms that are locked in diametric opposition to each other receive both reification and legitimacy in the Western popular imaginary. However, the epistemological foundation of the assumptions that animate this imaginary is inherently flawed.

According to Fred Halliday, "at the very core of this supposed challenge or conflict lie confusions: the mere fact of peoples being 'Islamic' in some general religious and cultural sense has been conflated with that of their adhering to beliefs and policies that are strictly described as 'Islamist' or 'fundamentalist.' It has been assumed, in other words, that most Muslims seek to impose a political programme, supposedly derived from their religion, on their societies."[123] Mohammad Arkoun makes a similar assertion:

> The misconceptions inherent in this imaginary go beyond current events. Although the problems of Muslim societies have indeed become knottier and more numerous since the emergence of national states in the 1950s and 1960s, another serious confusion—one that has contributed directly to the shaping of Western Imaginary of Islam—has also emerged in this short period of time. That is, all the political, social, economic, and cultural shortcomings of Muslim societies are hitched together and to Islam with a capital "I." Islam then becomes the prime mover of all contemporary history in a world that extends from the Philippines to Morocco and from Scandinavia, if we take account of Muslim minorities in Europe, to South Africa.[124]

Although, in reality, only a very small constituency of the highly variegated Muslim population in any location support Islamitic extremist groups of any form, these marginal groups have become instrumental in shaping current Canadian perceptions and understandings of Islam. The result of this is that these marginal groups become an index of the whole of Islam, thus perpetuating the false assumption that Islam and Muslims are a unified and monolithic entity that is constituted by one fixed and singular identity—an identity anti-Western in style and substance and predisposed to irrational violence. However, irrespective of the empirical reality that Islam and Muslims are not a monolith nor remain fixed by one transcendent identity, dominant representations of Islam and/or Muslims continually reproduce this mode of Western essentialism.

According to Armando Salvatore, essentialism, which is a "cognitive tool" of modernity, can only be "the result of the reciprocal knowledge, definition and cognitive domestication which take place between cultural universes capable of producing, as some time in history, and by virtue of inner impulses or external stimulation (or a combination of both), frameworks of universal reference."[125] As this author continues, "A prominent example of this phenomenon is the game of opposing essentialisms which has constituted such entities as the 'West' and 'Islam.'"[126] In effect, modern opposing essentialisms such as these enter a dialectical co-relationship where one essentialism depends on the other for its existence. Put in other terms, "the making of a generic Islam is strictly dependent on the making of the West."[127] Therefore, as Salvatore suggests, given that there does not exist any naturally occurring distinction between oppositional categories, essentialisms and their cognates, such as that of West/Islam and/or the Western man/Islamic man (the terrorist man), serve an epistemological and ontological function: to determine what something or someone is by what something or someone is not. This function is certainly evident in the Western construction of Islam vis-à-vis Orientalist discourse.

Orientalism, as conceptualized by Edward Said, is a style of thought based upon an ontological and epistemological distinction made between "the Orient" (East/Islam) and "the Occident" (West/Christianity).[128] Furthermore, as Said goes on to state, "Orientalism can be discussed and analyzed as the corporate institution for dealing with the Orient—dealing with it by making statements about it, authorizing views of it, describing it, settling it, ruling over it: in short, Orientalism as a Western style for dominating, restructuring, and having authority over the Orient."[129] As such, Albert Hourani outlines the three predominant implications of Orientalist discourse as it relates to Islam. The first is that this form of Western scholarship is reductionist and essentialist in nature: "that is to say, to explain all phenomena of Muslim societies and culture in terms of the concept of a single, unchanging nature of Islam and what it is to be a Muslim." The second implication of Orientalist discourse is that it has been politically motivated and is used to "justify domination over Muslim societies, by creating an image of Muslim societies (or oriental societies in general) as stagnant, unchanging, backward, incapable of ruling themselves or hostile." As Hourani continues, "fear of the 'revolt of Islam' haunted the mind of Europe during the imperial age, and has now come back to haunt it once more." Although Hourani describes this fear in the context of Europe, this fear is certainly applicable to North America as demonstrated by the events of 11 September 2001 and the previously documented reaction to this event by both the US and Canadian states. The third implication is, as Hourani identifies, "that western thought and scholarship have created a self-perpetuating body of received truths which have authority in intellectual and academic life, but bear little relation to the object of study on the ground."[130] As a consequence of the institutionalization and popularization of an Orientalist hermeneutic, specific representations, interpretations, and understandings of Islam have become so deeply naturalized and entwined in the Canadian, US, and Western European popular imaginary that Orientalist assumptions and essentialisms become consciously and/or unconsciously reproduced in both practical and popular discourse. As a result, a very particular Western composite of Islam and/or Muslims has been generated and subsequently imposed on Islam and Muslims: that of the *homo islamicus* and/or the *homo terrorismus*. The effect of the imposition of these composite identities is that artificial ontological and epistemological differences and divisions are established that enable Western states, including Canada, and elements of civil society to (re)produce themselves based upon imagined political, social, and/or cultural boundaries. Moreover, these same composite identities are used to designate and demarcate sources of both domestic and foreign threats and enemies in the war of terror.

Through the construction of the *homo islamicus* and/or the *homo terrorismus* and, as Maxime Rodinson suggests, the sealing off of these constructions in their own specificities, defining the Canadian nation-state and civil society along "civilizational lines" is made possible. As a consequence, racialized minorities associated with the "civilizational" Other, in this case domestic Muslim groups, become an abject enemy Other that once again represents an internal danger and threat to the Canadian nation-space. This internal danger and threat finds immediate spatial expression in urban areas like Toronto with large Muslim populations. As Katharyne Mitchell explains,

> Not only is racial difference associated with disorderliness and linked with particular places, but this stigmatization is accepted by residents 'of all races,' reflecting the impact of hegemonic stereotypes and their power at disciplining each other not just as different, but also as dangerous. Of course, hegemonic definitions shift and are frequently resisted, co-opted, and reworked, but their power in forming racialized perceptions of populations and spaces can have long-term effects.[131]

Indeed, some of these effects include increased surveillance of these groups by law enforcement and security apparatuses, the conscious or unconscious promulgation of anti-Islamic sentiment vis-à-vis practical and popular discourse, and the propagation of specific fearful imaginings regarding the Muslim presence in specific places (Fig. 2.1):

Fig. 2.1 "In Other News Today" (Although this political cartoon satirizes the media coverage following the arrests of the various members of the Toronto 18, the cartoon accurately captures the fear that has been inculcated into Canadian citizens by various state officials and institutions and the corporate media.) (*Globe and Mail*, 6 June 2006)

However, the most significant effect of the ontological and epistemological boundaries and divisions engendered by the *homo islamicus* and/or *homo terrorismus* and its concomitant civilizational divisions is that the emergence of both dominant and subversive discursive formations are made possible because of the perceived incompatibility and incommensurability of non-Islamic and Islamic social groupings (see Chap. 3). In other words, imagined civilizational divisions and differences, codified and popularized by works like Huntington's *clash of civilizations*, actually produce the ideological field necessary for a *clash* to be realized in place-specific contexts like the Greater Toronto Area (GTA).

Notes

1. Tuan, *Landscapes of Fear*, 209.
2. In the context of this argument, sacerdotal fear refers to a fear that is cultivated by both the repressive and ideological apparatuses (government experts, state intellectuals, and popular media) of the state through the continuous identification of an existential threat to the nation-state as a whole.
3. Tuan, *Landscapes of Fear*, 8.
4. Woods, 'It is better to kill too many than not enough,' A10.
5. Siddiqui, "Muslims and the Rule of Law," 1.
6. Ibid., 2.
7. Kalinowski, "Protesters oppose Muslim prayers in schools," *Toronto Star*, 25 July 2011.
8. Hume, "Islam a threat to Western freedom: Wilder," *National Post*, 9 May 2011.
9. Halliday, *Islam & the Myth of Confrontation*, 160. According to Halliday, anti-Muslimism "involves not so much hostility to Islam as a religion—indeed, few contemporary anti-Muslimists take issue with the claim of Muhammed to be a prophet, or with other theological beliefs—but hostility to *Muslims*, to communities of peoples whose sole or main religion is Islam and whose Islamic character, real or invented, forms one of the objects of prejudice. In this sense, anti-Muslimism often overlaps with forms of ethnic prejudice, covering peoples within which there may well be a significant non-Muslim element such as Albanians, Palestinians or even Caucasians," (160).
10. Ibid., 161.
11. Halliday, *Islam & the Myth of Confrontation*, 161.
12. Foucault, *Society Must Be Defended*, title of book.
13. Gramsci, *The Prison Notebooks*, 275–276. Joanne Sharp makes a similar observation as she states: "It has now become something of a cliché that with the decline of a communist threat at the end of the Cold War, conservative American culture has entered a period of crisis that had raised profound questions about both national identity and purpose" (Sharp, "Refiguring Geopolitics," 332).
14. Chomsky, *The Culture of Terrorism*, 3.
15. Chomsky, *The Culture of Terrorism*, 33.
16. Hunter, *The Future of Islam and the West: Clash of Civilizations or Peaceful Coexistence?*, 4. Certainly the replacement of the East-West conflict is ultimately made possible because the Other is always substitutable depending on the prevailing geopolitical conditions both internal and external to a given state.
17. Fukuyama, *The End of History*, xi.

18. Fukuyama, *The End of History*, p. 349.
19. Ibid., 349.
20. Ibid., 348. For examples of two other texts that offer a similar analysis of the supposed tensions between tradition, embodied by Islam, and Western modernity, embodied by liberal democracy and globalization, see Barber, Benjamin. (1995). *Jihad vs. McWorld*. New York: Random House., and Friedman, Thomas. (2000). *The Lexus and the Olive Tree*. New York: Anchor Books.
21. Lewis, "The Roots of Muslim Rage," 60.
22. For an online version of this lecture, see: www.youtube.com/watch?v=boBzrqF4vmo. Last accessed on 6 September 2011.
23. See, for example, Bonney, Richard. (2008). *False Prophets: The 'Clash of Civilizations' and the Global War on Terror*. Oxford: Peter Lang Ltd.; Said, Edward. (22 October 2001). "The Clash of Ignorance." *The Nation*; Said, Edward. (2003). "The Clash of Definitions," in Qureshi, Emaran & Sells, Michael. (Eds). *The New Crusades: Constructing the Muslim Enemy*. New York: Columbia University Press; Mottahedeh, Roy. (2003). "The Clash of Civilizations: An Islamicist's Critique," in Qureshi, Emaran & Sells, Michael. (Eds). *The New Crusades: Constructing the Muslim Enemy*. New York: Columbia University Press; and Halliday, Fred. (2003). "The "Clash of Civilizations"?, Sense and Nonsense," in Boase, Roger. (Ed.). *Islam and Global Dialogue*. England: Ashgate.
24. Bonney, *False Prophets*, 35.
25. Davies, "Clashing Civilizations or Conflicting Interests," 758.
26. Huntington, *Clash of Civilizations*, 21.
27. Huntington, *Clash of Civilizations*, 130.
28. Ibid., 128.
29. Ibid., 312.
30. Ibid., 209.
31. Ibid., 209.
32. Ibid., 211.
33. Ibid., 217.
34. Ibid., 258.
35. Said, "The Clash of Definitions," 70.
36. Nafissi quoted in Bonney, *False Prophets*, 35.
37. Huntington quoted in Trumpbour, "The Clash of Civilizations: Samuel P. Huntington, Bernard Lewis, and the Remaking of the Post-Cold War Order," 92.
38. Huntington, *Political Order in Changing Societies*, 3–9, 398–399 & see George, "The Discipline of Terrology," in *Western State Terrorism*, 88–89 for a synopsis of Huntington's ideas contained in the *Crisis of Democracy*.

39. Hunter, *The Future of Islam and the West*, 12.
40. Davies, "Clashing Civilizations or Conflicting Interests?," 759; and Hunter, *The Future of Islam and the West*, 12.
41. In addition to appearing in formal, practical, and popular discourse at the time, the codification "international terrorism" was used to describe this period in the history of terrorism by the terrorologist, David Rapoport (Rapoport describes the modern incarnation of terrorism as a succession of overlapping waves: Anarchist (1880s–1920); Anti-Colonial (1920s–1960s); International (1970s–1980s); and Religious (1970s–present)). As Rapoport states, "the term 'international terrorism' was used to describe the third wave partly because PLO training facilities were available. But there were other reasons. The revolutionary ethos created bonds between separate national groups, and targets chosen reflected international dimensions. Some groups conducted more assaults abroad than they did in indigenous territory; the PLO, for example, was more active in Europe than on the West Bank, and sometimes more active in Europe than European groups themselves," "The Fourth Wave: September 11 in the History of Terrorism," 421.
42. Chomsky, *Necessary Illusions*, 269.
43. Ibid, 114.
44. Reagan quoted in Chomsky, *Necessary Illusions*, 113.
45. Rapoport, "The Fourth Wave: September 11 in the History of Terrorism," 421.
46. Chomsky, *Necessary Illusions*, 113.
47. Rapoport, "September 11 in the History of Terrorism," 421.
48. Juergensmeyer, "Understanding the New Terrorism," 158.
49. Juergensmeyer, "Understanding the New Terrorism," 158.
50. Gerges, *America and Political Islam*, 23.
51. Alnasseri, "Die Konstruktion der orientalischen Feindbilder," 188–89. See, also, O' Tuathail, Gearoid & Agnew, John. (1992). "Geopolitics and Discourse: Practical Geopolitical Reasoning in American Foreign Policy." *Political Geography*, 11 (2): 190–204, for an analysis of Russia as an Orientalist construction.
52. Althusser, *On Ideology*, 159.
53. The import and strength of this meta-narrative are demonstrated by the emergence of what can be referred to as "clash" literature. Some examples of this literature include: Bawer, Bruce. (2006). *While Europe Slept: How Radical Islam is Destroying the West from Within*. Broadway Books: New York; Caldwell, Christopher. (2009). *Reflections on the Revolution in Europe: Immigration, Islam, and the West*. Doubleday: New York; Gabriel, Brigitte. (2008). *They Must Be Stopped: Why We Must Defeat Radical Islam and How We Can Do It*. St. Martin's Press: New York;

Geller, Pamela (2011). *Stop the Islamization of America: A Practical Guide to the Resistance*. WND Books: Washington, D.C.; Lindsey, Hal. (2011). *The Everlasting Hatred: The Roots of Jihad*. WND Books: Washington, D.C.; Laqueur, Walter. (2007). *The Last Days of Europe*. St. Martin's Press: New York; Spencer, Robert. (2008). *Stealth Jihad: How Radical Islam is Subverting America Without Guns or Bombs*. Regnery Publishing: Washington, D.C.; and Warraq, Ibn. (2003). *Why I am not a Muslim*. Prometheus Books: Amherst, New York.
54. Author's notes, 18 May 2010.
55. Bauder & Sharpe, "Residential Segregation of Visible Minorities in Canada's Gateway Cities," 204–205.
56. Preston et al., "Transnational Urbanism: Toronto at a Crossroads," 91.
57. James, Carl. "Introduction: Perspectives on Multiculturalism in Canada."
58. As previously cited, Peach's description of a Muslim "community of communities" more accurately encapsulates the Muslim presence in the Toronto CMA. There is a fallacious tendency in practical and popular discourse to refer to Muslims and/or Islam as a monolithic entity and/or group, which serves to conceal the diversity that exists within the communities that identify themselves as Muslim. Moreover, the use of the terminology Muslim diaspora is equally problematic because when subjected to close scrutiny what is revealed is the existence of a Muslim diaspora of diasporas.
59. D'Addario et al. "Finding Home: Exploring Muslim Settlement in the Toronto CMA," 4–5. The "South Asian" and "West Asian" categories utilized by Statistics Canada are problematic as these descriptive categories not only reproduce collective, homogeneous, reductive, and fixed identities that render opaque the inherent heterogeneity of those citizens who have origins in these diverse parts of the world but contribute to the racialization of particular groups through suggesting that those of South Asian or West Asian origin are culturally contiguous. See, for example, Ruppert, Evelyn. (2008). "'I Is. There I Am.' The Census as Practice of Double Identification." *Sociological Research Online*, 13 (4); and Kertzer D.I & Arel, D. (Eds.). (2002). *Census and Identity: The Politics of Race, Ethnicity, and Language in National Censuses*. Cambridge/New York: Cambridge University Press., for analyses of the use of the census as an instrument of identity formation and state power. Although information is available from the 2011 Canadian census on the religious landscape of the Toronto CMA, the reliability of this information is questionable as the long-form census that included questions relating to religious identity was made voluntary in 2010. Furthermore, for a social scientist to use the 2011 long-form census data is to tacitly endorse this irresponsible, if not reckless, policy decision of the Harper government.

60. In addition to the religious diversity of the South and West Asian populations, these groups are equally as ethnically diverse. As indicated in the 2001 census, the majority of the South Asian population was comprised of the following ethnic groups: East Indian, Pakistani, Sri Lankan, Punjabi, and Tamil, while the majority of the West Asian population was comprised of people who identified as being members of the following ethnic groups: Iranian, Armenian, Afghan, or Turkish.
61. Lindsay, Colin. "The South Asian Community in Canada." Statistics Canada, 1–18; and Lindsay, Colin. "The West Asian Community in Canada." Statistics Canada, 1–17.
62. www.salatomatic.com. Last accessed 21 November 2011. The actual amount of mosques/masjids in the Toronto CMA may actually be higher as "basement" mosques/masjids and other informal meeting spaces are not included in this tabulation.
63. Although many of the Muslim denominations are represented in Toronto, it is important to mention that certain members of the Muslim community of communities may not recognize some denominations as being Muslim. For instance, some denominational groups do not recognize the Ahmadiyya Movement in Islam as being valid and, therefore, perceive the Ahmadiyya Movement as heretical.
64. This figure was determined using LexisNexis Academic. The parameters used to conduct the electronic search included specifying the following search terms, "Muslim" or "Islam" and "Toronto"; identifying the newspaper, which, in this case, was the *Toronto Star*; and delimiting the time horizon to January 1990 and August 2001. The time horizon was used in order both to develop a sampling of the popular discourse emerging throughout the 1990s as the Muslim presence in the Toronto CMA was growing and becoming more pronounced and to ascertain the context in which Islam and Muslims were referenced and discussed prior to the events of 11 September 2001. The *Toronto Star* was selected as, arguably, it is the primary newspaper of record for Toronto and most closely represents the "common sense" attitudes and understandings of the mass populace. Furthermore, although 940 articles were identified through this electronic search, many of the articles listed were redundant as the same article appeared in different editions of the Toronto Star. Therefore, in actuality, the amount of articles identified that engage the issue of "Muslim" or "Islam" and "Toronto" is much smaller.
65. This event is important because it illustrates the latent prejudicial attitudes toward Islam that suffuse the North American popular imagination when acts of particular forms of violence are committed. As one individual commented in a letter to the editor entitled, "Maligning Muslims with Terrorism Label," in the *Toronto Star*: "Besides making the violent horror of terrorism all too real for Americans, the Oklahoma City

bombing showed the unseemly nature of prejudice against Arabs, Muslims, and Islam in North America" (26 April 1995, A18). Also see Hassan. Jamal. (1995, April 29). "Muslims were wounded by Crossfire in the Media." *Toronto Star*, E3.
66. Chaudhary, "Don't Link Terrorists with Muslim Beliefs," A26.
67. Lacina, "Why is Islam treated like a foreign faith?," A18.
68. Lacina, "Violence is extremely rare in Islamic Revival," D3.
69. Rabbani, "Pious Muslims are not violent or dangerous," A16.
70. Afaq Moin, "Muslim Fundamentalists not the same as terrorists," A14.
71. Hall, "Muslims Misunderstood, conference told stereotyped as terrorists, scholar says," A3.
72. Goraya, "Media make life difficult for Muslims," A32.
73. Turnbull, "Media called biased against Muslims Toronto Star worst offender, study by Islamic groups says," A28.
74. Although in 1998 the *Toronto Star* was found to be the most discriminatory newspaper in its reportage of Islam/Muslims, subsequent CIC reports found that the *Toronto Star* did improve. See http://www.canadianislamiccongress.com/cic2010/research/media-research/ (last accessed on 10 January 2012) for copies of the media reports dating between 2000–2004. Although the 1998 and 1999 reports are not digitally archived, summaries of the findings from these reports are available in any of the reports that are digitally archived.
75. Millward, "The Rising Tide of Islamic Fundamentalism (2)," No. 31. https://www.csis.gc.ca/pblctns/cmmntr/cm31-eng.asp (last accessed 10 January 2012).
76. Millward, "The Rising Tide of Islamic Fundamentalism (1)," No. 30. https://www.csis.gc.ca/pblctns/cmmntr/cm30-eng.asp (last accessed 10 January 2012).
77. Wilkinson, "Terrorism: Motivations and Causes," No. 53. https://www.csis.gc.ca/pblctns/cmmntr/cm53-eng.asp (last accessed on 10 January 2012).
78. Wilkinson, Paul. "Terrorism: Motivations and Causes," No. 53. https://www.csis.gc.ca/pblctns/cmmntr/cm53-eng.asp (last accessed on 10 January 2012).
79. https://www.csis.gc.ca/pblctns/prspctvs/200001-eng.asp (last accessed on 10 January 2012); https://www.csis.gc.ca/pblctns/prspctvs/200004-eng.asp (last accessed on 10 January 2012); and https://www.csis.gc.ca/pblctns/nnlrprt/2000/rprt2000-eng.asp. This report is not available in the Public Reports digital archive available on the CSIS website. Upon submitting a formal request for this report, I received a link to this document on 14 December 2011.
80. https://www.csis.gc.ca/pblctns/nnlrprt/2000/rprt2000-eng.asp

81. Transcript originally available at: http://www.whitehouse.gov/news/releases/2001/09/20010920-8.html. However, with the changing of the Administration, these releases are longer available. Therefore, see articles.cnn.com/2001-09-20/us/gen.bush.transcript_1_joint-session-national-anthem-citizens/5?_s=PM:US
82. Thorton, "Cold War II: Islamic Terrorism as Power Politics," 206–207.
83. Thorton, "Cold War II: Islamic Terrorism as Power Politics," 205.
84. Bassin, "Civilizations and Their Discontents: Political Geography and Geopolitics in the Huntington Thesis," 352.
85. Abrahamian, "The US Media, Huntington and September' 11," 531.
86. Abrahamian, "The US Media, Huntington and September 11," 532.
87. Huntington quoted in Aysha, "Samuel Huntington and the Geopoliltics of American Identity: The Function of Foreign Policy in America's Domestic Clash of Civilizations ," 127.
88. Ibid., 126–127.
89. Smith, "Scales of terror and the resort to geography: September 11, October 7," 631.
90. Ibid., 631.
91. Arat-Koc, "The Disciplinary Boundaries of Canadian Identity After September 11: Civilizational Identity, Multiculturalism, And the Challenge of Anti-Imperialist Feminism," 32. See Abu-Laban, Yasmeen. (2002). "Liberalism, Multiculturalism, and the Problem of Essentialism." *Citizenship Studies*, 6 (4): 459–482; Razack, Sherene. (2005). "Geopolitics, Culture Clash, and Gender After September 11." *Social Justice*, 32 (4): 11–31; and Karim, Karim H. (2003). *The Islamic Peril: Media and Global Violence* (2nd edition). Montreal: Black Rose Books, for varied analyses of how the *clash* paradigm has emerged in Canada not only in practical and popular discourse but in the security practices of the state.
92. Arat-Koc, "The Disciplinary Boundaries of Canadian Identity After September 11: Civilizational Identity, Multiculturalism, And the Challenge of Anti-Imperialist Feminism," 37.
93. Netherton & Seager, "Introduction: Framing In/Security," 4.
94. CPAC Special: 9/11 Reflections. Available at: http://www.cpac.ca/forms/index.asp?dsp=template&act=view3&pagetype=vod&hl=e&clipID=5938 (last accessed January, 2011).
95. Morton, "Canada's Asymmetrical War," 30.
96. Hassan-Yarri & Ousman, "Changes in Canada's Defence and Security Policy Since 9/11," 42.
97. Although the belief that the individuals involved in the 11 September 2001 attacks entered the USA via Canada is entirely fallacious (all of the individuals involved legally entered the USA from abroad under the

student visa program), this belief has become deeply entrenched in both the practical and popular imaginary of both countries. For instance, as Howard Adelman outlines in a book chapter entitled, "Governance, Immigration Policy, and Security: Canada and the United States Post-9/11," a 10 May 2002 Ipsos-Reid poll found that 77 % of Americans believed that the actors involved in 11 September 2001 attacks infiltrated the USA through Canada. Furthermore, the same poll revealed that 81 % of Canadians believed that the actors involved in 11 September 2001 infiltrated the USA through Canada (125). Despite the fact that the 9/11 Commission Report clearly indicates that these actors did not enter the USA via Canada, the persistence of this mythology is evident by the comments made by US Homeland Security Secretary Janet Napolitano in April 2009 when she repeated the widely held perception that the 11 September actors entered the USA via Canada.

98. Adelman, "Governance, Immigration Policy, and Security: Canada and the United States Post-9/11," 110.
99. Ronald Reagan quoted in Mamdani, "Good Muslim, Bad Muslim: A Political Perspective on Culture and Terrorism," 768.
100. Hassan-Yari & Outsman, "Incremental Changes in Canada's Defence and Security Policy Since September 11, 2001," 46.
101. Amery, "The Securitizatin and Racializatin of Arabs in Canada's Immigration and Citizenship Policies," 36.
102. Inge & Findley, "North American Defense and Security after 9/11," 25.
103. This scopio-spatial shift and the ensuing domestic war of terror facilitated the reconfiguration of the security apparatuses of many Western states. The rhetoric behind the reconfiguration of the security apparatuses was to ensure that these states had the capability to successfully target and contain domestic enemy Others that threaten the stability of these states. However, the effect of this incremental reconfiguration was the collective erosion of not only civil liberties and privacy rights but of democracy itself in the name of preserving freedom, liberty, and democracy. In the USA, for instance, the passage of the PATRIOT Act, the Homeland Security Act, the Military Commissions Act, the Violent Radicalization and Homegrown Terrorism Prevention Act, the FISA Amendments Act, and the National Defense Authorization Act has normalized not only the use of torture and targeted killing of US citizens but the normalization of invasive domestic surveillance and detention where *habeas corpus* and *posse comitatus* no longer apply to its citizenry. As Canada continues to emulate the draconian security measures of the USA and harmonizes its security configuration with that of the USA, which is the necessary outcome of the Canada-US *Beyond the Border Initiative*, the same erosion of democracy will continue in Canada. Although the rhetoric of the minority

as security threat is deployed to justify and substantiate the neo-fascist machinations of the governments in the USA and Canada, the reality is that these machinations are designed for the majority. In the context of Canada, the recent revelations of Edward Snowden demonstrate the extent of this scopio-spatial shift: the Communications Security Establishment of Canada (CSEC) is monitoring and collecting the domestic communications of Canadians in contravention of its mandate. Incidentally, as a result of its activities, the British Columbia Civil Liberties Association has filed a class action lawsuit against CSEC for violating the Canadian Charter of Rights and Freedoms.

104. Mansbridge, [Interview with Stephen Harper], 8 September 2011.
105. Engler, *The Ugly Canadian*, 158.
106. Ibid., 153.
107. Staeheli, "Migration, Civilizational Thinking, and the Possibility of Democracy," 750.
108. Smith, "Scales of terror and the resort to geography: September 11, October 7," 633.
109. Arat-Koc, "The Disciplinary Boundaries of Identity After September 11," 34.
110. Appadurai, *Fear of Small Numbers*, 45.
111. Ibid., 45–46. State violence against targeted minorities can manifest in a multitude of different forms. Although specific minority groups may be the object of actual physical violence, minority groups may also be the object of ideological, political, and discursive violence that can lead to social exclusion, rejection, isolation, and alienation from the larger national body.
112. For example, see Kordan, Bohdan & Mohovsky, Craig. (2004). *A Bare and Impolitic Right: Internment and Ukrainian-Canadian Redress*. Montreal: McGill-Queen's University Press.
113. For example, see Auger, Martin. (2011). *Prisoners of the Home Front: German POWs and "Enemy Aliens" in Southern Quebec, 1940–46*. Vancouver: UBC Press; Iacovetta, Franca et al. (Eds.). (2000). *Enemies Within: Italian and Other Internees in Canada and Abroad*. Toronto: University of Toronto Press; and Oikawa, Mona. (2012). *Cartographies of Violence: Canadian Women, Memory, and the Subjects of the Internment*. Toronto: University of Toronto Press.
114. Lockman, *Contending Visions of the Middle East*, 77.
115. Ibid., 88.
116. See Nashef, Hania. (2011). "The blurring of boundaries: images of abjection as the terrorist and the reel Arab intersect." *Critical Studies on Terrorism*, 4 (3): 351–368, for an argument that examines the abject

representation of terrorist actors in the media and film in the aftermath of 11 September 2001.
117. In a chapter entitled "The Discipline of Terrorology," Alexander George cites an article printed in the *International Herald Tribune* on 19 February 1987 written by William Buckley Jr. In this article, which Buckley entitled "The Way to Fight Terror, As Learned by Argentina," Buckley, as George cites, recommended "the establishment of an international agency charged with 'discovering and executing and directing offensive action against known terrorists and terrorist concentrations.' This international Murder Inc. 'would not traffic in live terrorists; only dead terrorists would serve its purposes, namely the extinction of a species'" (91). This metaphoric reference to the terrorist as a species that must be dealt with using extra-judicial strategies and tactics resurfaces in an argument developed by Amitai Etzioni (2011) in an article entitled, "Terrorists: A Distinct Species." *Terrorism and Political Violence*, 23 (1): 1–12. In this article, Etzioni advances the argument that terrorists should not be treated as soldiers or criminals but as a category of actor that is denied the institutional protections and rights afforded to military personnel or criminals as the current systems in place for dealing with these actors are not equipped to deal with this type of actor. As Etzioni states, "in short, terrorists are a distinct breed that requires a distinct treatment," 5. For an argument that attempts to partly explain a terrorist act at the biological level of the actor who is engaged in this activity, see Charlesworth, William. (2003). "Profiling Terrorists: A Taxonomy of Evolutionary, Developmental, and Situational Causes of a Terrorist Act." *Defense & Security Analysis*, 19 (3): 241–264.
118. See, for example, the following Orientalist scholars and texts that promulgate this image of Islam: Lewis, Bernard. (2002). *What Went Wrong? The Clash Between Islam and Modernity in the Middle East*. Perennial: New York; Lewis, Bernard. (2003). *The Crisis of Islam: Holy War and Unholy Terror*. Random House: New York; and Kepel, Gilles. *The War for Muslim Minds: Islam and the West*. Belknap Press of Harvard University Press: Cambridge, Mass.
119. Appardurai, *Fear of Small Numbers*, 70.
120. Al-Azmeh, *Islams and Modernities*, 81.
121. Rodinson quoted in Lockman, *Contending Visions of the Middle East*, 74. See also, *Europe and the Mystique of Islam*, 60 for the appearance of this quotation in its original form.
122. Lockman, *Contending Visions of the Middle East*, 74–75.
123. Halliday, *Islam & The Myth of Confrontation*, 107.
124. Arkoun, *Rethinking Islam*, 7.

125. Salvatore, *Islam and the Political Discourse of Modernity*, 72.
126. Ibid., 72.
127. Ibid., 68.
128. Said, *Orientalism*, p. 2.
129. Ibid., 3.
130. Hourani, *Islam in European thought*, 57–58.
131. Mitchell, "Zero Tolerance, Imperialism, Dispossession," 297.

CHAPTER 3

Through a Looking Glass Darkly: The Symmetry of Competing Discursive Formations

As Edward Said asserts, "just as none of us are outside or beyond geography, none of us is completely free from the struggle over geography. That struggle is complex and interesting because it is not only about soldiers and cannons but also about ideas, about forms, about images and imaginings."[1] Although the struggle over geography to which Said refers occurs at multiple scales and in different time-space conjunctures, the material manifestation of this struggle is apparent when one analyzes specific incarnations of the struggle over the representation, perception, experience, and meaning of place. More specifically, the struggle over place is pronounced in many of the world cities of the global north and south. However, these struggles are heterogeneous and are contingent[2] upon the actors involved. The heterogeneity and the contingency that the struggle over place engenders can be explained through Doreen Massey's conceptualization of place: "If space is rather a simultaneity of stories-so-far then places are collections of those stories, articulations within the wider power-geometries of space."[3] In this sense, place becomes a "relational assemblage" rather than an "isolated container" that is "always co-constituted by, mediated through, and integrated within the wider experiences of space."[4] The socio-political corollary is that the myriad articulatory assemblages (discursive and material) that collectively constitute place may or may not be conducive to socio-political coalescence and cohesion but rather socio-political divisions and antagonisms, as various articulatory assemblages may offer divergent or competing trajectories over the representation, perception, meaning, and experience of the places that both produce and are produced by those articulatory assemblages. Therefore, to develop an understanding of the socio-political divisions and antagonisms that are created through competing articulatory assemblages, one must first identify and foreground the different ideological positions informing the assemblage of articulations that constitute place. These different ideological positions and the struggle over the representation, perception, meaning, and experience of place are immediately recognizable when one assesses various incarnations of the phenomenon of Islamitic extremism.

According to Alexander Murphy,

> One of the most amorphous, yet important, dimensions of research on terrorism concerns how different spaces are understood. What places are of signal symbolic importance to different peoples? How do peoples view their places and their relationship to one another? Whatever may be said about the circumstances that precipitate terrorism, we cannot afford to see them in reductionist economic terms. To put it simply, if issues of ideology and space were not at play, the greatest centers of terrorism would be in places such as Burkina Faso and Haiti, which are facing even greater economic problems than the countries usually linked to terrorism (Pakistan, Malaysia, the Philippines, and so on).[5]

This contention is reinforced by Stephen Graham's assertion "that contemporary warfare and terror now largely boil down to contests over the spaces, symbols, meanings, support systems and power structures of cities."[6] In effect, these "contests" are animated by the competing articulatory assemblages that constitute place. As Graham goes on to state:

> Imaginative geographies tend to be characterized by stark binaries of place attachment. Not surprisingly, these tend to be especially potent and uncompromising during times of war. War mobilizes a charged dialectic of attachment to place: the idea that 'our' places are the antithesis of those of the demonized enemy. Often such polarization is manufactured and recycled through the discourses of the state, backed up by representations suited to popular culture. It sentimentalizes one's own place while stripping the humanity from the enemy's places. In building the political willingness to target and destroy the latter, binaried constructions are a crucial element.[7]

In the context of Domestic Islamitic Extremism, the competing articulatory assemblages of place and the concomitant ideological positions that inform these assemblages, i.e. the West/Islam *clash of civilizations* dichotomy, made the transit bombings in London, the bombing of the Boston

Marathon, the attack of a British soldier in the streets of London, and the plan to detonate various explosive devices in Toronto probable. Certainly, as these events demonstrate, "The 'clash of civilizations' is proving to be a clash at citified sites [.]"[8]

In the case of the so-called Toronto 18, two competing, or rather clashing, ideological positions and related articulatory assemblages are certainly evident as exemplified by the actions and practices of various members of the group. However, as stated previously, to understand the articulatory assemblage of the group, one must first understand the ideological position informing this assemblage. So, what are these ideological positions and how can one identify, foreground, and analyze the discursive form of these positions? Using a modified version of Tim Cresswell's *In Place/Out of Place* as a theoretical framework, two distinctive yet co-constituting ideological positions come into focus: dominant (*in place*) versus subversive (*out of place*). Furthermore, using this theoretical framework, one can then analyze and assess not only how the ideological construct of the *homo islamicus/homo terrorismus* (see Chap. 2) produces the discursive formation of the dominant position, but how this construct produces the discursive formation of the subversive position as well.

At multiple scales, real or imagined, political, social, and ideological boundaries are constructed to ultimately perform an ontological and epistemological function: to (re)produce the Self through the spatial delineation of the Other, a spatial delineation that is created through establishing demarcations between an inside (inclusion) and an outside (exclusion). Subsequently, as David Slater explains, "Behind the boundary we have our own world of community, membership, internal understandings, our morality, distributive mechanisms, democratic accountability, obligations, and allegiances. On the other side, outside our own constructed world, there would be alternative worlds of strangers, danger, external principles and uncertain moralities."[9] In a post-11 September 2001 context, the external threat of Transnational Islamic Extremism and internal threat of Domestic Islamic Extremism perceived by various Western states (e.g. Canada, the UK, and the USA) not only catalyzed the material hardening of the boundaries separating the respective inside from the outside but more importantly intensified the discursive boundaries used to reinforce normative political and social codes, orderings, and expectations of national bodies. However, how does one identify the discursive boundaries that are used to not only differentiate the normative (Self) from the aberrant (Other) but to condition the normative (Self) as normative and self-reflexively distinguish itself from the aberrant (Other)?

According to Cresswell, "Just as it is the case that space and place are used to structure a normative world, they are also used (intentionally or otherwise) to question that normative world."[10] The method Cresswell utilizes to demonstrate this assertion is to conduct an analysis of acts that are considered to have transgressed the sets of codes and behaviors expected to be followed in particular places and/or spatial configurations. As Cresswell states:

> One way to illustrate the relation between place and behaviour is to look at those behaviours that are judged as inappropriate in a particular location—literally as actions out of place. It is when such actions occur, I argue, that the everyday, commonsense relationships between place and behaviour become obvious and underlined. The labeling of actions as inappropriate in the context of a particular place serves as evidence for the already existing normative geography. In other words, transgressive acts prompt reactions that reveal that which was previously considered natural and commonsense. The moment of transgression marks the shift from the unspoken unquestioned power of place over taken-for-granted behaviour to an official orthodoxy concerning what is proper to what is not proper—that which is in place to that which is out of place.[11]

In effect, the "in place" and the "out of place" that Cresswell describes reveal that there are dominant ideological readings, interpretations, representations, and constructions of place and subversive ideological readings, interpretations, representations, and constructions of place. Therefore, "by acting in space in a particular way the actor is inserted into a particular relation with ideology. Importantly, the actor has the ability to recognize a particular spatial 'text' and react to it in a way that is antagonistic to a particular ideology."[12] In other words, to commit certain transgressive acts in space, an actor is not only tacitly aligning with a particular ideological position (dominant or subversive) but is articulating that position through the transgressive act itself. However, as Cresswell outlines, not all acts of transgression inherently embody resistance. Instead, one needs to assess the intentionality of the actor(s) and the concomitant transgressive act(s): "To have *transgressed* in this project means to have been judged to have crossed some line that was not meant to have been crossed. The crossing of the line may not have been intended. Transgression is judged by those who react to it, while resistance rests on the intentions of the actor(s)."[13] Consequently, as Cresswell continues, "Since transgressive acts are the acts judged to be 'out of place' by dominant institutions and actors (the press, the law, the government), they provide 'potentials' for resistance.

Intentional transgression is a form of resistance that creates a response from the establishment—an act that draws the lines on a battlefield and defines the terrain on which contestation occurs."[14] For instance, to illustrate the unintended versus the intended act of transgression, one can look at two different examples during the G20 held in Toronto in June 2010.

On 26 June 2010 a small group of so-called "black bloc" actors codified politically as anarchists engaged in intentional acts of transgression by vandalizing banks, store fronts, and decoy police cruisers to protest state repression and advance an anti-globalization and anti-corporatist message.[15] Obviously, these acts were judged to be "out of place" and resulted in a litany of acts of state violence. Conversely, during the same G20 Summit, hundreds and hundreds of innocent citizens unintentionally committed acts of transgression by virtue of either being in varying degrees of proximity to the security perimeter of the actual summit or engaged in peaceful demonstrations and marches. By virtue of being judged as "out of place," many of these individuals were victimized by various methods of state interdiction, such as forced identification and search and seizure of their individual person by police, mass arrest and detention, or forcible confinement by police through various tactics deployed for crowd control like the "kettling" technique used at the corner of Queen St. and Spadina Ave. on the last day of the G20 Summit. Although unintended transgressive acts are important in revealing the relationship between place and the (re)production of dominant ideological codes, behaviors, expectations, and practices, i.e. political and social quietude, passivity, conformity, compliance, acquiescence, and inactivity, the intentional acts of transgression as described by Cresswell bring into sharp relief the contest of differing and antagonistic ideological positions and related practices. To be sure, as intentional transgressive acts expose, "An ideology is not a harmonious structure of beliefs or assumptions; some of its beliefs militate against others, and some of its standards militate against our nature. An ideology is an aggregate of beliefs sufficiently at odds with one another to justify opposite kinds of conduct."[16] Indeed, the intentional transgressive practices of the actors involved in the so-called Toronto 18 unequivocally illuminate the existence of two conflicting yet co-constituting ideological positions and discursive formations that made the actions and practices of the group probable: a dominant (in place) ideological position and discursive formation versus a subversive (out of place) ideological position and discursive formation. These two positions and formations can be visualized using the following formulation (Fig. 3.1):

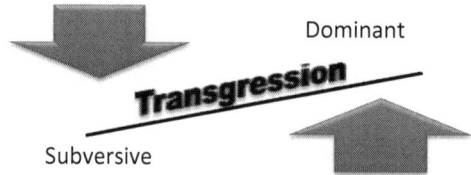

Fig. 3.1 "Dominant/transgression/subversive model"

Dominant (*In Place*)/Subversive (*Out of Place*) Formations

To begin the process of suturing together the dominant/subversive formations requires a brief return to the Western ideological construct of the *homo terrorismus*. In constructing the *homo terrorismus* as the "civilizational" Other, a Janus-faced creature was created. This creature is Janus-faced because it serves as the systole and diastole of both the dominant and subversive positions and formations. In effect, both the dominant and subversive rely upon the construct of the *homo terrorismus* to be brought into being. As such, the *homo terrorismus* functions as a perceptual figure that both the dominant (Self) and the subversive (Other) rely upon to catalyze and concretize their respective formations. In this sense, the *homo terrorismus* can be understood as functioning like the following reversible image (Fig. 3.2):

Fig. 3.2 "Young Man/Old Man" (Botwinick, "Husband and Father-In-Law: A Reversible Figure," 312–313)

However, rather than this image of the young man and the older man, the reversible image of the *homo terrorismus* is constituted by a stereotypical image of the man of "Western" civilization and a stereotypical image of the man of "Islamic" civilization.[17] Although both the dominant and the subversive set their gaze upon the same static image, the perceptual figure that emerges as their object is the cognitive distortion of each other's perceived opposite. In other words, the perceived interiority of the dominant is constructed through the perceived exteriority of the subversive and vice versa.[18] Therefore, in utilizing this construction as an imagistic referent, one can begin to identify the constellation of elements and articulations that in totality give expression to both the dominant and subversive ideological position and discursive formations.

As Slavoj Žižek, Ernesto Laclau and Chantal Mouffe, and S. Sayyid argue, the nucleus and identity of any ideological position and discursive formation are determined and sustained by what is varyingly referred to as the *point de capiton* (quilting point), nodal point, or master signifier.[19] Sayyid defines the master signifier in the following terms:

> In a totalized universe of meaning we find a multiplicity of nodal points operating to structure the chains of signification, but among them we find one specific signifier—the master signifier—which functions at the level of the totality (that is, it retroactively constitutes that universe of meaning as a unified totality). This master signifier is a paradoxical signifier in so far as it is a particularity that functions as a metonymy for the whole discursive universe. As such, it acquires a universal dimension and functions as the place of inscription for all other signifiers. It is the signifier of the totality that guarantees and sanctions that unity: it designates the whole by its very presence. It functions as the place of inscription for all other signifiers in that totality. The master signifier is a signifier to which all other signifiers refer, and are unified by—and it fixes their identity. It is the unique point of symbolic authority that guarantees and sustains the coherence of the whole ensemble.[20]

As Sayyid later continues:

> The master signifier functions as the most abstract principle by which any discursive space is totalized. In other words, it is not that a discursive horizon is established by a coalition of nodal points, but rather by the use of a signifier that represents the totality of that structure. The more extensive a discourse is, the less specific each element within it will be: it will become simply another instance of a more general identity. The dissolution of the

specificity and concreteness of the constituent elements clears the path for a master signifier becoming more and more abstract, until it reaches a limit at which it does not have any specific manifestation: it simply refers to the community as a whole and it becomes the principle of reading that community.[21]

In short, according to Žižek, the master signifier is a "signifier without the signified."[22] In effect, the master signifier can be conceptualized, to use the terminology of particle physics, as functioning like a God particle: an unseen and often unspoken signifier to which other signifiers stick and cohere to give the discursive formation its mass, its substance, its identity. However, if the master signifier often goes unseen and unspoken, how is it locatable? The answer is in identifying the constituent articulatory mechanisms (signifiers) that are metonymically contiguous with, and bound to, the master signifier in particular discursive formations. It is precisely in the shadow of these signifiers that the master signifier is made apparent.

To begin to map the articulations which in totality constitute the dominant discursive formation, it is necessary to first identify the positive content of this formation. Arguably, the positive content of the dominant formation is made manifest in a statement by Prime Minister Stephen Harper following the arrests of the individuals implicated in the Toronto 18 case. According to the *Globe and Mail*, Harper declared: "Their alleged target was Canada, Canadian institutions, the Canadian economy, the Canadian people [...]. We are a target because of who we are and how we live, our society, our diversity and our values—values such as freedom, democracy and the rule of law. The values that make Canada great, values that Canadians cherish."[23] These sentiments are reinforced by written comments made by two of the Supreme Court judges presiding over the court cases of some of the accused. In his *Reasons for Sentence* for one of the principal figures in this case, Justice F. Dawson stated:

> [...] there can be no doubt that terrorism offenses tend to undermine our democratic way of life. Democracy flourishes because it tolerates and values a diversity of views and protects the rights of those who hold views at odds with the majority. Such tolerance and recognition of value of diversity is founded on the principle that members of our society will not seek to effect change by violent means. Those who turn to terrorism to effect change break this fundamental compact. They are not only a threat to the physical safety of the populace but to the foundational principles of our civil society. Those who pursue terrorism seek to make all of us less free.[24]

Similarly, in his *Reasons for Judgement* for one of the secondary figures involved in the group, Justice Hill stated:

> In civilized societies committed to the rule of law, it is freedom of expression and democratic processes which advance public debate relating to political, religious, economic, and social issues. Regrettably, some persons or groups of like-minded individuals, on the basis of actual or perceived injustices, impatience with lack of desired changes, or discontent with the policies or structures of domestic or foreign governments, abandon civilized adherence to law in preference for violent means to further objectives of "making a statement", attempting to exercise extortive leverage through fear, or simply elimination of an "enemy" whether an identified victim or institution or symbol of the "opposition. So is the evil of terrorism."[25]

As these statements suggest, the positive content of the dominant discursive formation includes the signifiers "democracy," "freedom," "justice" and the "rule of law," "tolerance," "diversity," and "safety." However, as demonstrated not only by the context in which these statements were delivered but also by the actual references to terrorism, the content of the dominant discursive formation is not defined by the positive attributes of the above listed signifiers but rather by what Žižek refers to as their "positional-relational identity" with the negative content associated with these signifiers. That is, the positive content of the dominant discursive formation is only given meaning when in relation to its corresponding opposite, i.e. undemocratic, control, injustice and criminality, intolerance, uniformity, and danger, which, in the present time-space conjuncture, is embodied by the threat of the *homo terrorismus*.[26] Therefore, in effect, if the interiority of the dominant discursive formation is defined and given meaning only in relation to its perceived exteriority, then it is through the articulations of exteriority that the dominant discursive formation can be realized and actualized. In other words, the negative content displaces the positive content as the actual substance of the dominant discursive formation.

The negative content of the dominant discursive formation is made apparent through a sampling of various public statements and official documents of the Canadian state. For instance, in an interview conducted by the Canadian Broadcasting Corporation (CBC) for the 10-year anniversary of the 11 September 2001 attacks, Peter Mansbridge asked Prime Minister Harper the following questions: "Where is the major threat to us as a country right now? Where does it come from?" to which Harper responded:

> Well, you know Peter, there are a number of threats on different levels, but if you look at, if we're talking about terrorism, I mean the major threat is still Islamicism. There are other threats out there, but that is the one that I can tell you occupies the security apparatus most regularly in terms of actual terrorist threats. Now, as we have seen in Norway, terrorist threats can come out of the blue, they can come from something completely different, and there are other groups and individuals that, if given the chance, would engage in terrorism. But that one is probably still the major one. But it's diffuse: you know it ranges all the way, when people think of Islamic terrorism, they think of Afghanistan, or maybe they think of some place in the Middle East, but the truth is that the threat exists all over the world.[27]

Subsequent to Harper's identification of "Islamicism" and "Islamic terrorism" as the primary threat to Canada, both the Minister of Public Safety, Vic Toews, and the Minister of Foreign Affairs, John Baird, made public statements identifying terrorism as the single greatest threat facing Canada and the international community. For instance, at a meeting in New York in June 2012 to review the United Nation's global counter-terrorism strategy, Baird was reported as describing terrorism as "the great struggle of this generation and a phenomenon that knows no boundaries."[28] Similarly, albeit in a more explicit fashion, during a press conference in February 2012 which highlighted the release of Canada's first counter-terrorism strategy entitled *Building Resilience Against Terrorism*, Toews reiterated some aspects of the report, which characterizes and describes "violent Islamist extremism" in general and "homegrown Sunni Islamist extremists" in particular as the principal threat to Canadian national security.[29] As the report states, "While al-Qaeda affiliates may pose a threat of terrorist attacks from abroad, violent 'homegrown' Sunni Islamist extremists are posing a threat of violence within Canada."[30] These sentiments are echoed in a report prepared by the Standing Senate Committee on National Security and Defence entitled *Defence of North America: A Canadian Responsibility*. In this report, the threat to Canada is described in the following terms:

> Our great blessing is also a great danger. Peaceful thinking can become passive thinking. It has been nearly 60 years since Adolf Hitler forced Canadians to recognize that one cannot always appease those committed to the downfall of one's way of life. Even after the events of September 11, there remained a sense among many Canadians that "it can't happen here," just as there was a sense among many Canadians (and Canadian political

leaders) that World War I had ended all wars, and that there would never be a World War II.

They were wrong, and it would be wrong to think that Canada will never be a target of terrorists. Our lifestyle—so loathed by extremists in the Bin Laden mould—is similar to the lifestyle of Americans. Our economies are intertwined. In little over a decade these two countries have fought twice in a common cause—in the Persian Gulf and Afghanistan. Canada may not be the bull's eye in the sights of most extremists—the United States undoubtedly is. But Canada is clearly positioned as one of the inner rings on the target, and if our country is perceived to be much easier to penetrate than the United States, we will move closer to the centre.[31]

Moreover, in reference to the same threat, Andy Ellis, the assistant director of policy and strategic partnerships for the Canadian Security Intelligence Service (CSIS), was reported by the *National Post* as stating that, "cases such as the Toronto 18 show that radicalized individuals with a 'distorted version of Islam' are willing to conduct attacks inside Canada." He was then quoted as stating: "Frankly speaking, security agencies do not fully understand why and how seemingly young men or women can grow up in Canada yet come to reject the Western, liberal and democratic values that underpin Canadian identity—instead replacing them with the violent, anti-Western ideology of al-Qaeda."[32] So, what is the negative content that is brought into focus by these statements?

In aggregate, the statements referenced above enable one to extrapolate the following negative content: "terrorism," "Islamicism," "Islamic terrorism," "Afghanistan," "Bin Laden," "al-Qaeda affiliates," "a phenomenon that knows no boundaries," "homegrown Sunni Islamist extremists," "distorted version of Islam," "violent," and "anti-Western ideology." Although individually these dispersed articulations possess a diminished "experiential meaning potential,"[33] collectively these statements reveal a series of what Kenneth Burke refers to as "implicit equations" or "associational clusters"[34] that connect the articulations and produce a metonymically contiguous totality of mechanisms that ultimately give substance to the dominant discursive formation. As the above clustering of articulations reveal, each has assumed an associative identity so that, for example, terrorism is equated with Islamicism, which is equated with Islamic terrorism, which is equated territorially with Afghanistan, which is equated with Osama bin Laden, who is equated with al-Qaeda and al-Qaeda affiliates, which is equated with a phenomenon with a global reach, which is equated with the emergence of homegrown Sunni Islamist extremists, who are equated with Islam, which is equated with violence and the espousal of an anti-Western ideology. However, the aforementioned equations are not meant to imply that the series of articulations represented must follow a linear logic, i.e. a=b=c=d=e, and so on. Rather, each articulation is non-linearly connected to others in a rhizomatic structure or in what can be described as a metonymic constellation. Furthermore, these articulations are by no means exhaustive and do not represent the limits of this associative cluster. For instance, the principle of "resilience," which provides the conceptual impetus for the official counter-terrorism strategy of Canada, identifies minority community outreach and engagement by Canadian law enforcement and security apparatuses (e.g. the RCMP National Security Community Outreach program) to be an important dimension of preventing extremism. Although "pluralism"[35] is explicitly identified in the document as a fundamental Canadian value, the suspicion and securitization of diversity and multiculturalism (see Chap. 5), especially of minority communities identified as Muslim following 11 September 2001, demonstrate that diversity and multiculturalism are perceived as a source of threat to national security.[36] As such, pluralism, diversity, and multiculturalism become part of the negative content of the dominant discursive formation as terms that are metonymically contiguous with articulations such as "Islamist terrorism" and "Sunni Islamist extremism."[37] Now that the negative content of the dominant discursive formation has been established, one can look into the shadows of these articulations to identify the master signifier which gives this formation a unified coherence.

According to Greig Henderson, "words, for Burke, are agents of power; they are value-laden, ideologically motivated, and morally and emotionally weighted instruments of persuasion, purpose and representation."[38] Therefore, if one assesses the dialectical relationship between the discursive content and the extra-discursive situation, not only is the ideological function of the dominant discursive formation revealed but the master signifier is made apparent. In the current context of the war *of* terror, national security and law and order have become the predominant focus of the Canadian state. For example, following the events of 11 September 2001, the Rideau Institute, a think tank located in Ottawa, conducted a study and found that the Canadian government has spent approximately an additional $92 billion CAD (as of the 10-year anniversary of 11 September 2001) on the soft and hard infrastructure for counter-terrorism in Canada. For example, according to the report, military expenditures almost doubled, while security and public safety expenditures almost tripled. Some of these expenditures include: the creation of the Ministry of Public Safety (a Ministry which did not exist prior to 11 September 2001); a new $70 million CAD tower at CSIS headquarters in Ottawa; the increase of human capital in CSIS by approximately 1000 employees; the building of a $900 million facility for Canada's signals intelligence agency, the Communications Security Establishment (CSE), to accommodate for its growth in human capital by approximately 1000 employees; and the doubling of staff in the Royal Canadian Mounted Police (RCMP) assigned to national security criminal investigations.[39] However, despite this significant increase in spending RCMP, Assistant Commissioner Gilles Michaud is quoted as stating: "We've kept Canada safe from terrorist activities […]. However, are we safer? I'd be putting my neck on the line to say yes. Because at the end of the day what's still of concern is what the intelligence might not be picking up right now. And it's certainly not any easier to keep Canadians safe. The environment is constantly changing and evolving."[40] And, arguably, herein the ideological function of the dominant discursive formation is exposed: the inculcation of the threat posed by Islamitic extremism to the political, social, and spatial codes and orderings of the Canadian nation-state in the Canadian imaginary to legitimate the expansion of the Canadian national security state and to justify the introduction and use of authoritarian powers to maintain the collective security of Canada.[41] As William Purdue explains, "For in the National Security State, an ideological monopoly has taken form. The root of *security* is in the Latin *securus*, which means freedom from care, or more broadly, freedom from fear, anxiety, and danger. The National Security State turns this definition on end, promoting conceptions of safety rooted in its organized ability to inflict fear, anxiety, and danger."[42] Indeed, the use of fear as a strategy of state power was identified by Lawrence Martin in an article entitled "The fear card has been dealt—and Harper will play it," following the arrests of various members of the Toronto 18. As Martin writes:

> Having come this far, the Prime Minister can now go farther. Public support in this country for the war on terror will likely rise, giving him enough leeway to put himself firmly in league with the tough guys. We've heard his "cut and run" jargon. Now there will be additions. Lines like, "Our freedoms are at risk" and "Our very way of life is under threat." They will be

the rallying cries any time the government wants more support for policing, for security, for wars. The beauty of it politically is that no one will be able to say with certainty that Mr. Harper is wrong because no one can predict with certainty that there won't be an attack.[43]

Therefore, if the ideological function of the dominant discursive formation is to reinforce national consensus on values, behaviors, codes, and orderings through the inculcation of threat and fear vis-à-vis an external and internal enemy Other in the interest of state power, national *insecuritization* has arguably become the ontology of the political.

Unlike the concept of "ontological security" explicated by Anthony Giddens which, according to Samir Gandesha, refers to the desire of the self to maintain a stable, coherent, predictable, and dependable relation with the world which is in turn predicated on "the taken-for-granted patterns constitutive of everyday life,"[44] *insecuritization* refers to the assiduous manipulation of this desire of the self by the state to destabilize and disrupt these taken-for-granted patterns, whereby the security of the everyday becomes a state of exception that can only be tenuously guaranteed through the hyper vigilance and interdiction of a protector embodied by individuals, groups, and/or institutions that emerge from the self and purportedly operate on behalf of that self. However, the process of *insecuritization* can only be achieved through the use of what Kenneth Burke refers to as a "projection device"[45] or what is referred to above as an imagistic referent—in this case, the *homo terrorismus*. Without this imagistic referent as the locus of threat and fear, the prognostications of the state regarding national security would appear unconvincing to the social body and consequently would call into question the legitimacy of the claims made by the state. Therefore, the credibility of the state is contingent upon its ability to convince the citizenry that an existential danger to their personal safety exists in concrete form. Following the events of 11 September 2001, this requirement for *insecuritization* is easily satisfied because of the familiarity of the *homo terrorismus* in the Canadian popular imaginary.[46]

Although *insecuritization* remains unspoken and unnamed in dominant discourse, its unspoken and unnamed character reveals its ideological import: to speak and name *insecuritization* would be to identify, categorize, and codify this term thereby limiting and placing strictures on its political use value. Through remaining unspoken and unnamed, the political value of *insecuritization* is unlimited and can subsequently be utilized infinitely to support the political and its related discursive formations as circumstances dictate. As such, it is precisely the abstraction of *insecuritization* that enables it to assume the function of the master signifier. In effect, *insecuritization* unifies the dominant discursive formation and gives this formation its expressive coherence because without it the metonymic chain of signification could not be halted and would therefore be rendered formless and incoherent. As a consequence, this lack of form and coherence would oversaturate the discursive making it relatively devoid of meaning and thereby eliminate its practical function in maintaining and reinforcing a normative order predicated on particular political and social codes. Now that the elements and articulations of the dominant discursive formation have been established, this formation can be visualized in the following form (Fig. 3.3):

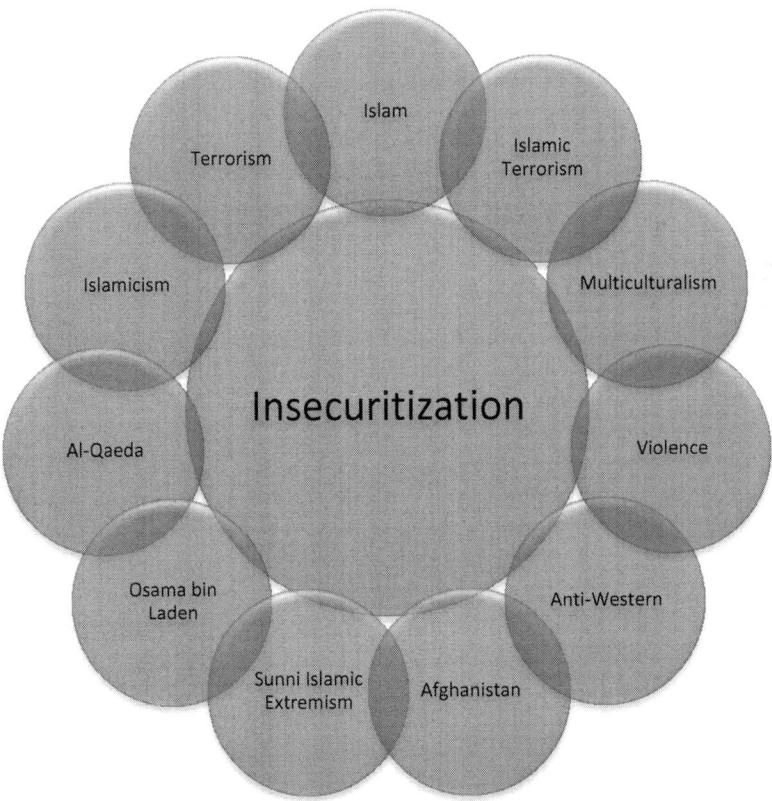

Fig. 3.3 "Dominant discursive formation"

Indeed, the same process that was used to construct the dominant discursive formation can also be used to construct the subversive discursive formation. However, to what body of articulatory material does one turn to properly identify and situate the ideological position and discursive formation of the subversive?

Currently, there is a multitude of ideological material written by an equally diverse group of ideologues that is utilized to support Islamitic movements and groups of all types: nationalist, secessionist, irredentist, transnational, and domestic. As a result of this miasma of material and figures, there has been a tendency, at least in formal discourse, to fetishize the works of some historical and more recent doctrinarians in an effort to explain the ideological genealogy and motivations of particular Islamitic movements and groups, especially al-Qaeda and/or movements and groups designated to be al-Qaeda affiliates. For instance, as Madawi Al-Rasheed observes, "Everywhere we find references to the medieval theologian Taqi al-Din Ahmad ibn Taymiyya (1263–1328) and the eighteenth-century founder of Wahhabism, Muhammad ibn 'Abd al-Wahhab (1703–92); we conclude that Salafi Jihadis draw on these sources, which in turn become part of the ideology of terror."[47] In other works, such as John Zimmerman's article "Sayyid Qutb's Influence on the 11 September Attacks," Sayyid Qutb (1906–1966) and Syed Abu A 'La Mawdudi (1903–1979) are identified as the principal ideologues of Islamitic extremism.[48] Additionally, others identify Ayman Al-Zawahiri as the principal ideological architect of contemporary Islamitic extremism.[49] Although the influence of these individual ideologues is certainly evident in a significant amount of the material used to inform, mobilize, and animate the activities of particular groups, the fetishization of one or two figures in formal discourse not only leaves the impression that to know these figures is to universally understand the ideology of Islamitic extremism but can lead to the oversimplification of a complex and nuanced ideological field. As Michael Watt identifies, "There is no unified body of Islamist thought and practice, and this holds true *a fortiori* for its most militant or terrorist forms of expression."[50] In reality, as even a cursory glance of the abovementioned ideologues demonstrates, the ideology of Islamitic extremism is not homogeneous but is highly variegated, is deeply intertextual, and is derived from a multiplicity of different sources.[51] Furthermore, the fetishization of particular ideologues can lead to the erroneous assumption that different Islamitic extremist groups, such as al-Qaeda, al-Qaeda affiliates, and/or al-Qaeda-inspired groups, rely upon the same ideologues and/or ideological material to animate their activities across space and time. However, this assumption is misleading as groups that appear to share ideological predispositions and affinities may rely upon different sources of inspiration to animate their activities. For example, whereas Ayman Al-Zawahiri directly relies upon Sayyid Qutb to inform dimensions of his ideological position,[52] the individual who acted as the principal ideologue of the Toronto 18, based upon the available evidence, did not directly rely upon the work of Sayyid Qutb or Ayman Al-Zawahiri to inform his ideological position and that of the group. Therefore, just as one should conduct a place-specific analysis to determine the conditions that make the ideological conditioning and political transformation of Islamitic social actors probable, one needs to identify and analyze the material each Islamitic formation relies upon to inform and animate its activities in order to more accurately understand the ideological field and discursive formation these actors occupy. As Madawi Al-Rasheed states, "There is no doubt that there is a set of global utterances, religious arguments, poetry, images, iconography and discourses that Jihadis themselves have circulated in global media and applied in real localities. Yet it is important to examine local contexts, and their relevance to the emergence of Jihadi groups."[53] As such, to construct as accurately as possible the subversive discursive formation to which some of the actors involved in the Toronto 18 transgressed and occupied, it is important to analyze the primary ideological material found in possession of various members of this group.

The following documents and materials were recovered in hardcopy form and/or from computer hard drives and/or memory sticks confiscated during the arrests of the various members of the Toronto 18:

- *Millat Ibrahim* (The Religion of Abraham) written by the Palestinian-Jordanian ideologue Abu Muhammad 'Asim Al-Maqdisi (1959-present).
- *Essay Regarding the Basic Rule of the Blood, Wealth and Honour of the Disbelievers* written by an anonymous ideologue associated with the online publisher: At-Tibyan Publications.
- *Fundamental Concepts Regarding Al-Jihad* written by the Egyptian ideologue 'Abdul-Qadir Ibn Abdul Aziz (1950-present).
- *Constants on the Path of Jihad* written by the Saudi ideologue Yusuf al-Uyayri (1967–2003) and translated into an English audio recording by the Yemeni-American ideologue Anwar al-'Awlaki (1971–2011).

(The English language recording was recovered during the arrests. Sections of this lecture were played during one of the *halaqahs* at the winter training camp in Washago, Ontario.)
- *39 Ways to Serve and Participate in Jihad* written by the Saudi ideologue 'Isa al-Awshin (assassinated 2004) under the pseudonym Muhammad bin Ahmad as-Salim.

Similar to the approach employed above, to identify the articulations which in totality constitute the subversive discursive formation, it is necessary to first identity the positive content of this formation. Arguably, the positive content of the subversive formation is revealed in the text *Millat Ibrahim*. In this text, al-Maqdisi argues that there is a knowable, singular, and authentic religion of Islam that is embodied by the concept of *Millat Ibrahim* to which Allah, according to al-Maqdisi, has lent his approval:

> And indeed We bestowed aforetime on Ibrahim his (portion) of guidance.... And He said: Truly, We chose him in this world and verily, in the Hereafter he will be among the righteous. And He approved his *Da'wah* for us and ordered the seal of all the Prophets and Messengers [i.e. Muhammad] to follow it and He made foolishness to be a description for everyone who turns away from his path and his methodology. And the Millah of Ibrahim is: Sincerity of worship to Allah alone, with everything that the phrase 'The Worship'(*Al-Ibadah*) encompasses in meanings.[54]

However, to bring his argument regarding the "righteous" and "sincere" of those that follow *Millat Ibrahim* into force, al-Maqdisi relies upon a positional-relational identification of the opposite, those deemed to be unrighteous and insincere, i.e. disbelievers and apostates, which he supports by quoting Surah 60 (Al-Mumtahanah), 4: "Indeed there has been an excellent example for you in Ibrahim and those with him, when they said to their people: 'Verily, we are free from you and whatever you worship besides Allah, we have rejected you, and it has become openly seen between us and you, hostility and hatred for ever, until you believe in Allah Alone.'"[55] Furthermore, the content of these two articulations represents the foundation of al-Maqdisi's conceptualization of *Millat Ibrahim*: the absolute and unequivocal loyalty to the worship of Allah and the active repudiation and denunciation, what al-Maqdisi refers to as "disavowal (*Bara' ah*)," of "disbelievers (*Kuffar*)" and "polytheists (*Mushrikin*)."[56] As Maqdisi states, which is quoted at length:

Yes, verily the *Millah of Ibrahim* holds one accountable for much. But in that, is tied the victory of Allah and the huge success. And with it, the people are differentiated into groups; the group of faith (*Iman*) and the group of disbelief (*Kufr*) and transgressions (*Fusuq*) and disobedience (*'Usyan*). And with it, the allies of The Most Merciful (*Ar-Rahman*) become distinguished from the allies of the Satan (*Ash-Shaytan*). Such was the *Da'wah* of the Prophets and the Messengers. They did not have these sick conditions, which we live with today from everything being all mixed up between the righteous and the unrighteous or the cozying-up to or sitting of the bearded people along with the people of transgression (*Fisq*) and wickedness (*Fujur*) and their honoring them and holding them above or ahead of the people of righteousness (*Birr*) and piety (*Taqwa*), despite the fact that those people openly show hatred and enmity towards the religion by several different means. Rather, their *Da'wahs* were clear disavowal (*Bara 'ah*) from their people who turned away from the legislation of Allah with open enmity towards their false deities, not compromising nor cozying-up nor making things nice in the conveyance of the legislation of Allah.[57]

In effect, as these statements reveal, the same relation between a conceived interiority and a conceived exteriority is being utilized to explicate the positive content of the subversive discursive formation. Therefore, just as the positive content of the dominant discursive formation relies upon its negative content in order for the dominant formation to be realized and actualized, the same is true of the subversive discursive formation. Subsequently, as in the case of the dominant discursive formation, the negative content of the subversive discursive formation displaces its positive content as the actual substance of this formation.

The negative content of the subversive discursive formation becomes apparent through the characterization of the current threat to Islam and the obligatory response by Muslims to these threats as variously articulated in the primary ideological material found in possession of the various members of the Toronto 18. For instance, as-Salim characterizes the threat to Islam and by extension Muslims in the following terms:

My noble brothers: the times in which we live are times of tribulation and estrangement for Islam that history has not witnessed before, where strangeness has become the norm and tribulation has become widespread, and where the entire Earth has become a stage for this conflict and for the expulsion of those who are firm upon their *Din* and hold onto it and defend it with their tongues and weapons… therefore, the entire world has announced its war on terrorism—or, rather, on *Jihad*—and its opposition to it and its various forms from being utilized by Muslims.[58]

Similarly al-'Awlaki describes the present era as one when "every government in the world is in line to fight Islam without exception."[59] According to al-'Awlaki, the entire world is mobilizing their "religious strength, political strength, economic strength, media strength, cultural strength, and popular strength" to fight against Jihad.[60] As a consequence of this current geopolitical condition, according to as-Salim, "*Jihad* today is the Ummah's only choice, as the enemy today has occupied the lands of the Muslims—one by one—as Allah the exalted said: '...And they will never cease fighting you until they cause you to turn back for your *Din*, if they are able to do so...' So, the Muslims today are left with no choice but that of *Jihad* and the language of weaponry."[61] In effect, as a result of these present circumstances, as Aziz argues, jihad has become the primary obligation of all Muslims: "Just as we see that the working of Muslims in any matter other than *Jihad* in the Path of Allah—in this time—as many of the Islamic groups do, is a betrayal of Allah and His Messenger and a betraying of this religion and losing it."[62] Aziz supports his argument by advancing three key considerations: the obligation of *Jihad At-Talab*, the obligation of *Jihad* as *Fardh 'Ayn*, and the obligation of fighting the nearest enemy.

According to Aziz, in the current geopolitical context, "the Muslim Nation is a *Mujahid* Nation" and must conduct itself accordingly. This includes not only engaging in *Jihad Ad-Dafa'* (defensive jihad) but engaging in *Jihad At-Talab* (offensive jihad).[63] As Aziz asserts:

> I say: And the Muslim must know that the belief that *Jihad At-Talab* is obligatory upon the Muslims, results in a clash with the modern international laws, which forbid the aggression of the countries against one another and prohibit the seizure of lands of others forcefully—these laws, whom the powerful ones who implemented them supersede them—but Allah, the Most High, said: Therefore fear not men but fear me...And He, the Most High, said: Verily, Allah will help those who help His (Cause).

Furthermore, in addition to arguing that offensive jihad is permissible, Aziz states that jihad is *Fardh 'Ayn* or is an individual obligation, and, as such, it is incumbent upon every Muslim to perform jihad: "I say: And the fact that the *Jihad* against those *Tawaghit* is *Fardh 'Ayn* is from the knowledge, which is obligatory to be spread amongst the general population of the Muslims, so that every Muslim will know that he is personally commanded by his Lord, Glory be to Him, to fight them."[64] As Aziz continues in a later section:

Verily, the *Jihad* presently, is *Fardh 'Ayn* upon the Muslims in most of the regions of the Earth. So the Muslim must perform *Jihad* in his country or must perform the *Hirjah* to support his *Mujahid* brothers in another country. And whoever is unable (with a valid excuse) from the (*Islamic*) legislation (*Shara'*), to do one or the other, then he must spend his wealth in the Path of Allah and must incite the believers upon the *Jihad*, and must strongly supplicate to Allah, the Powerful, the Majestic, to destroy the disbelievers and give the believers a near rescue and a quick victory.[65]

In addition to arguing that the present circumstances require *Jihad At-Talab* and that this jihad is *Fardh 'Ayn*, Aziz argues that it is obligatory to begin fighting the enemy that is closest in geographical proximity to the believers:

Ibn Qudameh said, "Topic: And Every People Fights Those Who Are Nearest to Them From the Enemy"—And the basic principle in this is His, the Most High's statement: O you who believe! Fight those of the disbelievers who are close to you… and because the nearest one is more harmful. And in fighting him, there is the repelling of his harm away from those who are directly facing them and away from those who are behind them.[66]

According to as-Salim, the failure to honor and actualize these obligations is to have committed a transgression against Islam. Quoting a scholar to support his position, as-Salim states:

The scholars have always considered the abandonment of *Jihad* to be from the greatest of sins. Ibn Hajar al-Haythami said: "The 391st and 392nd major sins: abandoning *Jihad* when it has become an individual obligation; when the enemy has entered into the lands of Islam, or took a Muslim as a prisoner that is capable of being rescued from them, or if the people abandon *Jihad* altogether, or if the people of the outskirts of the Islamic state abandon fortifying the frontlines, leaving them open to the attacks of the disbelievers." And because of this, the abandonment of *Jihad* and preparation for it is considered a sign of hypocrisy, as the Messenger of Allah (peace be upon him) said: "Whoever dies without fighting, or at least having the intention to fight, then he dies upon a branch of hypocrisy."[67]

However, just as there are those that support this particular construction of jihad, there are those that argue against it. Consequently, those from within Islam that argue against jihad represent an additional threat to the authentic Islam. Indeed, the ideological material found in possession of the various members of the Toronto 18 warns against these "hypocrites." As Aziz states, "And whomsoever from the scholars prevents the Muslims from *Jihad*, using these misconceptions, out of favoritism, and out of support for the disbeliever ruler; then there is no doubt concerning the *Kufr* of this scholar. He is an apostate, out of the religion of *Islam* and his ruling is the (same) ruling as his governing master."[68] Similarly, as-Salim asserts that these scholars represent the "extended arms of imperialism and Westernization" as they prevent "the *Ummah* from arming itself and they ask Muslims to live their lives in a state of "submission and humiliation."[69] Additionally, al-'Awlaki warns that some scholars are spreading misinformation regarding jihad. According to al-'Awlaki, Muslims "do not need jihad to be redefined by borrowing meanings from the East or the West because our heritage is sufficient for us to teach us what jihad means. We do not have to consult anybody on this issue because it's all clear in Qu'ran and Sunnah."[70] In effect, in this ideological material, jihad is presented as a test of faith, and those that deviate from or advocate the departure from this particular construction of jihad are considered to be inauthentic and insincere Muslims. So, what is the negative content that is brought into focus through the series of articulations outlined above?

Arguably, the following articulatory mechanisms reveal the negative content of the subversive discursive formation: "kuffar," "mushrikin," "war on terrorism," "war on jihad," "occupation of Muslim lands," "imperialism," "westernization," "submission and humiliation," "Jihad in the Path of Allah," "Jihad At-Talab," "Fardh-Ayn," "fight nearest enemy," "Millah of Ibrahim," "hatred and enmity," "hypocrisy," betrayal," and "apostasy." As conceptualized above, these individual articulations form a metonymically contiguous associational cluster which, in aggregate, provides the expressive substance of the subversive discursive formation. Now that the negative content of the subversive discursive formation has been established, again, one can look into the shadows of these articulations to identify the master signifier which gives this formation its unified coherence.

Similar to the analytical method employed above, conducting an examination of the dialectical relationship between the discursive content and the extra-discursive situation, not only is the ideological function of the subversive discursive formation revealed but the master signifier is made apparent as well. The discursive content of the subversive formation needs to be understood in relation to two distinct yet nonetheless interrelated and mutually reinforcing extra-discursive situations. The first relates to the active support of state repression and the coordinated efforts to prevent political and economic reforms in Southwest Asia by the USA and many of its allies from the Eisenhower administration through to the current Obama administration.[71] This situation and its attendant policies and practices are elucidated by Noam Chomsky who cites a US National Security Council (NSC) report 5801 released in January 1958 entitled *Long-Range U.S. Policy toward the Near East*. As Chomsky documents:

> President Eisenhower expressed his concern about "the campaign of hatred against us" in the Arab world, "not by governments but by the people." The reasons for the "campaign of hatred" were outlined by the National Security Council: "In the eyes of the majority of Arabs the United States appears to be opposed to the realization of the goals of Arab nationalism. They believe that the United States is seeking to protect its interest in Near East oil by supporting the status quo and opposing political or economic progress." Furthermore, the perceptions are accurate: "Our economic and cultural interests in the area have led not unnaturally to close U.S. relations with elements in the Arab world whose primary interest lies in the maintenance of relations with the West and the status quo in their countries," blocking democracy and development.[72]

As a result of the repressive policies and practices pursued by the USA and its allies in the region, a significant proportion of civil society throughout Southwest Asia has developed a very negative perception of Western involvement in this region. For example, according to a Pew Global Attitudes survey conducted in July 2011 that was designed to measure "Muslim-Western Tensions," approximately 53 % of the respondents surveyed identified US and Western policies as the predominant reason for the lack of prosperity in this part of the world. The second reason identified was government corruption and the third was lack of democracy. Incidentally, the reasons cited for the impairment of economic development in the region correlate directly with the USA and its allied policies.[73] This extra-discursive situation of Western-supported state repression and the negative perceptions it engenders is compounded by the second extra-discursive situation.

The second extra-discursive situation relates to the belligerent response of the USA and its allies to the events of 11 September 2001 as embodied by the war of terror. Indeed, the ill-conceived invasion of Afghanistan[74]; the condemnable occupation of Iraq[75]; the unlawful use of extraordinary rendition to apprehend and transfer suspects to detention and torture facilities around the world, such as Guantanamo Bay and other clandestine prison sites positioned in Eastern Europe, Central Asia, and Southeast Asia[76];

the abuse and torture of prisoners in Abu Ghraib[77]; the aggressive expansion of the war of terror into Pakistan, Yemen, Somalia, the Maghreb and Sub-Saharan Africa, Central Asia (Kazakhstan, Kyrgyzstan, Uzbekistan, Tajikistan, Turkmenistan) and Southeast Asia (southern Thailand, the Philippines, and Indonesia); the extrajuridical targeted killing of Islamitic extremist suspects; and the exclusionary socio-political rhetoric, policies, and practices experienced by Muslims living in Western Europe and North America create an impression that Muslims are under attack on a scale that is virtually global. As Christina Hellmich suggests, reacting to al-Qaeda with war has only reinforced the perception that the USA and its allies are a violent and oppressive force that causes suffering and pain to Muslims and that these same forces are at war with the Muslim world.[78] This perception is reflected in the findings of the Pew Global Attitudes survey referred to above. According to this survey, approximately 61 % of Muslim respondents believe the USA is hostile toward Muslims, and approximately 58 % of Muslim respondents believe Europeans are hostile toward Muslims.[79] In the context of these two extradiscursive situations, the ideological function of the subversive discursive formation becomes evident: the inculcation of the threat posed by Western powers to the political, social, and spatial codes and orderings of an imagined *Ummah* to galvanize a small segment of Muslims worldwide to synthesize the insurrectionary ideology of the subversive and actively participate in political violence to challenge the policies and practices of the USA and other Western allied powers. Therefore, similar to the dominant formation, if the ideological function of the subversive discursive formation is to generate threat and fear to achieve particular political, social, and spatial objectives, the same process of an ontological *insecuritization* animates the subversive and, ultimately, serves as the master signifier of this formation. Furthermore, just as the imagistic referent of the *homo terrorismus* makes the dominant formation possible, this same imagistic referent makes the subversive possible. The subversive relies upon the ideological construction of the *homo terrorismus* to not only reinforce a civilizational bifurcated worldview as conceptualized by Huntington but to demonstrate in the present time-space conjuncture that Muslims are under attack necessitating their mobilization to overcome real or imagined adversaries and in the process realize the authentic Islam—embodied by the *homo terrorismus*.

Now that the elements and articulations of the subversive discursive formation have been established, this formation can be visualized in the following form (Fig. 3.4):

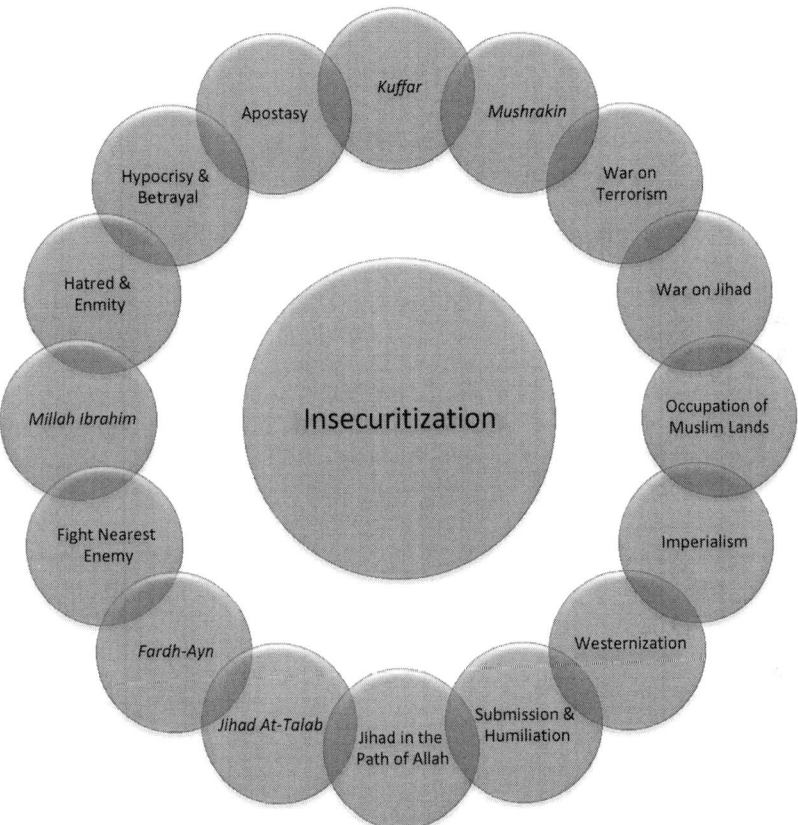

Fig. 3.4 "Subversive discursive formation"

The dominant discursive formation and the subversive discursive formation represent two competing and antagonistic ideological positions that provide divergent "frameworks for action."[80] However, the subversive discursive formation should not be understood as emerging outside of and in reaction to advanced Western modernity. On the contrary, the subversive discursive formation and the framework for action it makes possible arise inside of and are a product of advanced Western modernity.[81] In effect, each discursive formation ultimately informs differing representations, perceptions, meanings, and constructions of place while functioning in the same place-specific context.

The relationship between the dominant and subversive formations and the making of place can be understood when one considers the following proposition advanced by David Harvey: "Place, in whatever guise, is like space and time, a social construct."[82] As a social construct, place is always ideologically constituted. However, within any given social field circulate a multiplicity of ideational systems whose symbolic power is determined by the complex social processes and forces operating within that given social field. Therefore, as different social actors, in this case Islamitic social actors, become entangled within these social processes and forces, these actors begin to interpret and mediate their effective reality through ideational systems that strengthen and empower them in order to cope with and negotiate this same effective reality.[83] As a result, differing ideational systems necessarily inform different meanings of place in accordance with the needs and requirements of the social actors themselves. Although the social processes and forces through which place is constructed and conditioned are contingent and protean in character and change from context to context, place as a social construct is multilayered and is determined by the complex imbrications of ideological, institutional, and physical processes and forces.[84] In the context of this analysis, these different layers and processes and forces are expressed through the transnational sphere of influence (ideological), the state sphere of influence (institutional), and the group sphere of influence (physical).

A Janus-Faced Creature: Advanced Western Modernity and the Production of the Subversive

The production of the subversive is made possible because of two distinct yet interconnected generative moments that directly correspond to the foreign policy discourses, institutions, arrangements, alignments, and practices of the USA and other allied powers, including Canada. The first moment is discursive in character and the second moment is political in character. However, before continuing, it is necessary to establish how the concept of "foreign policy" is deployed in this context.

According to David Campbell, foreign policy is a boundary-making enterprise that is central to the production and reproduction of a national identity in whose name foreign policy operates and functions. Consequently, as the compound adjective "boundary-making" suggests, foreign policy is predicated on the process of political and social demarcation and differentiation between what a sovereign national body is versus what that sovereign nation body is not. Epistemologically, this demarcation and differentiation is realized through the dialectical friction created by dichotomous constructions, such as subject/object, inside/outside, self/other, order/disorder, West/East, rational/irrational, civilized/barbaric, modern/traditional, secular/religious, good/evil, inclusion/exclusion, center/periphery, and so on.[85] As Campbell identifies, in each instance of these dichotomous constructions, "the former is the higher, regulative ideal to which the latter is derivative and inferior, and a source of danger to the former's existence." As such, "in each instance, 'sovereignty' (or its equivalent) signifies a center of decision presiding over a self that is to be valued and demarcated from an external domain that cannot or will not be assimilated to the identity of the sovereign domain."[86] In effect, as Campbell goes on to assert:

> A notion of what "we" are is intrinsic to an understanding of what "we" fear. What this highlights is that there is an axiological level that proffers a range of moral valuations that are implicit in any spatialization. The construction of social space that emerges from practices associated with the paradigm of sovereignty thus exceeds a simple geographical partitioning; it results in a conception of divergent moral spaces. In other words, the social space of inside/outside is both made possible by and helps constitute a moral space of superior/inferior, which can be animated in terms of any number of figurations of higher/lower.[87]

In this sense, "foreign policy" is the register of evaluative equivalencies through which codes of normalization are transmitted to not only strengthen national identity as authorized by the state but to legitimize the projection of state force both domestically and internationally to uphold and protect that authorized identity. Although there are myriad fearful figurations through which these evaluative equivalencies are realized and actualized, the figuration that is most germane to the present boundary-making enterprise of "foreign policy" is embodied by the danger, threat, and fear of Islam and its violent by-products: Transnational Islamitic Extremism and Domestic Islamitic Extremism.

In a return to the first foreign policy initiative alluded to above, the epistemological production of the subversive is made possible through the evaluative equivalences used to reinforce the national identities of various Western states vis-à-vis the Western rationalist construction of Islam as received through and framed by Orientalist discourse. As a product of Western rationalism, Orientalist discourse is not only the expression of Western conceptions of modernity, political fears, social anxieties, and cultural unease but is a product of a process of translation through which the political, social, economic, cultural, and geographical characteristics of the spatial unit encompassing Southwest Asia and North Africa are filtered through a Western system of knowledge premised on and animated by the following system of equivalencies: rationality/irrationality, superiority/inferiority, and interiority/exteriority.[88] As a result of these Western rationalist equivalencies, several representations of the political, social, economic, and cultural geographies of Southwest Asia and North Africa have become deeply embedded in the North American and Western European imaginary. According to Edward Said, these representations include the following: that there is an absolute difference between the West, which is "rational, developed, humane, and superior," and Southwest Asia and North Africa, which is irrational, undeveloped, inhumane, and inferior; that Southwest Asia and North Africa are eternal, homogeneous, and incapable of change; and that Southwest Asia and North Africa are areas of the world to be feared because of the essential differences between this area of the world and the West, and the proclivity for violence that defines the culture of this area of the world. Therefore, as a consequence of these qualities, Southwest Asia and North Africa are represented and understood as regions that need to be controlled through research, pacification, intervention, development, and occupation when necessary.[89] Furthermore, this modality of interpretation and representation is supported, promulgated, and naturalized by a vast institutional infrastructure that is comprised of mutually reinforcing repressive and ideological apparatuses that share a common set of images, doctrines, scholarship, and vocabulary.[90]

The magnitude of this institutional infrastructure and related wellspring of materials creates the appearance that Western rationalism, as expressed through Orientalist discourse, is neutral, objective, and scientifically informed and supported.[91] Indeed, the scientific masquerade of Orientalist discourse enhances its appearance as a body of knowledge determined by scientific reason and fact rather than as a self-referential, vacuous, and propagandistic discourse predicated on an elaborate power/knowledge relationship that is supported by a system of equivalencies and a series of rhetorical tropes that serve elite geopolitical interests and power. As Edward Said explains:

> [Orientalism] brings opposites together as "natural," it presents human types in scholarly idioms and methodologies, it ascribes reality and reference to objects (other words) of its own making. Mythic language is discourse,

that is, it cannot be anything but systematic; one does not really make discourse at will, or statements in it, without first belonging—in some cases unconsciously, but at any rate involuntarily—to the ideology and the institutions that guarantee its existence. These latter are always the institutions of an advanced society dealing with a less advanced society, a strong culture encountering a weak one. The principal feature of mythic discourse is that it conceals its own origins as well as those of what it describes.[92]

In effect, the representational body of Orientalist discourse is a system of fabrications and myths whose validity is not guaranteed by the empirical manifold but by the ability to reproduce itself within an ideational matrix controlled by and limited to elite interests and opinions. Yet, despite the mythic character of Orientalist discourse, its efficacy as a legitimate and accurate body of knowledge persists and flourishes in both Western Europe and North America in a hegemonic fashion. Although the persistence of Orientalist discourse is indicative of the formidable character of the power/knowledge relationship, Jacques Lacan summarizes in rather succinct terms this type of epistemological arrangement and situation: "One can bullshit a lot over myths, because it is precisely the field of bullshitting. And bullshitting, as I have always said, is truth. They are identical. Truth enables everything to be said. Everything is true—on condition that you exclude the contrary—except that it nevertheless plays a role that it be like that."[93] Nevertheless, the currency of Western rationalism as expressed through Orientalist discourse, its circulation, and its consumption is not confined to the Western European and North American audiences for which it was originally intended. Instead, the influence of this discourse has spread globally, including into Southwest Asia and North Africa themselves with significant implications.[94]

The imbrications of Orientalist discourse in Southwest Asia and North Africa in its most acute form surface in the subversive discursive formation of Islamitic extremism. Whether consciously or unconsciously, the contemporary ideologues of Islamitic extremism have internalized many of the equivalencies, tropes, and methods of Orientalist discourse only to reproduce and rearticulate these same devices in a displaced form. For instance, al-Maqdisi's espousal of an authentic, unitary, timeless, and sincere Islam; al-'Awlaki's and Aziz's insistence that the use of violent action against disbelievers is inherent to Islamic legislation and that by extension this violent action is obligatory for all Muslims who are able to participate;

al-'Awlaki's advocacy of a philological method to understand and interpret Islam; and the overall presentation of the antagonisms between an abstracted West and Islam as a natural and irrevocable universal historical without any attempt to properly situate and contextualize these antagonisms beyond religious and cultural differences and incompatibilities all reflect the influence of Orientalist discourse and methods to inform and legitimate the position of Islamitic extremism. In effect, Islamitic extremist ideologues like those mentioned above, to use the terminology of Aziz Al-Azmeh, "re-orientalize themselves"[95] and the religion of Islam. As a result not only do these ideologues reify the Orientalist construction of the civilizational uniqueness of the Muslim *Ummah*, but they reinforce the Orientalist construction of the inevitability of a clash between the two "opposing essentialisms"[96] of the West and Islam. Ironically, the ideational matrix of the Orientalist enterprise and the attendant system of equivalencies and tropes that are utilized to construct the Islamic Other to reaffirm the national identity of the Western European and North American Self is the same system of equivalencies and tropes that informs, reaffirms, and empowers the supranational identity of the Islamitic extremist Other. Arguably, on an epistemological level, the subversive discursive formation of Islamitic extremism would not exist in its contemporary form without the borrowings of Orientalist discourse. In this sense, it is the boundary making of "foreign policy" and its figuration of the Islamitic Other that is integral to the production and constitution of Islamitic extremism.

The second generative moment that has made the production of the subversive discursive formation possible relates to the international deployment and operationalization of Western European and US "foreign policy" and its engagement of Islam during World War II and the subsequent Cold War period. In contrast to the belligerent engagement with Islam which followed the events of 11 September 2001, the mode of engagement was much more sanguine during World War II and the Cold War. Geostrategically, during these two periods, Western Europe, the USA, and its client powers actively cultivated and supported a relationship with particular Muslim actors located globally to engage by proxy the Soviet Union.[97]

During World War II, Nazi Germany developed through its Ministry for the Occupied Eastern Territories (*Ostministerium*) a strategy and supporting administrative infrastructure to mobilize Muslim minorities in Soviet-controlled Central Asia to expand Nazi territorial influence into this region of the world to not only militarily harass the Soviets but to help secure its geostrategic interests in the petroleum deposits located in and around the Caspian basin. Administratively, the success of this strategy relied upon the development of liaison offices to provide the military leaders harvested from the various ethnic groups of this region with some form of official representation within the Nazi establishment, however tenuous and superficial. As Ian Johnson explains, the success of this administrative strategy "depended on convincing soldiers in the field that these liaison offices were indeed quasi governments in exile. The offices held out the hope of independence to the various non-Russian ethnic groups, even if the Nazis had little intent of actually ceding it to them."[98] Ideologically, the success of this strategy relied upon Nazi Germany's ability to overcome ethnic divisions and unify potential recruits and soldiers through creating an imagined community of actors who shared a common identity. The perception of an imagined community among these actors was nurtured by inculcating them with the belief that their individual objectives were all interconnected with a broader and singular Islamic identity. To create this impression, as Ian Johnson outlines, not only did Nazi Germany recruit prominent Islamic leaders, such as the Grand Mufti of Jerusalem, Amin al-Husseini, to endorse the common identity, but a series of mosques/masjids and madrassahs were created around Germany to propagate this common identity and reinforce the identities of their common enemies.[99] Ultimately, the geopolitical instrumentalization of Islam and Muslim groups by the Nazis during World War II and its concomitant administrative infrastructure and ideological conditioning would serve as a model for the USA with the support of its allied puppet monarchies in Southwest Asia following the armistice of World War II and the onset of the Cold War.

At the beginning of the Cold War and as the contest over global space was beginning to take shape, the USA identified Islam as a weapon that it could utilize to strengthen its position and serve its geostrategic interests in various parts of the developing world. According to Ian Johnson, "Under Truman, U.S. intelligence reportedly was on the lookout for a charismatic figure who could rally Muslims in an anticommunist crusade."[100] However, under Eisenhower, the effort to geostrategically utilize and deploy Islam as a weapon was intensified. In 1953, a memorandum entitled "The Religious Factor" was crafted for Eisenhower that emphasized the importance of exploiting religion for political advantage. Incidentally, the issuance of this memorandum closely coincided with the passage of National Security Council Report 162/2 which defined the

Cold War strategy of the USA and its related policy formulations for its security apparatuses, including the mobilization of religious resources.[101] In 1957, the Operations Coordinating Board, which was an entity created to oversee the implementation of covert plans of various security apparatuses in the USA, issued a report that not only detailed various initiatives that should be undertaken to strengthen the relationships between various US agencies and foreign and domestic Islamic organizations but, more importantly, emphasized the need to ensure that all of the initiatives and relationships be as covert as possible so that the conscientious and deliberate manipulation of Islam for geopolitical purposes remained obscured.[102] Although the Vietnam War redirected US foreign policy strategy, the strategic use of Islam as a geopolitical instrument was revived following the Russian invasion of Afghanistan in 1979. Arguably, in fact, it is during this conflict that the manipulation and weaponization of Islam reached its apotheosis.[103]

According to Mahmood Mamdani, the primary objective of the USA during the Russian-Afghani conflict was "to unite a billion Muslims worldwide in a holy war, a crusade, against the Soviet Union, on the soil of Afghanistan."[104] To realize this objective, the Central Intelligence Agency (CIA), in conjunction with Pakistani and Saudi intelligence agencies among others, developed a labyrinthine network of recruitment nodes, training facilities, and madrassahs to both attract and produce the most extreme anti-communists to engage the Soviet Union in Afghanistan. As a result, Islamitic actors from, but not limited to, Algeria, Chechnya, Egypt, Kosovo, Indonesia, Saudi Arabia, Sudan, the UK, and the USA filtered through this network.[105] Mamdani describes the madrassahs as "politico-military training schools"[106] that integrated guerilla tactics with Islamic doctrine. According to Dilip Hiro, the predominant themes taught at these madrassahs included: "that Islam was a complete sociopolitical ideology, that holy Islam was being violated by atheistic Soviet troops, and that the Islamic people of Afghanistan should reassert their independence by overthrowing the leftist Afghan regime propped up by Moscow."[107] In addition to the ideological conditioning of the madrassahs that framed the conflict as an Islamic holy war, the training facilities, located in both Pakistan and the USA, instructed recruits in many of the advanced tactics and techniques currently utilized by contemporary Islamitic extremist groups and actors, such as infiltration/exfiltration; bomb making, including the sophisticated use of (remote) timers, detonators, and explosives;

small arms and ammunition, and so on. In effect, rather than constructing an infrastructure of emancipation, the USA and its partners constructed an "infrastructure of terror" whose durability and effectiveness was realized long after the formal cessation of hostilities against the form Soviet Union in Afghanistan.[108]

According to an investigation conducted by the *Los Angeles Times*, "the key leaders of every major terrorist attack, from New York to France to Saudi Arabia, inevitably turned out to have been veterans of the Afghan War."[109] Indeed, as has been widely documented, Osama bin Laden himself was a product of this infrastructure of terror. In short, the consequence of the operationalization of US "foreign policy" during the Cold War is succinctly summarized by the Algerian sociologist, Mahfoud Bennoune: "[The U.S. government] participated in creating a monster [.] Now it has turned against you and the world: 16, 000 Arabs were trained in Afghanistan, made into a veritable killing machine."[110] In creating this Frankenstein, the USA contributed significantly to the material perversion of Islam and provided the inspiration, ideological foundation, and practical training necessary for contemporary Islamitic extremism to exist in its current form.

Both the epistemological and material dimensions of US foreign policy reveal the complex conditions that have made the emergence of the subversive discursive formation and its attendant practices possible. On the one hand, US foreign policy contributed to the epistemological demonization of Islam and reified and institutionalized an Us/Them civilizational world view. On the other hand, the operationalization of US foreign policy led to the USA allying itself with the Muslim world, appropriating Islam, and weaponizing this religion for its own geopolitical advantage. It is as a result of this simultaneous demonization and allying instrumentalization of Islam that has produced the current incarnation of Islamitic extremism. As a result of these generative moments, Islamitic extremism cannot be interpreted as existing outside of and in reaction to advanced Western modernity but can be interpreted as existing inside of and as a product of advanced Western modernity. However, that being said, both the dominant and subversive discursive formations not only mutually reinforce an Us/Them dichotomy and worldview, but the dominant and the subversive serve as one another's "constitutive outside."[111]

Although the ideological position of the subversive and the generative moments that made its emergence possible have been established, what remains is an analysis of the conditions that make the transgression from the dominant to the subversive possible in the context of Domestic Islamic Extremism. This analysis is crucial as Domestic Islamic Extremist groups and/or actors do not a priori occupy a subversive ideological position nor are they predisposed to the actions and practices that these positions make probable. In the case of the so-called Toronto 18, a combination of conditions or spheres of influence conflated, converged, and condensed in that specific time-space conjuncture and facilitated the transgression from the dominant to the subversive position and made the articulatory trajectory of the group probable. Using Kevin Cox's conceptualization of "spaces of dependence" and "spaces of engagement" as an interpretive framework, it is possible to develop an understanding of how these spheres of influence came together and made the ideological conditioning and political transformation of the group probable.

"Dependence" and "Engagement": Constructing a Network of Scales

As Kevin Cox argues, political groups and/or actors rely upon two distinct spatial arrangements to realize their place-specific objectives: the space of dependence and the space of engagement. Cox defines these two distinctive spaces in the following terms:

> Spaces of dependence are defined by those more-or-less localized social relations upon which we depend for the realization of essential interests and for which there are no substitutes elsewhere; they define place-specific conditions for our material well being and our sense of significance. These spaces are inserted in broader sets of relationships of a more global character and these constantly threaten to undermine or dissolve them. People, firms, state agencies, etc., organize in order to secure the conditions for the continued existence of their space of dependence but in so doing they have to engage with other centers of social power: local government, the national press, perhaps the international press, for example. In so doing they construct a different form of space which I call here a space of engagement: the space in which the politics of securing a space of dependence unfolds.[112]

In other words, to secure the conditions through which the interests of local social actors can be realized, these actors construct a network of centers of social power that may exist both within and beyond the space of dependence. That is, the space of engagement of a particular social actor can be multiscalar in design, e.g. group, neighborhood, city, regional, national, and international. The space of engagement can therefore be understood as being constituted by a network of scales whose interconnectivity can both influence and support the political objectives of particular actors operating in place-specific contexts. However, the scalar arrangement of a space of engagement is entirely contingent on the political objectives of the actors involved.[113] For instance, "those who fought for black civil rights could never have accomplished what they did by constructing networks of influence within particular Southern cities or States. Rather a much broader network embracing federal officials and an alliance of civil rights workers throughout the country had to be put together. On the other hand, a school board issue may be fought out entirely with the local school district through the construction of networks among (e.g.) Parent Teacher Associations, teacher unions, local realtors and developers."[114] Furthermore, the space of engagement of a particular social actor is provisional and can shift and change as the objectives of the actor shift and change. In the context of Domestic Islamitic Extremism, the spaces of engagement of these social actors are equally contingent. Therefore, one needs to be sensitive to these contingencies when analyzing this phenomenon. For example, although the actors involved in the London transit bombings, the activities of the Toronto 18, and the Boston Marathon bombings are all incarnations of Domestic Islamitic Extremism, it would be mistaken to assume that the space of engagement for one group is the same as the other. As the space of dependence shifts so too does the space of engagement.

In the case of the Toronto 18, the space of dependence of the group is Toronto, and its space of engagement consists of a network of three spheres of influence operating at three distinct scales: the transnational sphere of influence (Chap. 4), the state sphere of influence (Chap. 5), and the group sphere of influence (Chap. 6). It is precisely these spheres of influence operating conjunctively in a network of scales that facilitated the transgression of the group from the dominant to the subversive discursive formation and made the ideological conditioning and political transformation of the group probable. The following three chapters (Chaps. 4, 5, and 6) offer an empirical demonstration of how these three spheres of influence lead to the transgression of various members of the Toronto 18.

Notes

1. Said quoted in Moore, "Remapping Resistance: 'ground for struggle' and the politics of place," 87.
2. The use of the term "contingent" in the context of this argument extends beyond its common meaning and usage: "dependent upon." Instead, contingent refers to a particular relation. As Andrew Sayer explains: "[a] useful distinction can be made between *external*, or *contingent relations* and *internal* or *necessary relations*" (89). This concept of contingency is further elaborated by Sabah Alnasseri who states that the success of any political project "is a complex question that depends on the balance and relation of forces, the forms of struggle, etc." However, as Alnasseri goes on to state, "to avoid the voluntarism and arbitrariness inherent in the concept of contingency, the latter can only be understood as a historical necessity, which means that it depends on the given conditions, not least on the structural selectivity of the state that limits the reach, impact, and implementation of [political] projects" (8). In effect, the concept of contingency draws attention to the historically specific and contextualized conditions that make particular forms of struggle, contestation, and subversion probable. The use of contingency in this sense is important because it invites an understanding that the material condensation of social relations is conjuncturally conditional rather than structurally fixed. As such, the conditions that make the emergence of particular social phenomena in one political/social structure probable do not mean that the same conditions will make the emergence of the same social phenomena probable in a different political/social structure. That is, the same conditions of existence in one political/social structure would have a different outcome in another political/social structure because of differing social relations and institutional forms.
3. Massey, *For Space*, 130.
4. Springer, "Violence sits in places? Cultural practice, neoliberal rationalism, and virulent imaginative geographies," 90–91.
5. Murphy, "The Space of Terror," 50–51.
6. Graham, *Cities Under Siege*, 36.
7. Ibid., 38.
8. Luke, "Everyday Technics as Extraordinary Threats," 135.
9. Slater, "Spatial Politics/Social Movements. Questions of (b)orders and resistance in global times," 261.
10. Cresswell, *In Place/Out of Place*, 9.
11. Ibid., 10.
12. Ibid., 17.
13. Cresswell, *In Place/Out of Place*, 23.

14. Ibid., 23.
15. It is worth noting that the "black bloc" was in many regards nothing but a state construction used as a mechanism to criminalize the political activities of those codified as Other. There is a considerable amount of evidence that reveals much of the destructive activity of the "black bloc" was state sponsored as these activities were orchestrated by *agent provocateurs*.
16. Burke, *Counter-Statement*, 163.
17. Huntington, *Clash of Civilizations*, 26–27.
18. In the context of this argument, interiority refers to the images, values, social codes, and behaviors that both the dominant and the subversive conceive as constituting the Self. Conversely, exteriority refers to the images, values, social codes, and behaviors that both the dominant and subversive conceive as constituting the Other.
19. See, for instance, Laclau & Mouffe, *Hegemony and Socialist Strategy*, xi, 105–115; Sayyid, *A Fundamental Fear: Eurocentrism and the Emergence of Islamism*, 41–49; and Žižek, *The Sublime Object of Ideology*, 95–110.
20. Sayyid, *A Fundamental Fear: Eurocentrism and the Emergence of Islamism*, 45.
21. Sayyid, *A Fundamental Fear: Eurocentrism and the Emergence of Islamism*, 47.
22. Žižek, *The Sublime Object of Ideology*, 103.
23. Chase, "Raids prove that Canada not Soft on terror, Day Says," A2.
24. Dawson, *Reasons for Sentencing*, R.v. Ahmad, 2010 ONSC 5874, 24–25.
25. Hill, *Reasons for Judgement*, R.v. Gaya, DR(F)2541/08, 43.
26. Žižek, *The Sublime Object of Ideology*, 109.
27. For a copy of the transcript of this interview, see http://www.cbc.ca/news/politics/story/2011/09/08/pol-harper-mansbridge-transcript.html. For a review of Prime Minister's characterization of the threat facing Canada, see: Siddiqui, Haroon. (2011, September 11). "PM's rhetoric stokes fires of division." *Toronto Star*, A23.; and Kennedy, Mark. (2011, September 8). "Harper putting too much focus on Islamic extremists: Rae." *National Post*, A14. Furthermore, for a sample of various letters to the editor submitted in response to this characterization, see: (2011, September 17). "Harper on Islamicism." *Toronto Star*, IN7.
28. The Canadian Press in the *Toronto Star*, "Canada adds $8 million to global fund against terror," A16.
29. Ministry of Public Safety, *Building Resilience Against Terrorism: Canada's Counter-Terrorism Strategy*, 4, 7–8.
30. Ibid., 8.

31. Standing Senate Committee on National Security and Defence, *Defence of North America: A Canadian Responsibility*, 23.
32. Quoted in Bell, Stewart & Carlson, Kathryn, "Tories Aim To Fill Terrorism Law Gaps," A7.
33. Kress, Gunther & Van Leeuwen, Theo, *Multimodal Discourse: The Modes and Media of Contemporary Communication*, 10.
34. Burke, *The Philosophy of Literary Form: Studies in Symbolic Action*, 20. As Kenneth Burke explains, "associational clusters" can be understood as the "what goes with what." For instance, as Burke elaborates, the writer will use particular associational clusters to describe "what kinds of acts and images and personalities and situations go with his notions of heroism, villainy, consolation, despair, etc" (20). Similarly, in this context, the Canadian state uses particular machinations to describe its notions of threats to national security and ultimately to the national consensus values embodied by the abstractions of democracy, freedom, justice, liberty, and so on.
35. Ministry of Public Safety, *Building Resilience Against Terrorism: Canada's Counter-Terrorism Strategy*, 10.
36. See, for example, Amery, Zainab. (2013). "The Securitization of Arabs in Canada's Immigration and Citizenship Policies." In Jenna Hennebry & Bessma Momani (Eds.), *Targeted Transnationals: The State, the Media, and Arab Canadians*, (32–53). Toronto: UBC Press.; and Abu-Laban, Yasmeen. (2013). "On the Borderlines of Human and Citizen: The Liminal State of Arab Canadians." In Jenna Hennebry & Bessma Momani (Eds.), *Targeted Transnationals: The State, the Media, and Arab Canadians*, (68–88). Toronto: UBC Press.
37. Following the arrests of the Toronto 18, the debate surrounding multiculturalism as a potential source of threat to the Canadian nation-state certainly emerged in popular discourse. See, for example, Grewal, San. (2006, June 7). "For Muslim students, school can alienate." *Toronto Star*, A10; Bonoguore, Tentille. (2006, June 7). "Diversity, faith stoke debate for Toronto-area educators." *Globe and Mail*, A6; Turley-Ewart, John. (2006, June 8). "Multicultrualism has its limits." *National Post*, A22; and Letters to the Editor. (2006, June 6). *National Post*, A15; and Collacott, Martin. (2006, June 6). "Keeping an eye on who gets in." *National Post*, A17.
38. Henderson, "Burke, Kenneth Duva," 269.
39. Bell, "The kind of security $92-billion buys," A1, A14.
40. Ibid., A14.
41. For a more elaborate analysis and discussion of how fear is manufactured by politicians and decisionmakers to increase state power while eroding

civil liberties, see, for example, Altheide, David L. (2006). *Terrorism and the Politics of Fear*. Maryland: AltaMira Press. For an analysis of the use of fear as a political strategy, see, for example, Robin, Corey. (2004). *Fear: The History of a Political Idea*. New York: Oxford University Press.
42. Purdue, *Terrorism and the State: A Critique of Domination Through Fear*, 20.
43. Martin, "The fear card has been dealt—and Harper will play it," A17. It is worth noting, however, that the inculcation of fear in the Canadian imaginary of an enemy Other by the Canadian state is not without precedent. According to Reg Whitaker and Gary Marcuse, "It was the state that most often played the crucial role in the establishment of the Cold War as a permanent force within Canadian life [.]" See Whitaker and Marcuse, *Cold War Canada: The Making of a National Insecurity State, 1945–1957*, 14.
44. Gandesha, "Ontological Insecurity and the Politics of Fear," 115.
45. Burke, "The Rhetoric of Hitler's "Battle"," 104. Burke defines the projection device as: "The 'curative' process that comes with the ability to hand over one's ills to a scapegoat, thereby getting purification by dissociation." Therefore, as Burke goes on to state, "if one can hand over his infirmities to a vessel, or 'cause,' outside the self, one can battle an external enemy instead of battling an enemy within. And the greater one's internal inadequacies, the greater amount of evils one can load upon the back of 'the enemy.'" As Burke continues, "This device is furthermore given a semblance of reason because the individual properly realizes that he is not alone responsible for his condition. There are inimical factors in the scene itself. And he wants to have them 'placed,' preferably in a way that would require a minimum change in the ways of thinking to which he had been accustomed" (104–105).
46. Although it is difficult to measure the degree of insecuritization experienced by the Canadian social body vis-à-vis Islamitic extremism, various polls provide an impressionistic understanding of the insecuritization felt by Canadians. For example, following the arrests of the suspects involved in the Toronto 18, a poll conducted by CanWest News Service/Global National poll found that 58 % of Canadians believe "the recent terror arrests are the 'tip of the iceberg' and new groups could be planning more attacks." In the same poll, 61 % of Canadians believed we were targeted by virtue of being a Western country (*National Post*, 10 June 2006, A6, A8). Another poll conducted by the Strategic Council following the arrests found that 71 % of Canadians believe an act of terrorism will likely take place in Canada in the next few years (*Globe and Mail*, 10 June 2006, A4). Furthermore, in a poll conducted by IPSOS REID to

measure the attitudes of Canadians toward particular ethnicities and faiths 10 years after 11 September 2001, the poll found that 59 % of Canadians felt that 9/11 gave them a negative impression of certain ethnicities and faiths, 74 % of Canadians believe our society has become less tolerant of others since 9/11, and 60 % of Canadians believe Muslims in Canada are discriminated against more than before (*National Post*, 8 September 2011, A14). Perhaps the most revealing findings to date are those documented in the final report of the *Bouchard-Taylor Commission* (2008) which concluded that Islamophobia is a persistent problem confronting Muslim communities and that this fear was fueled by both popular (media) and practical (institutional) discourse. More significantly, as Mohamed Kamel of the Canadian Muslim Forum identified, this was the first official government-sponsored document that affirmed that Islamophobia is a real force in Canadian society (Sharify-Funk, "Muslims and the Politics of "Reasonable Accommodation": Analyzing the Bouchard-Taylor Report and Its Impact on the Canadian Province of Quebec," 541, 546).
47. Al-Rasheed, "The Local and the Global in Saudi Salafi-Jihadi Discourse," 305. According to Al-Rasheed, for a caricature of this position see: Olivetti, Vincenzo. (2003). *Terror's Source: The Ideology of Wahhabi-Salafism and its Consequences.* Birmingham: Amadeus Books.
48. Zimmerman, "Sayyid Qutb's Influence on the 11 September Attacks," 222.
49. See, for example, Al-Zayyat, Montasser. Fekry, Ahmed (Trans.). Nimis, Sara (Ed.). (2004). *The Road to Al-Qaeda: The Story of Bin-Laden's Right-Hand Man.* London: Pluto Press.
50. Watts, "Revolutionary Islam," 186.
51. Lia, "'Destructive Doctrinarians': Abu Mus'ab al-Suri's Critique of the Salafis in the Jihadi Current," 285.
52. Zimmerman, "Sayyid Qutb's Influence on the 11 September Attacks," 241.
53. Al-Rasheed, "The Local and Global in Saudi Salafi-Jihadi Discourse," 307.
54. al-Maqdisi, *Millat Ibrahim*, 25.
55. Ibid., 11.
56. al-Maqdisi, *Millat Ibrahim*, 39.
57. Ibid., 72. For a comprehensive analysis of al-Maqdisi's conceptualization of *Millat Ibrahim* see: Wagemakers, Joas. "The Transformation of a Radical Concept: *al-wala' wa-l-bara'*" in Meijer, Roel. (Ed.). (2009). *Global Salafism.* New York: Columbia University Press.
58. as-Salim, *39 Ways to Serve and Participate in Jihad*, 5.

59. al-'Awlaki, *The Constants of Jihad*, audio recording.
60. Ibid.
61. as-Salim, *39 Ways to Serve and Participate in Jihad*, 5–6.
62. Aziz, *Fundamental Concepts of Al-Jihad*, 174. Incidentally, this position is reinforced by al-'Awlaki who suggests that Muslims whom do not follow jihad are following their own will and not the will of Allah.
63. Aziz, *Fundamental Concepts of Al-Jihad*, 64.
64. Ibid., 104.
65. Ibid., 174–175.
66. Aziz, *Fundamental Concepts for Al-Jihad*, 90.
67. as-Salim, *39 Ways to Serve and Participate in Jihad*, 54. The use of the "hypocrisy" trope is a defined feature of Islamitic extremist discourse. For more information regarding the use of this trope, see: Halverson, Jeffrey & Goodall, H. L. & Corman, Steven. (2011). *Master Narratives of Islamist Extremism*. New York: Palgrave Macmillan.
68. Aziz, *Fundamental Concepts for Al-Jihad*, 121.
69. as-Salim, *39 Ways to Serve and Participate in Jihad*, 27.
70. al-'Awlaki, *Constants on the Path of Jihad*, audio recording.
71. Chomsky, *Hopes and Prospects*, 193–195.
72. Ibid., 193.
73. Pew-Global Attitudes Survey, "Muslim-Western Tensions Persist," 2.
74. See, for example, Laxer, James. (2008). *Mission of Folly: Canada and Afghanistan*. Toronto: Between the Lines.
75. See, for example, Isikoff, Michael & Corn, David. (2006). *Hubris: The Inside Story of Spin, Scandal, and the Selling of the Iraq War*.
76. See, for example, Danner, Mark. (2009, April). "U.S. Torture: Voices from the Black Sites." *The New York Review of Books*, http://www.markdanner.com/articles/show/151.
77. See, for example, Giroux, Henry. (2005). *Against the New Authoritarianism: Politics After Abu Ghraib*. Winnipeg: Arbeiter Ring Publishing.
78. Hellmich, *Al-Qaeda: From Global Network to Local Franchise*, 161.
79. Pew-Global Attitudes Survey, "Muslim-Western Tensions Persist," 17.
80. Marc Howard Ross quoted in Funk & Said, "Islam and the West: Narratives of Conflict and Conflict Transformation," 3.
81. For an argument that advances that Islamitic movements emerge as a reaction to Western modernity, see, for example, Sivan, Emmanuel. (1990). *Radical Islam: Medieval Theology and Modern Politics*. New Haven: Yale University Press.
82. Harvey, *Justice, Nature, and the Geography of Difference*, 261.

83. Gramsci, *The Prison Notebooks*, 172.
84. Springer, "Violence sits in places?" 92–94 and Anderson, "The Idea of Chinatown: The Power of Place and Institutional Practice in the Making of a Racial Category," 580–581, 583–585.
85. Campbell, *Writing Security*, 65, 68.
86. Campbell, *Writing Security*, 65.
87. Ibid., 73.
88. Euben, *Enemy in the Mirror: Islamic Fundamentalism and the Limits of Modern Rationalism*, 22–23.
89. Said, *Orientalism*, 300–301.
90. Salvatore, *Islam and the Political Discourse of Modernity*, 157.
91. Euben, *Enemy in the Mirror*, 21.
92. Said, *Orientalism*, 321.
93. Lacan, *The Other Side of Psychoanalysis*, 111.
94. Said, *Orientalism*, 322.
95. Al-Azmeh, *Islams and Modernities*, 22.
96. Salvatore, *Islam and the Political Discourse of Modernity*, 67.
97. Although, in the context of this argument, the focus is on World War II and the Cold War, the use of Islam as a modern geopolitical instrument can be traced back to World War I. During this period, Germany sought to mobilize the Ottoman Empire against Allied powers under the aegis of jihad/"holy war" (Johnson, *A Mosque in Munich*, 14). Additionally, the British and the French also employed a similar strategy to advance their imperial interests in Southwest Asia and beyond.
98. Johnson, *A Mosque in Munich*, 26.
99. Ibid., 31–32.
100. Johnson, *A Mosque in Munich*, 68.
101. Ibid., 69–70.
102. Ibid., 127–128.
103. Following the Russian invasion of Afghanistan, the Pentagon commissioned the Rand Corporation to conduct an analysis of the Nazi exploitation of Muslims throughout World War II. Again, the Nazi model served as the framework for the US covert creation and deployment of the Afghani *Mujahideen* (Johnson, *A Mosque in Munich*, 177).
104. Mamdani, *Good Muslim, Bad Muslim*, 128.
105. Ibid., 126, 131, 132.
106. Ibid., 136.
107. Dilip Hiro quoted in Mamdani, *Good Muslim, Bad Muslim*, 136.
108. Mamdani, *Good Muslim, Bad Muslim*, 130, 138.
109. *Los Angeles Times* quoted in Mamdani, *Good Muslim, Bad Muslim*, 139.

110. Mahfoud Bennoune quoted in Mamdani, *Good Muslim, Bad Muslim*, 140. For a comprehensive analysis of the US activities in Afghanistan and its consequences, see, for example, Coll, Steve. (2004). *Ghost Wars: The Secret History of the CIA, Afghanistan, and Bin Laden, From the Soviet Invasion to September 10, 2001*. New York: Penguin Books.
111. Hall, "Who needs Identity?" 17.
112. Cox, "Spaces of dependence, spaces of engagement," 2.
113. Ibid., 4.
114. Cox, "Spaces of dependence, spaces of engagement," 17.

CHAPTER 4

A Condition of Transgression: The Transnational Sphere of Influence

The globalization of information flows made possible by advanced communication technologies and its supporting infrastructure has intensified the local/global nexus. For many constituencies with ready access to these communication systems, real and/or imagined transnational connectivities increasingly inform and influence social relations at the local level. Global geopolitical processes and practices are no longer incidental or tangential to local activities but are in many respects constitutive of them. In effect, the current accessibility of the geopolitical informs, reinforces, and sustains what Arjun Appadurai refers to as "local imaginings of power."[1] However, the localized social outcomes of this accessibility to the geopolitical are multidirectional. For instance, as the Arab Revolutions and the Occupy Movement demonstrate, the desired outcome is emancipatory, while Domestic Islamic Extremism advances on a trajectory of political provocation and agitation. Although traditional corporate media continue to perform an influential function in the framing and ultimate interpretation of global geopolitical events, processes, and practices, the advent and proliferation of advanced communication technologies, such as the Internet and World Wide Web, have reconfigured transnational circuits of communication and the production, dissemination, and acquisition of geopolitical knowledge and information.

One of the most salient features of the reconfiguration of the transnational circuits of communication is increased accessibility to geopolitical discourses, processes, and practices via subaltern sources of knowledge and modes of interpretation. As Paul Routledge explains, subaltern accounts of geopolitical processes and forces, or what he refers to as "anti-geopolitics," serve two functions: "First, it challenges the material (economic and military) geopolitical power of states and global institutions; and second, it challenges the representations imposed by political and economic elites upon the world and its differing peoples, that are deployed to serve their geopolitical interests."[2] As a result of these increasing forms of subaltern "anti-geopolitics," dominant geopolitical narratives are frequently threatened with collapse as these authorized narratives are much more difficult to sustain under the weight of the democratization of geopolitical knowledge and information and its concomitant heteroglossic and fragmentary counter-narratives. According to Bryan Turner, "The political implications of the new media for Western societies are [significant]."[3] As Turner continues, "While there has been a profound concentration of media ownership and power, no single corporation or state can control the global flow of information. The American invasion of Iraq is a classic illustration. Within the American commercial media, there was initially little critical analysis of the war, but there was a virtual storm of critical information and discussion available outside the commercial media."[4] Consequently, as influencing and controlling a dominant geopolitical imaginary become increasingly difficult in Western societies as a result of the democratization of geopolitical knowledge and information, the emergence of various forms of political consciousness and related subjectivities within the social body will continue to increase.

Although there is nothing intellectually, ideologically, culturally, ethnically, theologically, or spatially unusual and abnormal about the emergence of oppositional or dissenting political subjectivities, the political agency of particular social actors is constructed and construed as extraordinary and, therefore, is treated with suspicion and is subsequently monitored with an exceptional degree of scrutiny by law enforcement and security apparatuses. Currently, in the North American and Western European context, Muslim communities in general and Islamitic social actors in particular are constructed as possessing a political agency that always represents a potentiality to violence. For instance, during pretrial motions being argued by defense counsel for the only youth to face terrorism-related charges in connection with the Toronto 18, counsel outlined that in the Toronto GTA it is a commonly held perception among members of Muslim communities that if they express their opposition to Western foreign policies and practices, they are codified as radical, fundamentalist, or supporters of terrorism.[5] In effect, this perception reveals the racialization of political culture that has become one of the defining features of North American and Western European societies in the aftermath of 11 September 2001. This racialization constructs Islamitic social actors "[...] as the paradigmatic irrational rational actor, that is, the actor apparently rational enough to gravitate toward an ideology that is an effective and therefore appealing vehicle for essentially pathological reactionary sentiment."[6] These social actors are conceived as being predisposed to particular Orientalized characteristics including: "tyranny, servility to dogma, self-abnegation, superstition, and false religion."[7] Consequently, in North American and Western European contexts, Islamitic social actors are automatically relegated to and situated on the margins of a rational and non-violent political spectrum. Accordingly, this cultural relativist form of evaluative logic and rationality overdetermines, predetermines, and simplifies specific subaltern geopolitical knowledge and information and the impulses and motivations of the social actors who either produce or access it. Indeed, overdetermination, predetermination, and simplification are evident in how the virtual transnational information flows and ideational connectivities of Islamitic actors are interpreted and presented in dominant counter-terrorism discourse. Given the importance of virtual transnational information flows and ideational connectivities as a source of subaltern and democratized geopolitical knowledge and interpretation, it is imperative to develop an understanding of how virtual transnational information flows and ideational connectivities not only influence Islamitic social actors, but how this information and related ideas help to facilitate the mobilization of these actors in place-specific contexts. So, what function does the transnational sphere of influence serve in facilitating the transgression from a dominant to a subversive discursive formation in the case of the Toronto 18? However, before directly addressing this question, it is important to not only outline some of the problematic assumptions upon which counter-terrorism discourses and policies are predicated, but it is important to examine the transformative processes that are fostered and nurtured through (virtual) transnational information flows and ideational connectivities.

Fallacious Assumptions: The Internet and the Network

According to Scott Poynting and David Whyte, "if there is a core rationale or logic at the heart of contemporary counter-terrorism policies it is the eradication of political and socio-economic content from both state and sub-state political violence. In this logic, sub-state political violence in opposition to the state appears ideologically as irrational and driven by fanaticism."[8] Conversely, as they continue, "State political violence is presented as defensive, responsible, rational and unavoidable, rather than being motivated by particular ideological bias or political choice."[9] In line with this rationale or logic is the fact that geopolitical actors of the Islamitic nationalist, secessionist, irredentist, and transnational extremist type have a well-defined presence on the World Wide Web. These differing actors utilize this "information space"[10] as a communicative tool to promulgate and propagate the ideology, grievances, objectives, and accomplishments of their respective groups/movements, which is constructed in dominant discourse as a political aberration whose only coherence across space and time is a cosmologically inspired will to anti-Western violence. As a result, the virtual presence of these groups appears in abstraction with very little if any attempt to situate these groups in a geopolitical context that is sensitive to their historical genesis and the material conditions of their existence. For instance, Philip Seib and Dana Janbek argue that: "Extremist Web sites frequently provide links to one another, partly to convey a sense of common participation in a worldwide struggle. The site used by the Indonesian group Laskar Jihad, for example, has featured links to jihadist sites related to Palestine, Afghanistan, Chechnya, and elsewhere."[11] Although the authors appear to objectively observe that Islamitic actors/groups/movements establish virtual links to one another to create the appearance of a connected global struggle, the authors themselves present and reinforce this impression by disguising and omitting the distinctions, contexts, and realities of these actors/groups/movements through their wholesale and simplified categorization as "extremist" and "jihadist." In effect, these linkages and undifferentiated characterizations reproduce imagined geographies about particular regions of the world: Islamic spaces are unified through a culture of violence. In another text entitled *Terror on the Internet*, Gabriel Weimann explores how "terrorists" use the Internet to help them advance and achieve their respective objectives. Weimann describes the methodology he utilized to conduct his analysis in the following terms:

> The method used to study Web sites was content analysis, which is defined as "any technique for reaching conclusions by systematic and objective identification of defined properties of messages." To locate the terrorists' sites, we conducted numerous systematic scans of the Internet, feeding an enormous variety of names and terms into search engines, entering chat

rooms and forums of supporters and sympathizers, and surveying the links on other organizations' Web sites to create and update our own lists of sites. [...] The target population for the current study was defined as "the Internet sites of terrorist movements as they appeared in the period between January 1998 and May 2005." Using the U.S. State department's list of terrorist organizations [...], we found more than 4,300 sites serving terrorists and their supporters.[12]

Of the 4,300 websites identified by Weimann as serving terrorists and their supporters, he later asserts that as of 2006, al-Qaeda had a defined presence on more than fifty.[13] Again, although the analysis presented by Weimann masquerades under the auspice of objectivity, the argument presented and its related outcomes are predetermined by a reliance on a list of "terrorist organizations" developed by the US State department. Not only is this list highly politicized as it serves the interests of the US government and by extension those of its client regimes, but this list reduces highly complex and variegated political phenomena to the intellectually impoverished and pedestrian category of "terrorist."[14] Therefore, to use this list as a framework for identifying "terrorist organizations" is highly problematic. It requires that one accept that the entities listed are in fact "terrorist organizations." Furthermore, accepting this designation also requires that one dismiss the fact that "terrorist organizations" are a state construction used to delegitimize foreign and domestic political actors/groups/movements that oppose the interests of the state. As such, to uncritically use these lists is to accept a propagandistic exercise that advances the interests of the state while obfuscating the material conditions of existence of the actors/groups/movements listed, especially those of the Islamitic type. A corollary of this form of counter-terrorism logic and rationality is that Islamitic social actors who may access these types of virtual transnational information flows and ideational connectivities are presumed to endorse and support the ideology, objectives, and practices of various Islamitic actors/groups/movements. In effect, this presumption a priori situates Islamitic social actors in a subversive ideological system and discursive formation where enraged and irrational vessels of violence operate as undifferentiated parts in a theologically hypnotized totality. Moreover, homogenization of Islamitic actors/groups/movements can lead to the belief that these same entities are transnationally interconnected in what John Arquilla and David Ronfeldt envisage as a low-intensity, non-hierarchical, and networked mode of conflict they refer to as *netwar*.[15]

According to Colin Flint, netwar may be defined as "the network forms of organization, doctrine, strategy, and technology to engage in conflict."[16] As he continues, "the definition implies that there is a spatial manifestation of the network, but also a manner of thinking and implementing conflict."[17] Although certain forms of network building enabled by advanced communication technologies may appear to connect Islamitic actors/groups/movements operating in different jurisdictions around the globe, this appearance should not be used as evidence to support the conceptualization that geographically dispersed Islamitic actors/groups/movements, including al-Qaeda-affiliated groups and/or al-Qaeda-inspired groups, are transnationally linked in an all-channel network where each Islamitic actor/group/movement is connected to every other Islamitic actor/group/movement.[18] Rather, it is necessary to evaluate the qualities associated with any transnational linkage to determine what function that linkage serves for the actor/group/movement in question. For instance, in the case of the Toronto 18, some of the members of the group were connected to Islamitic actors operating in the UK. In the UK, the principal figure of the Scarborough group frequently communicated with Abid Hussain Khan who was arrested on terrorism-related charges in June 2006. Incidentally, Abid Hussain Khan was connected to Younis Tsouli whose online moniker was Irhabi007. According to Marc Sageman, Younis Tsouli was a frequent participant on various forums where he actively disseminated various forms of Islamitic propaganda and had connections to Islamitic actors/groups/movements in a variety of countries.[19] On the basis of these connections, Sageman asserts that: "The group involved in the Operation Osage case in Toronto was connected to groups in Copenhagen, Bosnia, London, and the United States."[20] However, very little evidence is provided that clearly outlines or details the nature and material outcome of these linkages beyond one commonality: that Islamitic social actors from various geographical jurisdictions happened to share an associative connection with one or two of the same virtual personalities. Nonetheless, the fact that these Islamitic actors shared a common associative connection appears to be a satisfactory performance indicator to deduce that these groups were connected across space and, as such, must share the same ideological orientation, sensibilities, and objectives.

Although the concept of a "network" has received a considerable amount of attention as an explanatory framework to help analyze and describe the contemporary manifestation and organizational structure of

Islamitic extremism, the use of this concept in interpreting and analyzing Islamitic extremism suffers from several deficiencies. First, the rise of this concept as a means of explaining the implications of advanced communication technology on economic and social organization and activity arguably achieved ascendancy in Manuel Castells' text (1996): *The Rise of Network Society. The Information Age: Economy, Society, Culture*. In this text, Castells provides a very complex and nuanced account of the concept of the "network." Similarly, the concept of the network is used to inform analyses of the complicated recursive and dynamic processes and relationships associated with immigration and migration.[21] Conversely, the transplantation of this concept into terrorism research betrays the origins (economic and social) and complexities of the concept through decontextualizing the concept of network from its origins and more importantly simplifying its meaning. Second, as a result of this decontextualization, one assumes that the concept of the network can be used to adequately explain the political in general and Islamitic extremism in particular. Third, the simplification of its meaning enables one to present a conspiratorial character of Islamitic extremism that divorces these actors/groups/movements from their place-specific material conditions of existence and objectives. The effect of these deficiencies in aggregate is that the term network becomes a form of terminological and ideological violence that superimposes a coherence onto Islamitic actors/groups/movements that materially does not exist in any substantive form. Therefore, to avoid repeating the presumptive fallacies that Islamitic extremism exists in a transnationally linked and organized decentralized network structure, it is important, as Antonio Gramsci states, "to resist the tendency to render easy that which cannot become easy without being distorted."[22]

Political Transformation and the Transnational

Within any dominant symbolic order, there are competing interpretations of social reality. As Gramsci states, "Various philosophies or conceptions of the world exist, and one always makes a choice between them."[23] Subsequently, "in acquiring one's conception of the world one always belongs to a particular grouping which is that of all the social elements which share the same mode of thinking and acting."[24] However, the conceptions of the world to which Gramsci refers are dynamic and contingent upon the constellation of moments influencing and shaping a particular social formation. Furthermore, choosing a conception of the world is a transformative process that results from complex decisionmaking made by rational actors in specific time-space conjunctures.²⁵ Therefore, the conscious acceptance by a social actor of a specific conception of the world requires persuasion and consent vis-à-vis ideological conditioning. Additionally, the transformative process requires that the ideological find articulation through practice as it is through practice that the ideological materializes.²⁶

The articulation of ideology through political action and practice requires a multitude of variables to be operating in conjunction to make the concretization of ideologically motivated action and practice probable. These variables include: the aims and objectives of the actors/group/movement; the strength of the leadership; the organizational sophistication of the respective entity; the amount of resources available to and at the disposal of a particular entity; and, most importantly, the existence of an asymmetrical relation of power between a particular social formation and a conceived opponent or contentious situation precipitated by acts of state violence (ideological, institutional, or actual, i.e. war). However, the presence of these variables does not guarantee the articulation of ideology through action and practice. In most circumstances, this process of articulation and the political transformation it engenders is complex, "difficult," and "full of contradictions" and includes both "advances and retreats."²⁷ Therefore, the right constellation of moments or, in the context of this argument, spheres of influence need to be in place in a particular time-space conjuncture to make not only the articulation of ideology through action and practice possible but the political transformation of social actors probable. One such sphere of influence is that of the transnational, which can serve as a powerful source of the ideological conditioning necessary for a political transformation to occur.

Transnational Information Flows and Ideational Connectivities

In the case of the "Toronto 18," a group that did not have any formal connections to al-Qaeda but who, according to the principal figure of the Scarborough group, claimed to be inspired by al-Qaeda,²⁸ transnational information flows and ideational connectivities served a necessary function in the political transformation of the group. The function of the transnational sphere of influence in this case is threefold. Firstly, the transnational served as an important conduit for knowledge transference through providing members of the group with access to materials that helped to inform, influence, and frame the group's geopolitical imagination. For instance, the vast majority of doctrinal and propagandistic materials accessed by the principal figures and other members of the group were downloaded from two web-based resources: a non-aligned repository of Islamitic doctrine, the London-based *At-Tibyan Publications—Discover the Truth* (www.tibyan.co.cc)[29] and the San Francisco-based multimedia library www.archive.org.[30] Through the virtual repository, various members of the Toronto 18 accessed a variety of documents, such as *Blood, Wealth, and Honour of the Disbelievers*; *39 Ways to Serve and Participate in Jihad*; *The Religion of Ibrahim*; *Fundamental Concepts Regarding Al Jihad*; the *Constants of* Jihad; and *Islam is our Citizenship* (see Chap. 3 for an analysis of the material that informed the activities of the group). Additionally, through this particular multimedia library, group members accessed images of Osama bin Laden; images of Shamil Basayev and other Chechen rebels; images of unidentified Islamitic actors carrying weapons or engaged in combat; images of Islamitic actors who have died while engaged in conflict; videos of Islamitic actors fighting in Chechnya, Afghanistan, and Iraq; videos of the detonation of improvised explosive devices (IEDs) targeting occupying forces; and footage of occupying forces destroying infrastructure and killing or wounding unarmed civilians and non-combatants including women and children.[31] For example, a documentary entitled "The Return of the Crusaders" was discovered and seized by Canadian law enforcement officials during the arrest and detention of the various members of the Toronto 18. This documentary frames the US-led invasion of Afghanistan and occupation of Iraq as a crusade of the Christian West against the Islamic East through using the following rhetorical mechanisms: highlighting Islamophobic and/or anti-Muslim comments made by various ultra right-wing Christian evangelical figures; portraying US military personnel engaged in Christian religious practices; providing footage of the destruction of mosques; depicting the victimization of non-combatant citizens, including men, women, and children in Iraq and Afghanistan by US military personnel; and the recounting of the abuses suffered by Muslim detainees in Guantanamo Bay and Abu Ghraib.[32] Cumulatively, these materials provide an ideational and representational framework through which a particular ideological position and concomitant geopolitical conception of the world are communicated. Indeed, this worldview is clearly expressed in comments made by Osama bin Laden, which were included in the documentary described above: "Bush was right when he said you are either with us or with the terrorists.

You are either on the side of the Crusaders or on the side of Islam."[33] Virtual transnational information flows and ideational connectivities also enabled other forms of information sharing that made the articulation of ideology through action and practice possible. This form of knowledge transfer is explicated through the web-based research conducted by one of the principal figures involved in the Toronto 18.

The principal figure in the Mississauga group utilized the information-sharing capacity of the virtual to research and conceptualize a plan to detonate explosive devices at the CSIS office in downtown Toronto, at the Toronto Stock Exchange (TSX), and at an unidentified military installation located between the cities of Toronto and Ottawa. Through virtual transnational channels, this figure acquired the information needed to assemble the ingredients to create explosive devices similar to those that were detonated at the Alfred P. Murrah Federal Building in Oklahoma City on 19 April 1995. For instance, on 22 March and 3 April 2006, this same figure entered the Meadowvale Public Library in Mississauga, Ontario, to research the ingredients necessary to manufacture explosive material. On both occasions, members of the Ontario division of the Integrated National Security Enforcement Team (INSET), whose responsibility it is to investigate the activities like those carried out by the Toronto 18, confiscated the hard drives of the computer terminals used by this figure. They found that the following web-based searches had been performed: "ammonium nitrate in agriculture," "nitric acid," "rocket fuel," "fuel tablets," "buy nitric acid," "fertilizer," "explosive," and "ways of getting ammonium nitrate."[34] In addition to utilizing the Internet to research the manufacture of explosives, he also consulted the following: a photograph of hexamine containers; various photographs of chemicals such as hexamine fuel tablets; a video containing information about RDX—an explosive substance that can be synthesized from hexamine and nitric acid—and hexamine with instructions on how to mix and cook the chemicals; videos of the detonation of various explosive devices; detailed instructions for the manufacture of explosives out of a variety of substances; and detailed instructions for the assembly of a cellular-based remote control for use in a light-sealed enclosure.[35] On 30 March 2006, the principal figure of the Mississauga group also placed an order with vistaprint.ca for business cards emblazoned with the title "Student Farmers."[36] The business cards were designed to divert suspicion and confer legitimacy on the actors when purchasing ammonium nitrate fertilizer and other chemical compounds. However, one should exercise analytical caution and avoid interpreting these activities using an instrumentalist mode of logic. Contrary to interpreting the accessing of this material as evidence that this Islamitic social actor had already assimilated an Islamitic extremist ideology and was acting in accordance with that dictum, the accessing of this material represents only one aspect of the ideological conditioning required in the process of a political transformation.

Secondly, the transnational provided various members of the Toronto 18 with the opportunities to interact with and engage in ideational exchanges with like-minded Islamitic social actors outside Canada, whereby particular ideological positions and geopolitical hermeneutics were debated and ultimately reinforced. Although there are a variety of methods and platforms through which people can communicate and interact in a virtual environment, e.g. websites, chat rooms, and message boards, web-based forums provided an interactive environment where like-minded yet geographically dispersed individuals could congregate, engage in discussions, and exchange ideas. For instance, one prominent forum that was utilized by Islamitic social actors in, but not limited to, Canada, the USA, and the UK was www.clearguidance.com. In the case of the Toronto 18, certain members of the group initially came into contact with one another through this particular web-based forum. This forum also became an important source of ideational exchange for various members of the group. In fact, this forum served a seminal role in shaping the ideological position of the group's principal figures. As Mubin Shaikh, the undercover agent that infiltrated the group, explained: "the forum is very significant primarily because of its role as an echo chamber where like-minded in-group members could solidify their views with one another or amongst other members."[37] Incidentally, this forum is where various members of the Toronto 18 established a relationship with Abid Khan—an Islamitic actor based in the UK—and with Syed Haris Ahmed and Ehsanul Sadequee, two Islamitic actors from Atlanta, Georgia. Other web-based forums, such as paltalk.com, enabled various members of the Toronto 18, such as the principal figure in the Scarborough group and some of the young offenders associated with the Toronto 18, to interact with one another and engage in ideational exchanges. These web-based forums are significant as the connectivities these interactive platforms facilitate enable Islamitic social actors to not only discuss particular ideological systems and positions but receive validation from other participants in the forums. However, it is important to note that ideational exchanges and the platforms that enable these interactions can serve as a space of political catharsis and expression for Islamitic social actors and rarely become the sole avenue through which Islamitic extremism materializes.[38] For instance, as Seib and Janbek outline, there is no evidence to date directly linking the Internet to the recruitment of individuals to extremist groups.[39] Participation in virtual forums and the related exchange of ideas represents only one aspect of the ideological conditioning experienced by various members of the Toronto 18.

Thirdly, virtual transnational information flows and ideational connectivities served as a consensus-building mechanism enabling domestic Islamitic social actors to develop and establish an imagined sense of connection and a collective purpose with other Islamitic groups operating in various jurisdictions around the world. This imagined sense of geopolitical solidarity is achieved by accessing documentary/propagandistic materials, news reports, and other media regarding the activities of Islamitic groups. For instance, the principal figure in the Scarborough group and other adult members of the Toronto 18 frequently made reference in intercepted conversations to regions where Muslims were involved in conflict, such as Afghanistan, Bosnia, Chechnya, Eritrea, Iraq, Kashmir, Palestine, Somalia, and Waziristan.[40] For example, in a conversation between the principal ideologue and another adult member of the group, which was recorded by Canadian law enforcement officials on 27 February 2006, several of these conflicts are referred to in an effort to establish a sense of collective purpose and connection between the members of the Toronto 18 and other groups in various spaces of conflict. The following are a series of comments made by the principal ideologue during that exchange:

> *Principal figure in the Scarborough group*: [...] the fact that they are attacking Afghanistan, right? We're peacemakers, peacemakers. [...] Okay, fine. Perhaps you're doing some good things inside Kabul, okay. Other than the fact that you start opening these nudie bars, and this and that, you know what I mean? [...] You are no longer peacemakers. Now you guys are front liners, fighters, blah, blah, whatever. [...] You didn't get involved in Iraq, okay, so why are your airplanes there? Why is your technology there? Why are your engineers there? [...] So the covenant as far as it goes with the non-believers, bottom line is, they attack one country. We don't have to ... like Iran, that's the other thing. Islamic citizenship is not a border. These borders are only drawn on pages by some non-believers. Muslims never draw these border lines. [...] So, the fact that you see a ... we're attacking Afghanistan and Pakistan is not but yet Waziristan is a maybe, slash, we did against that village. So that village is not allowed to look at us. It doesn't

work like that. You attack Afghanistan, you attack the Muslims that is it. You attack Iraq, you just attacked Muslims in another area. [...] Just like Russians, they're all our enemies for still being in Chechnya. It doesn't matter where you are. Because, that's another thing ah … it's not uh … from the Sunnah to say that, if … a people are my enemy, they're only my enemy in a certain part of the land. That's not right. If they're your enemy, they're your enemy everywhere you see them.[41]

Arguably, the abovementioned conflicts figure prominently in the geopolitical imagination of the Toronto 18 for the following two reasons. First, as Oliver Roy suggests, the sources for most Islamitic extremist materials regarding these various conflicts, such as websites, chat rooms, web forums, bulletin boards, and multimedia repositories, are predominantly Western-based and are widely and readily accessible to North American and Western European Islamitic social actors. Secondly, many of these conflicts have attracted North American and European Islamitic extremist actors and as a result have been romanticized as destinations where foreign actors are not only welcome but where foreign actors can actively participate. For example, during the Bosnian war, many second-generation Islamitic social actors from the UK and other Western European countries traveled to Bosnia to participate in the conflict, including le gang de Roubaix which, incidentally, was linked through Said Atmani to Ahmed Ressam in Montreal, Canada. Similarly, in the context of the irredentist struggle in Chechnya, several Islamitic extremist actors from France and Germany were either detained or killed while attempting to engage, or while engaged, in hostilities.[42] The fact that these foreign conflicts resonate with and inform the geopolitical imagination of domestic Islamitic social actors is demonstrated in the case of the Toronto 18. During the paintball games at their winter training camp, the principal figure of the Scarborough group not only likened the actions of the attendees to those of the resistance fighters in Chechnya but also regaled the attendees with exhortations of being brave and proud warriors like those in Chechnya.[43] Moreover, the same transnational information flows and ideational connectivities that served to establish an imagined sense of connection and collective purpose between domestic Islamitic social actors and other geographically dispersed Islamitic actors/groups/movements are also conduits through which information is communicated and shared regarding the atrocities to which Muslim non-combatants are subjected in disparate geopolitical conflicts and struggles.

The conversations intercepted by security and law enforcement officials between many of the members of the Toronto 18 frequently included references to violent injustices committed against non-combatant citizenry by Western military apparatuses and/or governments in various jurisdictions, including Afghanistan and Iraq. For instance, as Justice Dawson states in his *Reasons for Sentence* of the principal ideologue of the group, "He prepared and distributed collections of fundamentalist Islamic videos advocating violence towards and hatred of non-believers in Islam, and depicting atrocities against Muslims and retaliating violence against western forces in Iraq and Afghanistan."[44] Furthermore, in his *Reasons for Sentence* for the oldest adult member of the group to stand trial in connection to the bomb plot, Justice Dawson describes an encounter between the accused and the second undercover agent tasked with infiltrating the Mississauga group[45] where reference is made to the plight of Iraqi citizens: "In mid April 2006, the accused underwent heart surgery. When [the agent] visited the accused in the hospital on April 17, 2006 [the accused] indicated that he had thought about the plan and said that he had decided to assist [the leader of the Mississauga group]. He made reference to the fact that the United States embargo of Iraq had caused the deaths of one million children."[46] As the previous quotation indicates, transnational information flows and ideational connectivities can provide access to geopolitical knowledge and information which, under specific conditions, is capable of motivating domestic Islamitic social actors to actively participate in specific non-constitutional political actions and practices. However, access to geopolitical knowledge and information does not guarantee that these flows and connectivities will result in physical violence to achieve a particular geopolitical objective. Therefore, it is important to develop an appreciation of how transnational channels encourage Islamitic social actors to politically mobilize in a place-specific context.

Transnational Information Flows and Geopolitical Affectivity

In the case of the Toronto 18, information from transnational sources served as an effective recruitment tool—something that was certainly recognized by the principal figures as well as other senior members of the group. As Mubin Shaikh testified at the trial of the only youth to face terrorism-related charges under the Criminal Code of Canada in this case, a recruitment technique of the principal ideologue was to distribute CDs depicting atrocities against Muslim citizens in a variety of contexts and later approach the prospective recruit to discuss what this individual thought of the material.[47] During this trial, Shaikh described in his testimony his experience of being recruited into the group. Shortly after establishing contact with the individuals he was tasked with targeting, the individual who would later become the leader of the Mississauga group provided him with two publications: *Fundamental Concepts of Jihad* and *The Community of Ibrahim*. Subsequent to receiving these documents, the principal figure of the Scarborough group approached Shaikh and presented him with the following publication: *Blood, Wealth, and Honour of the Disbelievers*, a text that Shaikh described as justifying the killing, stealing from, and defamation and derision of people identified as non-Muslim.[48] Although Shaikh was tasked with infiltrating the group and as a result the effectiveness of this recruitment technique cannot be accurately gauged by his experience, the usefulness of this recruitment technique, albeit in variation, is demonstrated by the recruitment of one of the adults accused who participated in the bomb plot as described by Justice Hill in his

> *Reasons for Judgment*:
> [The accused acknowledged his first meeting with [the leader of the Mississauga group on] March 22nd, 2006 at McMaster University. He recalled the meeting as involving "motivational type of conversation". Reference was made to troops in Afghanistan. [The leader of the Mississauga group] was attempting to recruit him—"he was trying to tell me you know…that I am [a] special type guy, I was chosen…things like that". The applicant recalled [the leader] suggesting that "whatever happens he would "be a hero" and that "there's a really big goal in mind" and "it's our duties…you know try to like do something about it.""[49]

These ideas are elaborated in an interview between the accused referenced above and a Canadian law enforcement official following the arrest of this individual in June 2006 which is reproduced at length:

> **Applicant**: … things are permissible or not… so like… some, some like hold a little more… like different views, just in case and they uhm… what he said and he said this the first day, when I met him in _____ that like whatever we're gonna do, he's like I'm gonna make sure that you guys all agree with it. Right… he said that I'm gonna try to… I'm gonna try to make sure that you guys don't feel as if like I… I'm doing things like… in… in our religion, it's called uh *consultation*, it means like asking for advice, right… so he

kinda said that like... he's like what I'm gonna try to do at the end is like... it's like things will be open so you know, you guys can like think about it and I was like oh... what is that mean? You know what I mean?...... so...I don't... like... I...I don't know how to explain it to you but... to me, something big like didn't have to be the worse consequence that, that we talked about like... I'm sure...

Detective: It didn't have to be.

Applicant: Yeah, it didn't have to be the worse consequence that we're thinking of, you know what I mean... could've been something like... something like... maybe hopefully didn't involve people themselves, like who knows... but at the end of the day, like it was his choice, right... I don't know, right... that was his thing so... that's... that's what I mean, like this stuff was there for and... I was told, like... there's a lot of like, uh... like helping out the bigger cause, like there's a lot of good in doing that (Stutters) like, you know, uh he was saying like... like how one person, only one person, you can like, like change like so many thousands of lives uh like... like for all the other people are being oppressed... you're that one person that was chosen that's gonna make a difference so maybe you should help out... things like that, so...

Applicant: ...and... and as much as I think, say, yeah, civilians aren't being hurt we hear about stories coming out of the blue every single time. Just, like, two days ago I was watching Anderson COOPER on CNN like they're talking the whole ____ but, like, they were saying massacres of civilians and innocent people in A... recently in Afghanistan. There was, like, umm... like... a whole village was bombed for no reason.

Detective: A whole...

Applicant: Whole village.

Detective: ...village?

Applicant: Yeah. And like all these civilians and kids were there. And, like, it's... I don't know, I just think it's not fair. And... and I really, really, really don't think that Canada has anything to do with, or should have anything to do with that. Like, uhm... I... know they're pressurized because the United States and stuff... the United States ____ we have to ____ 'cause we do depend on the United States a lot.

Detective: Yes.

Applicant: And I understand that. Like, I don't know, it's a world of politics and that's the way it works, but I... you know, we're Canadians and we stand up for our own morals and ____. And, like, it's not only... like, it's not only, like us Muslims that are against it. There's enough people against it over here. And you know you have to... like, we have to see that. And, like, I just... I... I just think it's unjust. And for, like, what, for what? Like, ____ the whole western, like, civilization stands for, it's not always gonna

_____. And... and... that's... that's my point of view. And the fact... I was just... and when I heard there's a way to make a difference. And that's you got one person who can change, like, everything. And it just kinda, I don't know, like, I... I follow this like... it seems if you _____ Muslims _____sort of like way of like fixing things.[50]

Moreover, the atrocities and crimes committed by invading and occupying powers in jurisdictions such as Afghanistan, Iraq, and Guantanamo Bay were routinely mentioned and actively deployed to reinforce the injustices being faced by many Muslims around the world and to help legitimize the need for action. In effect, representations of genuine state violence, particularly crimes perpetrated against civilians and other non-combatants, support and give credence to the lines of argumentation in the materials found in the possession of various members of the group. For instance, the attendees at what was described as a winter training camp in Washago, Ontario, in December 2005 were invited to participate in three halaqahs (gatherings). The first halaqah consisted of listening to an audio recording of *The Constants on the Path of Jihad* translated and presented by Anwar al-Awlaki. According to testimony provided by Mubin Shaikh, the explicit message of this recording was that engaging in violent hostilities is a religious obligation and that theological study is not required prior to participating in conflict. This recording also advised listeners that one should resist peaceful co-existence with unbelievers and that it is a religious obligation to kill unbelievers wherever they are found. Following the presentation of this audio recording, the principal ideologue of the group then reinforced its message by displaying images and video footage of atrocities committed against citizens in Iraq.[51] Similarly, following the winter training camp, members of the Toronto 18 would meet informally in various cafes and restaurants located in the Greater Toronto Area (GTA) and would review multimediated forms of material depicting not only atrocities committed against non-combatants but the actions of Islamitic actors purportedly fighting on behalf of those being victimized by the occupying forces. Ultimately, these popular geopolitical materials were used to strengthen and fortify a particular conception of the world and to build consensus among various members of the group regarding a specific geopolitical hermeneutic through amplifying the affectivity of these experiences. However, before elucidating the affect these popular geopolitical materials had on the collectivity of the group, it is necessary to briefly explain affect and its relationship with geopolitical rationalities.

According to Sean Carter and Derek McCormack, "affect is by no means reducible to the subjective qualities of personal emotion, but designates something both more and less; a kind of vector of the intensity of encounter between bodies (non-human and human) of whatever scale and consistency."[52] However, the vector of intensity to which affect refers is not devoid of emotion. Rather, the expression of emotion is the register of a vector of affective intensity.[53] So, what is the significance of affect? As Brian Massumi argues, "affect is crucial to any understanding of the operation and proliferation of different modalities of power and politics in the contemporary world, providing the conditions of the emergence of virulent forms of ideology and discourse."[54] As Carter and McCormack elaborate, "In particular, incorporating affect into accounts of the geopolitical moves us to think more about how highly mediatised practices and performances generate what Linda Kitz call *resonance*, a kind of intensification of politically charged passion."[55] As they later continue, "Importantly, in the context of geopolitical intervention, resonance is not only the effect of performative repetition of particular ideological mantras or discursive scripts. It also depends on the capacity to capture and amplify particular vectors of affect."[56] The relationship between affect and the geopolitical is evidenced by the events of 11 September 2001 and the subsequent war *of* terror. As Jason Dittmer outlines, the "affective reservoir" that was generated as a result of the attacks shaped, and was shaped by, various state apparatuses and was used to justify and legitimate military interventions, e.g. Afghanistan, by the USA and other allied countries.[57] Indeed, this affective reservoir was also used to justify other practices associated with the war *of* terror, such as extraordinary rendition and indefinite detention, torture, the expansion of the war *of* terror to other countries, targeted killing, and so on. However, just as affect shaped, and was shaped by, state actors and informed geopolitical thinking and practices, it can also shape, and be shaped by, non-state actors and inform responses to that same geopolitical thinking and practice.

In the case of the Toronto 18, multiple modes of popular geopolitical discourse for the conveyance of the suffering of non-combatants and the very real indignities and injustices that non-combatants were enduring in different contexts were used as a tool not only for amplifying the affect of these materials but for increasing their resonance with those that reviewed the materials. Although it is difficult to identify and measure the affective impact these materials had on the collectivity of the group, one performance indicator of affect was the generation not only of a sense of imagined collectivity with other geographically dispersed Islamitic actors/groups/movements but of a sense of collectivized disempowerment as a result of the varying degrees of suffering of various Muslim populations at the hands of North American and Western European powers. For example, in an intercepted conversation that took place in February 2006 between the principal ideologue, the undercover informant Mubin Shaikh, and some of the other group members, this imagined sense of collectivity is conveyed. As the principal ideologue states: "Now it's basic law. The whole nation—you harm one part, the whole body feels it. You harm one Muslim, the whole Muslim nation has to defend that person.... Islamic citizenship is not a border. These borders are only drawn on paper by some non-believer. Muslims never draw these border lines."[58] Furthermore, the sense of collectivized disempowerment is revealed during an interview between a law enforcement official and an adult member of the group in June 2006:

> **Applicant**: Yeah. It's also because... it's a feeling of helplessness that like... Yeah, like, since I'm a kid I've told everyone ____ was even ____. Like I... like since I'm a kid I've been taught at, right now, like, Prophet Mohammad *peace be upon him* said he wants us at like... the whole Muslim nation is, like one body. So, like, if the head is hurting it affects the heart. If the leg is hurting it affects the heart. If the leg is hurting if affects the heart. So no matter it hurts it has to affect their Muslim ____. And like that was it, I was ____ that, like, even that I'm not ____ I'm not related to them by blood... I'm not related to other Muslims by blood but they're still Muslims, right. And there are still other people that like I'm supposed to love them the way I love myself. And... and if I'm not doing all that I can to help them there's a feeling of guilt that rightly comes into me. Because I'm not doing my duty, right.[59]

As these statements help to illuminate, popular geopolitical materials that expose the atrocities of war can affectively produce imagined collectivities that contribute to the legitimacy of a particular geopolitical hermeneutic and ideological position. However, the collectivized intensity, emotion, resonance, and overall experiential meaning of popular geopolitical materials are marked by impermanence, temporariness, and contingency. Therefore, the affectivities made possible by transnational information flows and ideational connectivities must be positioned within a constellation of other ideological practices in order to sustain the ideological conditioning of Islamitic social actors.

Although the transnational sphere of influence served a necessary role in the political transformation of the members of the Toronto 18 through the ideological conditioning made possible by knowledge transfer, ideational exchange, and consensus building, this sphere of influence was not sufficient to facilitate the transgression from the dominant to a subversive discursive formation and its related modality of political action. As Valerie Preston, Audrey Kobayashi, and Myer Siemiatycki explain, "the form, intensity, and impact of transnational social fields reflect processes operating at various spatial scales. The policies and practices of nation-states frame transnational ties and the social fields that result, just as the experiences of daily life [...] inevitably influence the actions of [specific social groups and actors]."[60] In other words, one needs to develop an understanding of the multiscalar processes and forces that not only implicate the transnational sphere of influence but are implicated by the transnational sphere of influence. In the case of the Toronto 18, this necessitates an analysis of the state sphere of influence.

NOTES

1. Appadurai, *Fear of Small Numbers*, 136.
2. Routledge quoted in Dittmer, *Popular Culture, Geopolitics & Identity*, 134.
3. Turner, "Religious Authority and the New Media," 121.
4. Ibid., 121.
5. Author's notes, 9 April 2008.
6. Euben, *Enemy in the Mirror*, 24.
7. Ibid., 34.
8. Poynting & Whyte, "Introduction: Counter-Terrorism and the State," 9.
9. Ibid., 9.
10. Dodge & Kitchin, *Mapping Cyberspace*, 3
11. Seib & Janbek, *Global Terrorism and New Media*, 41.
12. Weimann, *Terror on the Internet*, 5.
13. Ibid., 67.
14. For example, whereas the Iranian group Mujahedin-e-Khalq (MEK) was previously listed as a "terrorist organization" by the US Department of State, in October 2012, this group was delisted as a "terrorist organization" and is now considered a legitimate political oppositional group/movement. This maneuver coincides with the efforts of the USA to destabilize the current Iranian regime and develop conduits through which clandestine action can be exacted.

15. Arquilla & Ronfeldt, *Networks and Netwars*, 2–3.
16. Flint, "Netwar, the Modern Geopolitical Imagination, and the Death of the Civilian," 38.
17. Ibid., 38–39.
18. See Burke, Jason. (2004). *Al Qaeda: The True Story of Radical Islam*. New York: I.B Tauris, 1–21., for an analysis that dispels commonly held perceptions of the global al-Qaeda network and puts in perspective the actual reality of these types of actors/groups/movements.
19. Sageman, *Leaderless Jihad*, 119–120.
20. Ibid., 121.
21. See Walton-Robert, Margaret. (2003). "Transnational geographies: Indian migration to Canada." *The Canadian Geographer*, 47 (3): 235–250; Hyndman, Jennifer. (2003). "Aid, conflict and migration: the Canada-Sri Lanka connection." *The Canadian Geographer*, 47 (3): 251–268; and Glick Schiller, Nina. (2005). "Transnational Social Fields and Imperialism: Bringing a Theory of Power to Transnational Studies." *Anthropological Theory*, 5 (4): 439–461.
22. Gramsci, *Prison Notebooks*, 43.
23. Gramsci, *Prison Notebooks*, 326.
24. Ibid., 324.
25. Although vestiges of the belief that extremism and acts of terrorism are the province of those suffering from a form of psychopathology can still be found in dominant formal, practical, and popular discourse, this belief has been largely discredited and found to be without any analytical substance. As Andrew Silke states, "An act of extreme violence does not in itself show that the perpetrator is psychologically distinct from the rest of humanity. Although a few psychologists believe terrorists are mentally abnormal, their conclusions are based on very weak evidence. Psychologists who have met terrorists face to face have nearly always concluded that these people were in no way abnormal, and on the contrary they had stable and rational personalities" (Silke, 2008, 104). These same conclusions were reached following the psychiatric evaluations of the various members of the Toronto 18 to stand trial for their actions—all were found to not suffer from any form of psychopathology. However, in the absence of psychopathology as the explanatory agent of extremist behavior and action, a surrogate explanatory agent has been created: Islam. In effect, the religion of Islam, as interpreted through an Orientalist prism, is constructed as effectively pathological, and therefore those that self-identify as Muslim are rendered inherently irrational. Consequently, the use of theology as an explanatory agent of the activities of Islamitic actors denies these actors a political rationality for their actions whether extremist or not.
26. Gramsci, *Prison Notebooks*, 197, 326.

27. Gramsci, *Prison Notebooks*, 334.
28. Author's own notes, 9 June 2008.
29. Although many Islamitic social actors located in various North American and Western European jurisdictions have accessed similar materials to that of the various members of the Toronto 18 from this virtual repository, it is important to note that this repository, as outlined by Trevor Aaronson, has not been linked to al-Qaeda or any of its purported affiliates. See Aaronson, *The Terror Factory*, 108.
30. Author's own notes, 26 May 2010.
31. Author's own notes, 3 May 2010 and 18 May 2010.
32. Author's own notes, 26 May 2010.
33. *The Return of the Crusaders*, http://archive.org/details/ReturnOfTheCrusadersDivX. Last accessed on 10 November 2012.
34. R.v. ZA, *Agreed Statement of Facts*, 4–5.
35. R.v. SK, *Agreed Statement of Facts*, 6 and R.v. ZA, *Agreed Statement of Facts*, 13.
36. R.v. ZA, *Agreed Statement of Facts*, 5.
37. Private communication between author and Mubin Shaikh, 17 October 2012.
38. Bjelopera, "American Jihadist Terrorism: Combating a Complex Threat," 21.
39. Seib & Janbek, *Global Terrorism and New Media*, 60.
40. Author's notes, 18 January 2010 and 19 April 2010.
41. Author's notes, May 2010
42. Roy, *Globalized Islam*, 312–314. However, it is important to note that not all Islamitic social actors who participate in foreign conflicts are motivated by an Islamitic extremist ideology. Many combatants may have an attachment to these countries through their parents or relatives and may be motivated to engage in hostilities for complex reasons, such as long-distance nationalism and other recursive forces, which have nothing to do with Islamitic extremism.
43. Author's notes, 16 June 2008.
44. R.v. FA, *Reasons for Sentence*, 9.
45. The use of undercover agents as an investigative technique in these types of cases is very controversial. In effect, as agents of the state who helped facilitate the activities of the group, the state itself could be considered a co-conspirator not only in the development of the group but in the construction of the threat certain members of this group posed to society. Furthermore, without the penetration of these undercover agents and their involvement with the group, would various members of the group, especially the members of the Mississauga group, have undergone a political transformation oriented on a violent trajectory? See Chap. 5 for an elaborate discussion of the state sphere of influence.

46. R.v. SA, *Reasons for Sentence*, 7.
47. R.v. NY, *Reasons for Judgment*, 5. This same technique was also utilized by the oldest adult to stand trial in connection to the bomb plot. When this individual approached the second agent tasked with infiltrating the Mississauga group and to assist in the acquisition of bomb-making materials because of his background in agricultural science, he began discussing the topic of "jihad" and presented the second agent with "violent jihadist videos" to determine how receptive the second agent was to such ideas (R.v. SA, *Reasons for Sentence*, 5).
48. R.v. NY, *Reasons for Judgment*, 4–5.
49. R.v. SG, *Reasons for Judgment*, 20.
50. R.v. SG, *Reasons for Judgment*, 25–26.
51. R.v. NY, *Reasons for Judgment*, 8.
52. Carter & McCormack, "Film, geopolitics and the affective logics of intervention," 234.
53. Ibid., 234.
54. Massumi quoted in Carter & McCormack, "Film, geopolitics and the affective logics of intervention," 230.
55. Ibid., 241.
56. Ibid., 241.
57. Dittmer, *Popular Culture, Geopolitics & Identity*, 94.
58. Author's own notes, 15 April 2010.
59. R.v. SG, *Reasons for Judgment*, 26.
60. Preston, Kobayashi & Siemiatycki, "Transnational Urbanism: Toronto at a Crossroads," 93.

CHAPTER 5

A Condition of Transgression: The State Sphere of Influence

"Be true! Be true! Be True! Show freely to the world, if not your worst, yet some trait whereby the worst may be inferred"

—Nathaniel Hawthorne, The Scarlet Letter.

From September to December 2010, the Canadian Security Intelligence Service (CSIS) conducted a study using the twenty-four people charged and/or convicted under provisions contained with the Anti-terrorism Act (ATA) as a control group to analyze the factors that led to the political transformation of these individual actors. This study, which is entitled "A Study of Radicalisation: The Making of Islamist Extremists in Canada Today," reaches some of the following conclusions: the majority of Domestic Islamitic Extremists demonstrate a high degree of integration in mainstream Canadian society; these same actors possess heterogeneous ethnic, family, and socio-economic backgrounds; the majority of these actors are highly educated and have no history of violent criminality; and, ultimately, that there is no reliable profile of Domestic Islamitic Extremist actors.[1] As a result, according to this study, the identification of readily discernible "patterns and trends on radicalisation remains elusive."[2] Subsequent to the public release of this study, Doug Saunders, in an article entitled "We're looking for terrorists in all the wrong places," makes the following observation after synthesizing the findings of the CSIS report and similar reports conducted by MI5 and the New York Police Department (NYPD):

There are important conclusions we can draw from these findings. The first is that immigrants, and immigrant communities, have little directly to do with terrorism. They are among those very unlikely to become radicalized. It's not a matter of people bringing foreign attitudes and beliefs to Canada; extremists gained their political ideas here, often from local influences. As a result, revoking the citizenship of people convicted of terrorism—as Immigration Minister Jason Kenney proposed this week—will do little to combat or deter extremism. Nor will spying on communities of ordinary religious Muslim immigrants, as the New York Police Department admitted it had done for six years (and it didn't find a single piece of actionable evidence after investigating thousands of people). As the CSIS report grimly concludes, it's not that easy.

Saunders goes on to conclude that "This doesn't make things easy for police or governments. It's a criminal tendency, neither imported nor theological, not rooted in communities or faiths. At the very least, we now know where we shouldn't bother looking."[3] Therefore, if one knows where not to look, the question remains as to where one should direct their gaze? However, to answer this question requires establishing an understanding of the limitations of the formal and practical analytical spectrum that informs most research into the ideological conditioning and political transformation of domestic Islamitic social actors.

To date, there is a propensity in formal and practical analysis to overemphasize the micro-social relations that make the ideological conditioning and political transformation of Islamitic social actors probable. Moreover, there is a tendency to attempt to explain the process of ideological conditioning and political transformation through the schematic categorization of linear developmental stages. As Michael King and Donald Taylor identify, four out of the five primary models of radicalization that have been developed since the events of 11 September 2001 varyingly describe this process in a linear succession of stages.[4] For instance, Randy Borum presents a model where social actors progress through the following stages: social and economic deprivation, inequality and resentment, blame and attribution, and stereotyping and demonizing the enemy. Alternatively, Quintan Wiktorowicz proposes that social actors undergo the following process: cognitive opening, religious seeking, frame alignment, and socialization. As a final example, the NYPD has developed a model that describes the radicalization process using the following sequence: preradicalization, self-identification, indoctrination, and jihadization.[5] Although these types of schematizations are attractive for descriptive and analytic purposes, the inherent danger is that these models not only simplify what is in practice a very complex and non-linear process but myopically focus on the subjectivization of the process of ideological conditioning and political transformation, e.g. age, gender, marital status, socio-economic status, education, familial dynamics, and peer group. Therefore, in an effort to avoid the dangers that can result from overly subjectivizing this process and too narrowly focusing on micro-social relations as the primary explanatory framework for the ideological conditioning and political transformation of Islamitic social actors, the field of engagement needs to be expanded.

As previously stated, the predominant focus on the relationship between micro-social relations and subjectivity tends to overly individualize the process of political subject formation. As a result, the broader conditions that influence and shape political subjectivities are generally neglected or are treated as tangential to the political transformation of the social actors in question. However, as Karl Marx argues, the subjectivity of a social actor is an ensemble of that actor's social relations.[6] Similarly, as Louis Althusser suggests, the subjectivity of a given social actor develops in response to being interpellated by social institutions.[7] Therefore, if one accepts and takes these propositions seriously, it is necessary to consider the broader conditions that make the political transformation of Islamitic social actors probable.[8] Although in the case of the Toronto 18, several conditions or spheres of influence operated in conjunction to facilitate the ideological conditioning and political transformation of the group, one of the most important to consider is the state sphere of influence.

A serious and productive analysis of the ideological conditioning and political transformation of Islamitic social actors requires that one engage the issue of state violence. As Simon Springer argues, although violence in its institutional forms is often obscured because of a predisposition to apprehend violence as something that can be seen through overt expression, these less visible forms of violence must be taken into account if one is to understand what might otherwise appear, or be construed, as irrational acts.[9] Arguably, to ignore the catalytic function of state violence in the transformation of the Islamitic subject is to embark on a quixotic adventure where concrete realities become ferocious giants and where reason is replaced with a vulgate of propagandistic treatise and lore. As Frantz Fanon explains, "The existence of an armed struggle is indicative that the people are determined to only put their faith in violent methods. The very same people who had it constantly drummed into them that the only language they understood was that of force, now decide to express themselves with force."[10] In effect, the use of state violence to neutralize the perceived nascent and nefarious Other can become the moral oxygen of the potentiality to violence of the Other. However, as previously mentioned (see Chap. 4), state violence can manifest in a multitude of forms. More specifically, in relation to Islamitic social actors, respective governments and the apparatuses that operate on their behalf must recognize that, consciously or unconsciously, the foreign and domestic policies and practices they pursue in the interest of counter-terrorism may actually contribute to the process of political transformation that can occur in place-specific contexts. In the case of the Toronto 18, three different forms of state violence—when operating in conjunction with the other spheres of influence—made the political transformation of the group probable: physical violence, institutional violence, and ideological violence. These three forms of state violence contributed to the transformation of the group through serving as a source of ideological consensus building.

Consensus Building Through Canadian Foreign Policy

Just as William Shakespeare's Friar warns Romeo and Juliet that "These violent delights have violent ends,"[11] the same warning applies to the relationship between the violent foreign adventurism of the Canadian state and the potentiality of domestic acts of extremism perpetrated in response to these policies and practices. As Brooke Rogers states:

> The apparent difficulty or unwillingness on the part of the policy makers to situate Western foreign policy within an account of violent radicalization deprives us of a means of objectively assessing the contribution that Western foreign policy makes to the radicalization process. Instead, dialogues of integration and multiculturalism abound, resulting in a lack of understanding about the impact of foreign policy on violent radicalization.[12]

In actuality, the empirical manifold suggests that the political transformation of Islamitic social actors and the material manifestation of Domestic Islamitic Extremism are organically linked to the foreign policy of the country within which these actors emerge, mobilize, and function. For instance, the 7 July 2005 transit attacks in London and the more recent attack on a British soldier in the streets of London were both directly correlated with the British government's involvement in Afghanistan and Iraq. Similarly, in the case of the Toronto 18, the activities of this group were organically linked to Canada's involvement in Afghanistan. However, before demonstrating this linkage, it is important to contextualize Canadian military involvement in Afghanistan.

Following the tragic spectacle of 11 September 2001, the Canadian government offered immediate and unequivocal support to the US government as its military and intelligence apparatuses prepared to inaugurate a global war *of* terror that would begin in Afghanistan in October 2001 under the auspices of the American-led Operation Enduring Freedom. According to Jerome Klassen, the reasoning that was utilized to inform and motivate the decision to involve Canada in the US-led interdiction of Afghanistan was predicated on the following political calculations as shared with Klassen in interviews conducted with key Canadian cabinet ministers: [...] "the primary considerations were fighting terrorism, supporting a NATO ally, and appeasing Canada's largest trading partner. According to these interviews, Canadian politicians hoped to gain favour with the Bush administration through a series of 'early in, early out' deployments."[13] However, as Greg Albo elaborates, participating in the war on terror was also strategically utilized by the Canadian government as a framework to structurally reorganize and reorient the Canadian state:

> Before 2001 the international branches of the Canadian state already incorporated neoliberal norms and US primacy strategies into their organizational structures. However, with the United States' revamping of security measures after 9/11, a further reorganization of the Canadian state took place, linking national security to continental integration and a forward military force projection. This structural transformation was organized and directed by the central agencies of the state without public mandate through election manifestos or extensive parliamentary debate. The core decision was to incorporate 'imperial security' norms directly into the Canadian state, and thus to pattern Canada's administrative and policy response after Washington's.[14]

As a result of the imperial repositioning of the Canadian state, the Canadian government initially supported the military intervention in Afghanistan not only through deploying Canadian Special Forces soldiers in conjunction with hundreds of regular troops but through sending one-third of the Canadian navy to the Persian Gulf. Following this initial military contribution, in 2002 the Canadian government deployed an additional two thousand troops to southern Afghanistan where Canadian soldiers were to help secure transportation routes and supply lines as well as engage in hostilities. From 2003 to 2005, the Canadian government deployed approximately two thousand soldiers to the capital city of Kabul where their mission was to protect the Karzai government. In 2005, the Canadian government assumed a much more bellicose role in counter-insurgency operations by relocating to and leading these efforts in Kandahar province where approximately twenty-five hundred soldiers directly engaged Taliban forces. Initially, the Kandahar deployment was designed to last two years; however, the Canadian government, under the leadership of Stephen Harper, decided to extend the troop deployment until 2011.[15] As a consequence of the repositioning of the Canadian state not only as a US client with imperial ambitions but as an increasingly belligerent power in the global order, the Canadian nation by extension automatically assumed responsibility for all of the intended and/or unintended outcomes of this Faustian arrangement, including all atrocities committed in Afghanistan by the Canadian military. In effect, the imperial fantasies of the Canadian state rendered the Canadian nation more vulnerable, less secure, and ultimately less free.

As Neta Crawford states, exact figures for the total deaths of Afghani civilians caused by the US-led Operation Enduring Freedom are very difficult to ascertain as "there is no long run tally, no 'Afghanistan body count,' or similar independent public accounting of civilian injury or death caused by all combatants since 2001."[16] However, using publicly available data, Crawford conservatively estimates that between 12 500 and 14 700 innocent civilians, including men, women, and children, have been killed since the conflict began in October 2001.[17] Although various Canadian generals have justified the military's involvement in the war *of* terror in general, and in Afghanistan in particular, through positioning the Canadian military as being effectively engaged in a noble enterprise to kill "'detestable murderers and scumbags' who are 'insidious by their very nature,' 'detest our freedoms,' and want to 'break our society,'" the Canadian military has been accused of being involved not only in the deaths of innocent civilians but complicit in the torture of prisoners transferred to Afghani military and security apparatuses.[18] Consequently, these atrocities and crimes have not only resulted in protests within Afghanistan but have resulted in protests within Canada regarding the decision of the Canadian government to participate in this conflict. Although in the Canadian context the vast majority of the subversive activity regarding the war in Afghanistan has relied upon non-violent and constitutional methods to challenge the elite position on the war, two notable examples exist where violent and unconstitutional methods were utilized in protest to Canada's military involvement in Afghanistan. The first example is encapsulated by the bombing of a military recruitment center in Trois-Rivieres, Quebec, on 2 July 2010 by members of the group *Initiative de Resistance Internationaliste*. The second example is encapsulated by the so-called Toronto 18. Now that Canadian military involvement in Afghanistan has been contextualized, the connection between the Toronto 18 and Canadian foreign policy vis-à-vis Afghanistan can be explicated.

The evidence of the organic linkage between the ideological conditioning and political transformation of the Toronto 18 and the involvement of the Canadian military in Afghanistan is explicitly demonstrated through excerpts from a dialogue between the principal ideologue of the group; the undercover agent, Mubin Shaikh; one of the adult accused to stand trial in connection with the Scarborough group; and an individual referred to as "Talib" who was approached by some members of the group to help them procure money to help finance their activities. (Talib, who later testified in the trial of some of the adult accused, was approached by various members of the group because of his expertise in identity theft and fraud.) In this conversation, the individuals present explained to Talib the geopolitical forces and practices that informed and shaped their ideological position. Furthermore, through this conversation, the use of physical violence by the Canadian state as a consensus-building mechanism is revealed. The following is a series of successive excerpts taken from a dialogue captured in an intercept dated 3 March 2006:

> Principal Ideologue: It's a global fight. It's not just a specific country and a specific battlefield. I mean they attacked you in Afghanistan right.
> Pg. 14:
> Principal Ideologue: Doesn't mean every single Muslim, if you want to fight the Americans you have to go strictly to Afghanistan to fight them.
> Principal Ideologue: If you wanna fight the Americans, you fight them wherever you find them. Because it's a global fight. I mean we're not the ones that declared…although from Afghanistan okay fine. But the…for the people who say well it could be interpreted this way or that way find okay with this. Bush himself declared it.
> Principal Ideologue: You're with us in Afghanistan right.
> Principal Ideologue: You're with the good or the evil terrorists right.

Principal Ideologue: And who's the evil terrorists?

Principal Ideologue: Yeah, so it's like they hate us and they do things to us. I mean okay fine, it's okay that you go and you killed a man right. That's okay. You go and carpet bomb entire villages and, and there has been.

Adult Accused: Yeah.

Principal Ideologue: I can prove you some videos. It shows them just carpet bombing the hell out of an entire village, nobody survives.

Pg. 15:

Talib: So what's your mission to kill them?

Adult Accused: Uh it's, it's not just…I mean I know you heard just a few things right now. The reasons why this Jihad is necessary and what preparations are…are necessary. Um, but don't just think we just go one or two things: oh Bush said this now we have to put a big Jihad team together.

Adult Accused: There's a lot of things like…

Mubin Shaikh: The proof is in the…Prophet, may God's prayers and peace be upon him, that uh the nation is like the body. When one part of the body suffers the whole body suffers, right. And it follows that if one one part is hurt, you're gonna employ the rest of your body part to help that part heal.

Mubin Shaikh: To relieve the hurt from that part of the body.

Mubin Shaikh: Right. And like here, we live, we made an equivalent Rome right or as the Rastas they keep saying Babylon, Babylon.

Mubin Shaikh: Right, they mean Rome.

Mubin Shaikh: In Babylon, it's the same, the same thing, they symbolize the same thing right. The source and the fountain of the oppressor that is causing all these things elsewhere. It makes sense that if Rome is sending troops to Turkey, to Syria, to Egypt….

Pg. 17:

Mubin Shaikh: It makes sense that you attack Rome.

Mubin Shaikh: If you are in Rome, you attack Rome. If you're in Syria you attack the Romans in Syria.

Mubin Shaikh: Right. It's logical, it makes sense. Like this is basic warfare strategy.

Principal Ideologue: There is, there's an obligation to attack the near enemy, than the far enemy.

Principal Ideologue: So you look around, I mean these same soldiers that are training in their military bases here are gonna go to Afghanistan and fight there.

Principal Ideologue: So it doesn't make sense to go to Afghanistan and fight them when they're already prepared for you.

Principal Ideologue: Where let's say you make one attack and maybe you'll shoot a soldier or two what not.

Principal Ideologue: While you're here and what are they going to do. They'll carpet bomb their own country…population?

Principal Ideologue: No. Another thing is these same soldiers are fighting you there, so why can't you attack them here?[19]

Indeed, further evidence of the organic linkage between the political transformation of the Toronto 18 and Canadian foreign policy is revealed by comments made by Justice Dawson in the *Reasons for Sentencing* document he prepared for the sentencing of the principal ideologue of the group:

> According to the presentence report, when [the principal ideologue] was at the mosque he began to interact with individuals who believed Islam was under attack and that Muslims everywhere needed to stand up for their faith and for those Muslims whose countries were being attacked by the United States and its allies. At the same time [the principal ideologue] began to spend more time on the Internet, including sites making claims that atrocities were being committed against Muslims by western forces overseas. He became convinced it was his duty to assist the Afghani people and his faith by becoming involved in the conflict.[20]

Similarly, Justice Durno in his *Reasons for Sentencing* for one of the adult accused associated with the Mississauga group identified the Canadian presence in Afghanistan as the primary agitating force of the individuals involved in the case of the Toronto 18. As Justice Durno states, "In the spring of 2006, a group of young men were involved in a plan to detonate bombs in Toronto and elsewhere in Ontario. Their objective was to influence Canada's policy in Afghanistan."[21] Justice Durno goes on to elaborate the motivation of the individual in question: "It was not contested that the plot to acquire explosive substances and cause explosions was for a religiously-inspired political purpose. The offender's motivation was to pressure Canada into withdrawing troops from Afghanistan, the religious aspect being to protect a Muslim country from attack."[22] In effect, as the abovementioned comments suggest, the physical violence of the Canadian state significantly contributed to the ideological conditioning and political transformation of the various members of the Toronto 18. However, the organic link between foreign policy as expressed through physical state violence and the political transformation of Islamitic social actors is not the only relationship that one needs to evaluate. Another important relationship is the linkage between domestic security policy and the ideological conditioning and political transformation of Islamitic social actors.

Consensus Building Through Canadian Domestic Security Policy

Following the events of 11 September 2001, the Canadian government responded to the perceived nascent and nefarious threat of Transnational Islamitic Extremism by hurriedly developing legislation that would enhance and fortify the anti-terrorism framework of the Canadian state. Subsequently, Bill C-36 or the *Anti-terrorism Act* (ATA) was submitted to Parliament and received royal assent in December 2001. According to a report entitled "Fundamental Justice in Extraordinary Times: Main Report of the Special Senate Committee on the *Anti-Terrorism Act*," the passage of Bill C-36 was, as the title of the report suggests, extraordinary: "Rarely has such a complex omnibus bill proceeded so rapidly through the legislative process. Given the perceived necessity to respond quickly and comprehensively to the threat of terrorism, a majority of parliamentarians were willing to support this key element of the government's anti-terrorism plan. Parliament accordingly expedited both the study and passage of the Act."[23] As a result, several contentious and draconian measures were introduced to the Canadian counter-terrorism repertoire of strategies and tactics, including but not limited to investigative hearings, preventative arrest, and administrative detention (incarceration without charge). Invariably, given the zeal with which the ATA and other security-related legislation was passed in conjunction with the revelation that the threshold required for passing government legislation that potentially violated the Charter of Rights and Freedoms was set so low as to be virtually non-existent,[24] authoritarian abuses of state power and concomitant crises of legitimacy followed. For instance, in its comprehensive review of the provisions and functions of the ATA, the Special Senate Committee on the Anti-terrorism Act alluded to the crisis of legitimacy precipitated by this legislation by using the following terms and examples:

> It is clear, both in international and our own domestic law, that all rights are of equal value, and that one right cannot be sacrificed in the name of preserving another. However, when dealing with the threat of international terrorism, how best to protect and preserve our rights, obligations and values becomes a complex question for Canadian society and its lawmakers to answer. Our government and courts have already been struggling with this challenge, as demonstrated in the context of the Commission of Inquiry into the Actions of Canadian Officials in relation to Maher Arar and by the constitutional challenges to the *Immigration and Refugee Protection*

Act's security certificate process, which were heard by the Supreme Court of Canada in June 2006. As stated by former Supreme Court of Justices Frank Iacobucci and Louise Arbor in a challenge to the *Anti-Terrorism Act's* investigative hearing provisions, "a response to terrorism within the rule of law preserves and enhances the cherished liberties that are essential to democracy." This is the goal of our counter-terrorism legislation. Much thought must therefore be given to constructing an appropriate framework, capable of ensuring that physical security is protected and civil liberties respected.[25]

Although domestic security policies, especially domestic anti-terrorism policies, are presumably designed to enhance public safety and security, these same policies and related practices can actually have the opposite effect. As Frederic Volpi elaborates and explains:

> By trying to make 'objective' defensive gains against perceived terrorist threats, governments deploy security policies that induce other social and political players to view their own security and insecurity in a particular way. Consequently, regardless of its initial intention, the process of deploying policies with pervasive (and often unintended) implications does not simply address pre-existing threats, but also shapes what would count as a threat subsequently.[26]

Therefore, evaluating the relationship between domestic security policy and the political transformation of Islamitic social actors, the Canadian state and its relevant policy practitioners require self-reflexively considering the intended and/or unintended consequences of the state violence produced by particular anti-terrorism policies and practices. In the case of the Toronto 18, the relationship between domestic security policy and the ideological conditioning and political transformation of the actors involved in the group is certainly evident vis-à-vis the Canadian government's security certificate program. However, before elaborating on the linkage between the security certificate program and the political transformation of the various Islamitic social actors involved in the case of the Toronto 18, it is pertinent to briefly describe the Canadian Security Regime and then contextualize the background, usage, and implications of the security certificate program.

The Canadian Security Regime is multilayered and is comprised of a multitude of interconnected and interrelated entities. The following chart provides a visual summary of the constituent entities that in totality comprise the Canadian Security Regime:

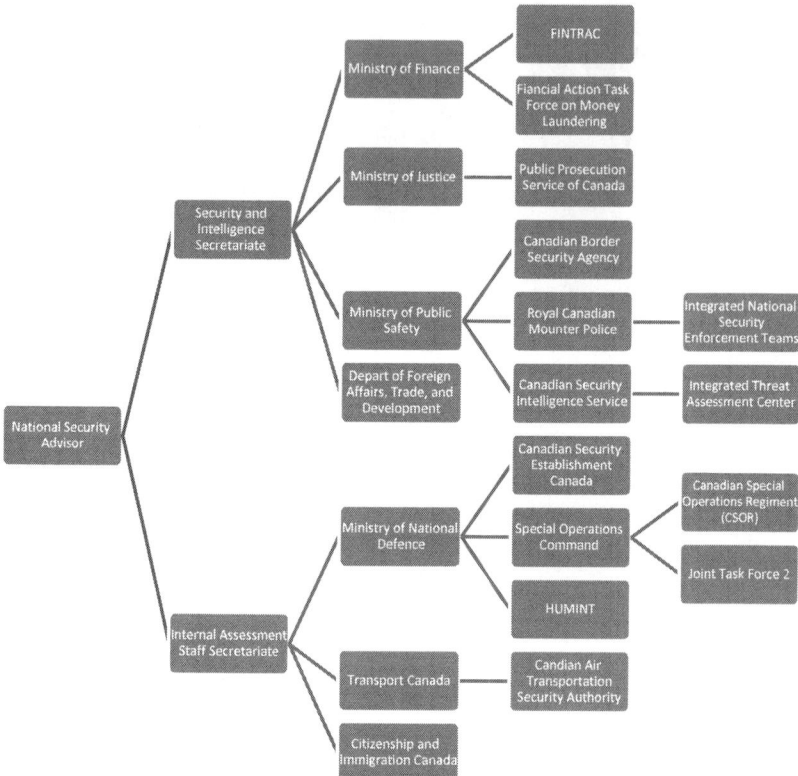

Fig. 5.1 "The Canadian Security Regime" (For a more elaborate description of the roles of various Canadian governmental entities involved in the national security of Canada, see the Canadian Department of Justice website at: http://www.justice.gc.ca/eng/cj-jp/ns-sn/role.html)

Although all of these entities perform a function in the Canadian Security Regime, the law enforcement and intelligence apparatuses are the systole and diastole of Canadian counter-terrorism initiatives and investigations. These two apparatuses include: national security investigators from the Royal Canadian Mounted Police (RCMP), who also work conjointly with local law enforcement officials depending upon the jurisdiction; intelligence officers from the Canadian Security Intelligence Service (CSIS); and intelligence analysts from the Communication Security Establishment of Canada (CSEC). Following the events of 11 September 2001, the funding and expansion of human capital in these state apparatuses quickly increased as did their power to gather intelligence and conduct investigations regarding threats to national security, such as Transnational Islamitic Extremism and Domestic Islamitic Extremism. One of these enhanced powers was the reintroduction of the security certificate program as a counter-terrorism tool.

The security certificate program was introduced into Canadian immigration law in the late 1970s. Approximately a decade later, it was added to the *Immigration Act* (1988) and was reincarnated in the *Immigration and Refugee Protection Act* (2002) as an important aspect of the Canadian government's anti-terrorism framework. Initially, the security certificate regime could only be applied to personages with non-citizenship status; however, the reincarnated version expanded this provision to include personages with permanent residence status.[27] Robert Diab describes the security certificate regime in the following terms: "Section 34 of the *Immigration and Refugee Protection Act* states that a permanent resident or foreign national is 'inadmissible' to Canada 'on security grounds' for a number of possible reasons, including 'engaging in terrorism' or being involved in an organization that is engaged in terrorism or 'being a danger to the security of Canada.'"[28] As Diab explains, Section 77 of the *Act* enables the Minister of Citizenship and Immigration, in conjunction with the Minister of Public Safety and Emergency Preparedness, to declare a permanent resident or foreign national inadmissible to Canada for national security concerns and sign a certificate that effectively becomes a warrant for the arrest and detention of the named individual. Following the detention of an individual, a hearing is scheduled in a Federal Court of Law where a judge reviews the evidence presented by the Canadian state against the individual and determines whether or not deportation proceedings should begin.[29] Although there are a litany of problems associated with the security certificate regime, Diab outlines the following dimensions of the security certificate regime as the most problematic. First, the detainee is not shown all of the evidence being brought against them by reason of national security and has no way of refuting or challenging the evidence brought against them. Second, the information that the judge may consider is so broad as to include untrustworthy information obtained through torture or other methods that would call into question the veracity or reliability of the evidence. In effect, the evidentiary threshold is significantly lower than what one would expect under ordinary judicial conditions. Third, as the proceedings are held in camera and the majority of the evidence is withheld from the detainee and his or her legal representative, the detainee is denied the ability to mount a proper legal defense. Lastly, if it is determined that an individual is inadmissible to Canada, but could face cruel or unusual punishment, torture, or death if returned to their respective country of origin, the individual could be imprisoned indefinitely with very little legal recourse.[30] However, the negative implications and embodied impact of the security certificate regime extend far beyond judicial concerns. In effect, the bodies on which the security certificates are written become metaphors for the institutional racialization of security in Canada.

As Jacqueline Flatt observes, "the use of security certificates has, until recently, been largely hidden from the general public. The development of the 'war on terror' has produced a dichotomy between security and rights that has compromised human rights in favour of security."[31] However, as Flatt goes on to assert, "the use of security certificates has not only produced human rights abuses but has also been a form of hidden racism."[32] As Sherene Razack states, "Security certificates did not begin with the 'war on terror,' but they have become the 'front-line tools' used by Canada to fight terrorism, and their usage is now primarily directed at Arabs and Muslims."[33] As a result, according to Flatt, "Arab and Muslim individuals are placed outside of what is normalized, reinforcing racialized boundaries between who is and who is not seen as citizen and as belonging to Canada."[34] In effect, as Temitope Oriola suggests, the broader implications of the security certificate regime are the reification and reinforcement of difference as an object of risk and potential danger: "by having a distinct provision for trying aliens—permanent residents and foreign nationals—the Canadian state dispenses *alien justice*. Here, the alien is a 'frightening symbol of the fact of difference.' Such an individual is not necessarily the new comer, but one for whom assimilation remains a perpetual mirage by virtue of socially constructed difference."[35] Consequently, through the production of an extraordinary legal space of administrative detention that situates particular racialized detainees on the margins of a democratic judicial framework, the Canadian state by extension situates targeted suspect communities on a social margin where they effectively occupy a space of social detention. As a result, the body of the detained and the social body of the targeted suspect community become one and the same. As a result, the Canadian state generates a socio-political gravitational force with a field of affectivity that extends from the body of the detained to the social body of the targeted suspect community. The socio-political affect of the security certificate regime is certainly evident in the case of the Toronto 18.

On 27 November 2005 various members of the group attended a public lecture at the Taj Banquet Hall in Toronto.[36] This public lecture was sponsored by the Muslim Inmate Assistance Program and concerned the detention of Muslims under the auspices of the Canadian security certificate regime. The significance of this event is threefold. First, according to Mubin Shaikh, an important element of the public lecture concerned the humanitarian grievances generated by the security certificate process.[37] The grievances expressed at the lecture illustrate the perceived and/or real injustices felt by certain segments of the communities in question as a result of this form of institutional violence. Second, this policy and practice of the Canadian state helped to catalyze the political transformation of the group by reinforcing the perception that Muslims are under attack not only outside the Canadian nation-state but within it as well. Indeed, the CSIS building in downtown Toronto was selected as a target precisely because of the perception by members of the group that Muslims were being unfairly harassed and targeted by CSIS. Third, the institutional violence to which Islamitic social actors and other segments of civil society react is the very modality of violence that makes the infiltration of the Toronto 18 by an agent of the state possible. As Justice Sproat outlined, CSIS instructed Mubin Sheik to attend the Taj Banquet Hall lecture in order to make contact with and obtain more information about the principal figures of the group.[38] In other words, without the presence of institutional violence as expressed through the security certificate regime, the opportunity to infiltrate the group would have been significantly diminished and quite possibly altogether neutralized. By producing spaces of extraordinary institutional violence, the state creates spaces where the use of extraordinary non-state violence becomes possible. In effect, in the context of this group, the security certificate regime served a self-fulfilling prophesy of violence. Although institutional violence and physical violence are important dimensions of the ideological consensus building required for the ideological conditioning and political transformation of the group, another important dimension of state violence is ideological violence.

Consensus Building Through Ideological Violence

In a post-11 September 2001 milieu, multiculturalism has become a very contested, if not a highly controversial, subject of engagement. Although the official narrative in Canada positions multiculturalism as a source of strength for the nation-state, some, especially in the law enforcement and security apparatuses of North America and Western Europe, conceive of multiculturalism as a source of vulnerability for the nation-state.[39] As Vivienne Jabri observes:

> Multiculturalism has long been viewed as presenting a challenge to liberalism and the liberal state. Articulated mainly in normative discourses around the question of citizenship, the tension highlighted is between liberalism's primary attachment to individual autonomy and the question of group rights in multi-ethnic liberal societies. With the advent of the so-called 'war against terrorism', multiculturalism has increasingly been associated with insecurity; that cultural difference as such is potentially a source of threat and danger.[40]

As a consequence, particular communities in North America and various Western European jurisdictions, such as the UK, France, the Netherlands, and so on, that are believed to be susceptible to the influence of Islamitic extremist ideology and related activity have become objects of state suspicion and, by extension, spaces of state interdiction:

> What is significant in the present political context is the construction of the particular other as threat, so that it is the Islamic, the Asian, or he or she who hails from the Middle East, that is constituted in discourse as the existential threat and is hence subjected not simply to practices of exclusion, but to a whole panoply of interventions that seek to re-shape, re-form, re-design the very subjectivity of this other in the name of security.[41]

Although the various forms of "intervention" and interdictory policies and practices enacted by the state are presumably designed to detect, deter, and/or prevent the transformation of violent subjectivities among Islamitic social actors, paradoxically, if not ironically, the opposite of these desired outcomes can occur in communities targeted by the state:

> The paradox for government is that, despite efforts in the form of published declarations or policy frameworks aimed at the elimination of racism and xenophobia, the substantial content of the government of social relations is targeted at the Muslim subject perceived and constructed as the potentially 'radicalized' other. Both categories, Muslim and radical, utilized in the identification of citizens, come to constitute those citizens exactly in these terms. The paradox of such interpellations is all too clear; governmental discourses aimed to combat 'radicalization' actually radicalize.[42]

In effect, the securitization of multiculturalism, which is a form of ideological violence, can contribute to the ideological consensus building of

Islamitic social actors and the shaping of particular political subjectivities. However, in what way does this modality of state violence serve a catalytic function in the transformation of Islamitic social actors?

The securitization of multiculturalism and the concomitant targeting of suspect communities produce an atmosphere of racialized persecution that creates, reifies, and reinforces cultural difference, social division and exclusion, and political antagonism. It is precisely this atmosphere that helps to make particular political transformations probable under specific conditions. The production of this atmosphere is certainly evident in the Canadian context. Although, officially, the Canadian state and its law enforcement and security apparatuses deny and disavow the practice of racial profiling, the unofficial reality is that the practice of racial profiling represents a dimension of the decisionmaking calculus utilized in national security-related initiatives. For instance, the official report of the Special Senate Committee on the *Anti-terrorism Act* states:

> With respect to racial profiling, and more specifically its avoidance, the Committee was told by the federal government that racial profiling does not occur and that discriminatory practices, including the targeting of minorities, have no place in law enforcement and security and intelligence work. However, we did note an evolution in the views of police, security and intelligence agencies as our work progressed and community members were given the opportunity to express the unease and anxiety they were feeling. By the end of our study, government representatives acknowledged that, despite the fact that racial profiling is not officially condoned, certain groups nonetheless feel that they have been the targets of racial profiling.[43]

The report later goes on to note:

> Although efforts have been made on the part of government to ensure that racial profiling does not take place, many witnesses who appeared before the Committee as representatives of community organizations or to address civil liberties matters asserted that racial profiling had occurred and was still occurring. They also explained that the perception of certain communities that they are being targeted or singled out for increased scrutiny and investigation is a strong one, and that a culture of fear has been created, particularly among Canada's Muslim and Arab groups.[44]

Indeed, both the Royal Canadian Mounted Police (RCMP) and the Canadian Security Intelligence Service (CSIS) have been directly implicated in this form of practice. As Temitope Oriola identifies, "A study commissioned by the Royal Canadian Mounted Police confirms that Muslims are being racially profiled in Canada."[45] Similarly, Shaista Patel identifies a report issued by the Canadian Council on American-Islamic Relations (CAN-CAIR) that found the same type of activity being conducted by CSIS. According to a survey sponsored by CAN-CAIR of members of Muslim communities, a disturbing degree of racial profiling emerged. Of the 467 respondents, 8 % report being interviewed by CSIS. Of this 8 %, 89 % were between the ages of 18 and 35 and were either of Arab, South Asian, Persian, or African background. Furthermore, 85 % of those interviewed by CSIS were Canadian citizens.[46] However, the securitization of multiculturalism extends beyond the practice of racial profiling perpetrated by national security investigators and finds institutional expression in two further forms.

The first institutional expression of the securitization of multiculturalism is demonstrated through the development of the Cross-Cultural Roundtable on Security in 2004. The development of this initiative was announced in the first official national security policy released by the Canadian government in April 2004 shortly after the Madrid transit bombings. Operating under the auspices of the Ministry of Public Safety and Emergency Preparedness, this initiative is described in the following terms: "The Cross-Cultural Roundtable on Security was created to engage Canadians and the Government of Canada in a long-term dialogue on matters related to national security. The Roundtable brings together citizens who are leaders in their respective communities and who have extensive experience in social and cultural matters. It focuses on emerging developments in national security matters and their impact on Canada's diverse and pluralistic society."[47] The representatives of the roundtable came from a variety of ethnocultural and religious communities from across Canada and were meant to advise the Minister of Public Safety and Emergency Preparedness and the Minister of Justice on the prevention of terrorism, the promotion of tolerance, and the impact of national security policies and practices on certain minority communities. Incidentally, as Kent Roach and Liette Gilbert separately identify, representatives from the two largest Muslim communities in Canada (Toronto and Montreal) were initially excluded from the advisory committee even though the communities were subject to a high degree of state scrutiny and discrimination.[48] The inaugural meeting of the Cross-Cultural Roundtable took place in March 2005 and since then has reconvened several times per annum to discuss a multitude of issues relating to national security with a notable emphasis on border security and radicalization.[49] However, as Roach suggests, the credibility of the Cross-Cultural Roundtable on Security as an effective liaison between the government and minority communities has been compromised as the Roundtable serves a conflicting dual function: it is meant to serve an advocacy role for those who have been or are being wrongfully profiled and subjected to anti-terrorism legislation, while also serving as a mechanism through which the Ministry of Public Safety and Emergency Preparedness and the law enforcement and security apparatuses that operate under the aegis of this Ministry can disseminate information to these communities. Consequently, the danger is that the Cross-Cultural Roundtable could serve more as a Public Relations group for the government and as a conduit through which to gain access to communities of interest.[50] Indeed, the latter rather than the former appears to be the guiding ethos of the Cross-Cultural Roundtable on Security as evinced by the focus of the Roundtable on inculcating the zero tolerance of terrorism in particular communities without advocating the zero tolerance of the practice of racial profiling by law enforcement and security apparatuses and by the members serving as liaisons between the various communities represented and the government in order to establish outreach activities relating to various national security issues as per the June 2008 meeting of the Roundtable entitled, "Radicalization Leading to Violence."[51] Arguably, in effect, the Roundtable is a unidirectional, top-down initiative that is designed to facilitate access to communities of interest and enable the government to develop its capacity for resilience rather than that of the communities in question.

The second institutional expression of the securitization of multiculturalism is demonstrated through the development of the "Citizens Academy" and other outreach programs that are administered through the RCMP in conjunction with other local law enforcement services, the various regional offices of the CSIS, and the Canadian Border Security Agency (CBSA). During an interview between the author and a senior officer with the RCMP who was in charge of national security investigations in the province of Ontario, the officer, who, incidentally, implemented the "Citizens Academy" program, described the initiative in the following terms:

> The Citizens Academy was not really new; it was new for us. After 9/11 the Muslim community felt that they were under siege and under attack. People were looking at them differently because they dress differently and people were drawing connections between the hijackers and bombers. There was a great deal of interest from the Muslim community to get information and facts and to set the record straight. So, I started attending a lot of meetings and town hall meetings and there were a lot of perceptions that were

completely false. Some examples are when Canada passed the ATA that the government gave the police extraordinary powers including arrest without charge and secret trials. So, I thought to myself how do we inform people that we have the Charter of Rights, people will get a fair trial, if they can't afford representation the government will pay for it, and that we don't discriminate against people based upon religion. So, having attended a number of very large meetings and getting consistent feedback, I started looking at what other organizations were doing. Some organizations call it the "Community Consultative Group" and others call it the "Chiefs Advisory Board." We decided to create a "Citizens Academy" and we would invite people from a wide range of communities and we are going to host a program that is eight weeks in length and 3 hours per week at the INSET office.

We started with the history of the RCMP, how we recruit people into our organization, the type of training we receive, and walked them through a quick session where each speaker had one hour to go over their material. We brought in our partners, including municipal police forces, Ontario Provincial Police (OPP), Canada Border Services Agency (CBSA), CSIS, to discuss what their roles are and to help remove the myth of how we operate and to be completely transparent. Certainly in Ontario the RCMP is not as well known as we are in other provinces where we are the police force of jurisdiction. In Ontario there is kind of this mystique where we work undercover and other things. So, that is what the Citizens Academy was created for. As feedback, all we were looking for was the community leaders to go back to their respective communities to help educate people on an informal basis about the role of the RCMP or CSIS and dispel these myths. We then encouraged the community liaisons that if they had a particular interest in any area that we would help facilitate and put together subject matter experts to give them further information on whatever the topic may be— radicalization of youth was one. That is how the Citizens Academy was born and it has been very successful, but it is a slow process and I often make the analogy of going back to the early 80s when I worked in drug enforcement. Back then we created a program called "Drug Awareness" and we partnered with professional sports personalities to educate young people to just say no to drugs. Fast forward 20 years and young people are much more aware of the issue of drugs then they were in the early 80s. Hopefully, over time, as a number people go through they can help to educate their communities.[52]

The Citizens Academy program began in 2005, and at the time of the interview eight of these sessions had been administered in the city of Toronto.
Although the stated objective of the Citizens Academy may be to educate communities that are considered vulnerable to particular forms of

extremist ideation and activities about the roles and functions of Canadian law enforcement and security apparatuses, these same apparatuses need to be self-reflexively aware of the implications of engaging these communities using this type of strategy. For instance, during a similar outreach initiative that is designed to facilitate the access of law enforcement and security officials to select schools throughout the Toronto GTA and beyond, the RCMP brought banners to an Islamic elementary school in Hamilton that read the following: "National Security—A Shared Responsibility."[53] Arguably, the impetus for this initiative is driven by an ethos that the children and adolescents of suspect communities are susceptible to particular forms of messaging. As one RCMP official states, "You know, we've had experiences where kids have been disenfranchised for one reason or another that have been susceptible to influence and taken up causes."[54]

This ethos is further reinforced by two documents released by CSIS. The first document is a *Memorandum for the Prime Minister* entitled, "Intelligence Briefing On Radicalization and Jihad In The West." This was prepared for the Prime Minister of Canada shortly after the arrests of the Toronto 18. According to this document, "Anyone in the community is potentially at risk of becoming radicalized: those born in Canada, immigrants, or converts."[55] The second document is an *Intelligence Assessment* entitled, "Venues of Sunni Islamist Radicalization in Canada."[56] According to this report, prisons, family settings, travel abroad, and virtual environments are all places where "radicalization" is occurring. As the report concludes, "As radicalization is usually a social process, it can occur wherever humans interact, in the real world or virtual ones."[57] As these documents suggest, any Muslim socializing in any venue is potentially vulnerable to an Islamitic extremist ideology. As a result, a climate of suspicion is produced where interpellations like those described above are considered important and necessary to prevent this messaging from actively shaping the beliefs and activities of this suspect community. Therefore, branding an event using "National Security—A Shared Responsibility" as the slogan of choice encodes that these communities, by virtue of their ethnocultural and religious orientation, occupy what Mustafa Dikec has described as the badlands of the city and therefore require the attention of law enforcement and security services as they live within but effectively exist outside the Canadian nation-state irrespective of status.[58] As one participant asked at a Citizens Academy held in the basement of a mosque in the city of Mississauga, "How can we work together when the system itself is against Muslims?"[59]

Although the securitization of multiculturalism is a result of a variety of complex processes that are inherent to the mandates guiding the policies and practices of law enforcement and security apparatuses in Canada, two formative and co-constituting moments make this approach to security possible. The first moment refers to the general knowledge deficit that exists within the security and law enforcement apparatuses of Canada regarding Islam. For example, during an interview the author conducted with a senior intelligence analyst with the CSIS, when asked how well the security service understood Islam, this individual offered the following evaluation: that the knowledge of Islam within the service was getting better and that there is a concerted push to elevate their knowledge capacity to increase understanding of cultural mores in order to engage and not alienate. As part of their knowledge-building strategy, the CSIS has been actively and aggressively hiring Canadian Muslim citizens to reflect the diversity of Canada.[60] Similar sentiments were expressed in an interview the author conducted with the senior officer in the RCMP who was responsible for national security investigations in Ontario. When asked how well law enforcement understood Islam, this individual offered the following evaluation:

> Probably not that well. I mean there are people who have an interest and have taken the time to do their own personal research to establish their own basic understanding of Islam. But, the vast majority have a very limited level of information on it. For example, over the years we've brought people in and put on workshops and seminars on Islam, but that is because we were working in the area.[61]

However, when asked if further developing the knowledge capacity of the RCMP regarding Islam was an important initiative, this individual answered in the affirmative and explained that this was an important component of the RCMP's approach to law enforcement:

> Yes. However, it is not only Islam. Canada is a very diverse country so depending on where you are and what you are working on the RCMP is an organization that is continuously learning. A significant part of successful policing is understanding various cultures. In the 80s I was working in the area of heroin and I had to develop a good understanding of the Chinese culture because it was a source country for heroin. So you have to educate yourself about how they operate to develop strategies to combat it. Terrorism and national security are no different.[62]

Indeed, this knowledge deficit is recognized by the suspect communities themselves.

In an interview, a former Executive Director of the Canadian Arab Federation (CAF) identified the Canadian government in general, including law enforcement and security apparatuses, as possessing a very underdeveloped understanding of Islam and/or Muslim communities. When asked if the Canadian government understands Islam and/or the Muslim communities of Canada, this individual clearly stated "no" and elaborated by suggesting that the government and law enforcement and security services do not interact with communities as partners but, rather, interact to spy or inform. As this individual suggests, this impression was felt most acutely following the events of 11 September 2001. According to this individual, the initial response by the government was harsh, repressive, threatening, intimidating, and coercive.[63] As reported in the *Toronto Star*, these sentiments are echoed by Ally Hindy, an Imam at the Salaheddin mosque located in the city of Scarborough: "Hindy claims police and the spies unfairly target Muslims, and that their invasive tactics have dissuaded many in the community from co-operating with federal authorities."[64] A concrete example is evidenced by an encounter between a Muslim student in the Crime, Deviance, and Law program at the University of Toronto and a representative of CSIS: "I, personally, had a visit from CSIS at my house. They want you to go to the mosque, look and see if there is anything suspicious, and come back and report to them. They basically think that if you are not willing to do that, you must have something to hide."[65] In another interview the author conducted with the former and founding president of the Canadian Islamic Congress (CIC), this individual described the Canadian government's understanding of Islam and/or Muslim communities in the following terms: the "Harper government" does not understand communities and does not want to understand. This individual also described the increased scrutiny to which Muslim communities were subjected by law enforcement and security apparatuses following the events of 9/11. However, this individual did indicate that the understanding of Islam and/or Muslim communities by Canadian law enforcement and security apparatuses was "getting better." He indicated, for example, that he had spoken with senior officials from both the RCMP and the CSIS and provided them with a history of Canadian Muslim communities and articulated the concerns of these communities.[66]

Finally, Muhammad Robert Heft, who is an individual that not only went to Iraq following the American-led bombing and occupation of the country but who opened the Paradise Forever Islamic Centre (P4E) to counsel wayward Muslim youth who demonstrated strong sympathies for Islamitic extremist ideology and practices after his return to Canada,[67] characterized the understanding of Islam and/or Muslim communities by Canadian law enforcement and security apparatuses during an interview in the following terms:

> I would give them a passing grade given the scramble they had to go through over the past several years to get to know these communities. I mean they're making mistakes still, but they are trying. I think they are trying to make an effort to reach out and understand. I tell the RCMP and CSIS this: I believe there are people in the policing agencies who are so right wing that they will tell you: "Don't believe anything a Muslim said, they are dangerous and they are all bad." I believe there is a small percentage who believe that. I believe that there is a small percentage who think we are being picked on and that the whole thing is exaggerated. And then I believe that the vast majority are in the middle working 9-5 just trying to figure out who the bad guy is and who the good guy is and how can we solve the problem. I say this to government and I say this to my own community. And I say this because if we don't give everybody the benefit of the doubt and live in a black and white society we are going to stereotype people who might otherwise be our friend or an ally or an asset. The vast majority of people are just trying to do their jobs [...]. You have to pre-empt what they have been told and you can't assume that they know the answer. You have to give them an answer that is sufficient for them to say, "That makes sense." This way you quiet the right wing in government and government agencies, and you win the hearts and minds of the majority. This is why RCMP, CSIS, and the police are calling me for outreach, because I think that I am a decent guy and they trust that I want to help them to progress to make Canada a safer place. Overall, they are doing a good job but they have a long way to go.[68]

Although the sentiments expressed in the final interview referenced are the most sympathetic in describing the understanding of Islam and/or Muslim communities by Canadian law enforcement and security services, cumulatively the interviews identify the knowledge deficit that currently exists within the governance structure of the Canadian state. As a result, the second moment that makes the securitization of multiculturalism in Canada possible emerges.

The second moment refers to an epistemological problematic that is endemic to the current dominant interpretation of both Transnational

Islamitic Extremism and Domestic Islamitic Extremism. As previously argued in detail (see Chap. 2), a neo-Orientalist framework for interpreting this phenomenon has become so deeply entrenched and naturalized in dominant discourse and the security imaginary of the state so as to become what Antonio Gramsci has termed "common sense." Consequently, in the absence of a comprehensive and robust knowledge reservoir—in other words, where a knowledge deficit exists—common sense interpretations are utilized to inform, in this case, the security policies and practices of the state. However, this form of common sense is predicated on fallacious assumptions, racist rationalities, and Eurocentric/ North American-centered negative projections. Therefore, to inform state policies and practices utilizing a neo-Orientalist mode of logic inevitably results in counter-productive, exclusionary, and injurious outcomes. This is not to suggest that apparatuses of the state malevolently and consciously choose to adhere to this mode of logic. On the contrary, in most instances, the opposite is actually the case. As the law enforcement and security apparatuses of the state are not prediscursive and do not exist outside a dominant "regime of truth,"[69] unconsciously these apparatuses enact strategies and practices informed by neo-Orientalist thinking without necessarily being self-reflexively aware that their decisionmaking calculus and concomitant actions are built on a foundation of false dichotomies and antagonisms. Therefore, even though law enforcement and security apparatuses receive "cultural sensitivity and/or diversity training" to engage more responsibly with members of minority communities,[70] the approach of law enforcement and security apparatuses to Muslim communities is epistemologically predetermined in such a way that the replacing of vulgar suspicion with polite suspicion does not negate the overall suspicion as the initial suspicion of these communities remains confirmed as per neo-Orientalist precepts. As a result, the securitization of multiculturalism remains intact. In effect, law enforcement and security apparatuses engage in ideological violence without necessarily being aware of the fact that they are committing this form of violence and unconsciously enter a vicious cycle of their own design.

The aforementioned formative and co-constitutive moments create a vicious cycle that leads to the securitization of multiculturalism through the following system: the knowledge deficit that exists in Canadian law enforcement and security apparatuses regarding Islam and/or Muslim communities precipitates reliance on "common sense" as an explanatory framework, which, in turn, is used to neutralize the knowledge deficit. As a consequence, the knowledge deficit is exacerbated through the reliance upon neo-Orientalist logic as a mode of apprehension. As a result, these apparatuses become locked in a negative feedback loop that makes the securitization of multiculturalism appear prudent while simultaneously undermining their own efforts. The overall impact is that the securitization of multiculturalism produces an atmosphere of racialized persecution in which the majority may begrudgingly accept this form of ideological violence, but, a minority, under certain conditions, may perceive ideological violence as an example that further exemplifies an Us/Them bifurcated worldview. This atmosphere can reinforce an Islamitic extremist narrative thereby contributing to the ideological conditioning and potential political transformation of Islamitic social actors. For instance, as verified by Mubin Shaikh, in the case of the Toronto 18, the regional office of the CSIS located in Toronto was selected as a target precisely because of the perceived persecution of Muslim communities by CSIS officials.[71]

In totality, the three modalities of state violence—physical, institutional, and ideological—discussed above contributed to the ideological conditioning of the various members of the Toronto 18 through serving as consensus-building mechanisms. In effect, when taken in aggregate, these forms of state violence were used to illustrate that Islam and/or Muslims were manifestly under attack by the Canadian state both internationally and domestically. Consequently, the use of violence as a mode of resistance was presented as legitimate and justified as per the dictates of the specific Islamitic ideological material found in possession of various members of the group. However, again, the state sphere of influence, even when operating in conjunction with the transnational sphere of influence (see Chap. 4), is necessary but not sufficient for the political transformation experienced by the various members of the Toronto 18. As such, one needs to understand the group sphere of influence (see Chap. 6) in order to fully appreciate the conditions that made the political transformation and transgression of this group probable.

Notes

1. CSIS, "A Study on Radicalisation: The Making of Islamist Extremists in Canada Today," 1–15. This report was made available through an Access to Information request made by Colin Freeze of the *Globe and Mail* in his article entitled, "Canadian extremists more likely homegrown: secret CSIS report," http://www.theglobeandmail.com/news/national/canadian-extremists-more-likely-homegrown-secret-csis-report/article8149887. Last accessed on 2 February 2013.

2. Ibid., 16.
3. Saunders, "We're looking for terrorists in all the wrong places," 9 February 2013.
4. King & Taylor, "The Radicalization of Homegrown Jihadists," 605.
5. King & Taylor, "The Radicalization of Homegrown Jihadists," 607.
6. Marx, *Theses on Feuerbach*, http://www.marxists.org/archive/marx/works/1845/theses/theses.htm.
7. Althusser, *On Ideology*, 42–51.
8. It is important to emphasize that although particular macro-social relations and structures make the political transformation of Islamitic social actors probable, this probability should not be confused with inevitability.
9. Springer, "Violence sits in places?" 92.
10. Fanon, *Wretched of the Earth*, 42.
11. Shakespeare, *Romeo and Juliet*, II.vi.9.
12. Rogers, "The psychology of violent radicalization," 41.
13. Klassen, "Introduction: Empire, Afghanistan, and Canadian Foreign Policy," 11.
14. Albo, "Fewer Illusions: Canadian Foreign Policy since 2001," 254.
15. Albo, "Fewer Illusions: Canadian Foreign Policy since 2001," 263.
16. Crawford, "Civilian Death and Injury in Afghanistan, 2001–2011," 2. http://costsofwar.org/sites/default/files/articles/14/attachments/Crawford%20Afghanistan%20Casualties.pdf (last accessed on 6 March 2013).
17. Crawford, "Civilian Death and Injury in Afghanistan, 2001–2011," 1.
18. Klassen, "Introduction: Empire, Afghanistan, and Canadian Foreign Policy," 9.
19. Author's own notes, 9 June 2008.
20. R.v. FA, *Reasons for Sentence*, 14–15.
21. R.v. SG, *Reasons for Sentence*, 2.
22. R.v. SG, *Reasons for Sentence*, 2.
23. Special Senate Committee on the *Anti-terrorism Act*, "Fundamental Justice in Extraordinary Times: Main Report of the Special Senate Committee on the Anti-Terrorism Act," 1.
24. In December 2012, Edgar Schmidt, a former senior Canadian Justice Department lawyer, launched a lawsuit against the Canadian government for failing to properly evaluate whether or not proposed pieces of legislation violated the Canadian Charter of Rights and Freedoms. According to this courageous whistleblower, as long as there was a 5 % chance ("credible argument") that a proposed piece of legislation would withstand a Charter challenge in court, the Minister of Justice and by extension Parliament were not to be notified.
25. Special Senate Committee on the *Anti-terrorism Act*, "Fundamental Justice in Extraordinary Times: Main Report of the Special Senate Committee on the Anti-Terrorism Act," 2.

26. Volpi, "Constructing the 'Ummah' in European Security: Between Exit, Voice and Loyalty," 454–455.
27. Diab, Guantanamo North, 70; Coalition Justice for Adil Charkaoui, http://www.adilinfo.org/en/what-is-a-security-certificate.
28. Diab, *Guantanamo North*, 70.
29. Ibid., 70–71.
30. Ibid., 70–71.
31. Flatt, "The Security Certificate Exception," 244.
32. Ibid., 244.
33. Razack quoted in Flatt, "The Security Certificate Exception," 244.
34. Flatt, "The Security Certificate Exception," 245.
35. Oriola, "Counter-terrorism and alien justice: the case of security certificates in Canada," 267. The construction of suspect communities and the use of racialized security practices to protect the Canadian nation from communities perceived to be a fifth column or enemy within are not an anomaly in the context of Canada. On the contrary, these types of xenophobic security practices have a long history in Canada. In effect, as the treatment of these different suspect communities demonstrates, "Orientalized" security practices are intrinsic to the Canadian state and reflect prevailing geographic reference points of real or imagined threats and/or dangers. As such, the targeting of a suspect community by the Canadian state in the war *of* terror is actually a continuation and not a departure from past practices.
36. R.v. NY, "Summary of the Crown's Anticipated Evidence," 1.
37. Author's own notes, November 2012.
38. Sproat, "Ruling—Defense Motion For Stay Of Proceedings Based Upon Abuse of Process," 5.
39. For example, see Banting, Keith & Kymlicka, Will. (2010). "Canadian Multiculturalism: Global Anxieties and Local Debates." *British Journal of Canadian Studies*, 23 (1): 43–72. Although formal Canadian immigration literature suggests that second-generation immigrants in Canada experience greater difficulty with integration and perceive higher degrees of discriminatory and prejudicial practices in Canadian society (see Reitz, Jeffrey and Banerjee, Rupa. (2007). *Racial Inequality, Social Cohesion, and Policy Issues in Canada*. Canada: Institute for Research on Public Policy.), there is no evidence to suggest that these were aggravating factors in the case of the Toronto 18. In fact, as Jeffrey Reitz and Rupa Banerjee reveal, the religious practices of minority immigrant groups do not serve as a barrier for integration into Canadian society (712). Again, as this evidence suggests, the inherent cultural and religious incompatibilities advanced by the *clash* paradigm are predicated on false assumptions. Therefore, any perceived incompatibilities are socially constructed vis-à-vis state practices.

40. Jabri, "Security, multiculturalism and the cosmopolis," 44.
41. Ibid., 46–47. See, for example, Hickman, Mary et al. (2011). *'Suspect Communities'? Counter-terrorism policy, the press, and the impact on Irish and Muslim communities in Britain* (RES-062-23-1066). London: London Metropolitan University. Although this report focuses on the British context, the findings are germane to the Canadian experience as Canadian counter-terrorism policy and practices are in many regards derivative of the British framework as encapsulated by their PREVENT strategy.
42. Jabri, "Security, multiculturalism and the cosmopolis," 47.
43. Special Senate Committee on the *Anti-terrorism Act*, "Fundamental Justice in Extraordinary Times:" 21–22.
44. Special Senate Committee on the *Anti-terrorism Act*, "Fundamental Justice in Extraordinary Times," 22–23.
45. Oriola, "Counter-terrorism and alien justice: the case of security certificates in Canada," 265.
46. Patel, "The Anti-terrorism Act and National Security: Safeguarding the Nation against Uncivilized Muslims," 281–282.
47. http://www.publicsafety.gc.ca/prg/ns/ccrs/index-eng.aspx.
48. Roach, "National Security, Multiculturalism, and Muslim Minorities," 411–412, and Gilbert, "Legitimizing Neoliberalism Rather than Equality: Canadian Multiculturalism in the Current Reality of North America," 24–25.
49. http://www.publicsafety.gc.ca/prg/ns/ccrs/mtngs-eng.aspx.
50. Roach, "National Security, Multiculturalism, and Muslim Minorities," 412.
51. Ibid., 411 and http://www.publicsafety.gc.ca/prg/ns/ccrs/mtngs-eng.aspx#a10.
52. Interview with Senior Officer for National Security Investigations—Ontario Division (RCMP), 12 August 2010.
53. Freeze & Hammer, "Mounties ask to be allowed into schools—to teach, not spy," 18 June 2012.
54. Ibid.
55. CSIS, "Intelligence Briefing On Radicalization and Jihad In The West," 2.
56. *Intelligence Assessment* made available through Bell, "Islamist extremists radicalizing Canadians at 'a large number of venues,' secret report reveals," 3 January 2013, http://news.nationalpost.com/2013/01/03/islamist-extremists-radicalizing-canadians-at-a-large-number-of-venues-secret-report-reveals/.
57. CSIS, "Venues of Sunni Islamist Radicalization in Canada," 8.
58. Dikec, *Badlands of the Republic*, 1–14.

59. Javed, "RCMP, Muslims build bridges, break barriers," 7 December 2009, http://www.thestar.com/news/gta/2009/12/07/rcmp_muslims_build_bridges_break_barriers.html.
60. Interview with Senior Intelligence Analyst (CSIS), 17 April 2009. The author has reproduced the interviewee's response to this question from the notes taken during the interview as accurately and fairly as possible. However, a direct quotation was not possible as the author was asked to record the interview in note form as per the security protocol of the CSIS.
61. Interview with Senior Officer for National Security Investigations—Ontario Division (RCMP), 12 August 2010.
62. Ibid.
63. Interview with a former Executive Director of the Canadian Arab Federation (CAF). The author has reproduced the interviewee's response to this question from the notes taken during the interview as accurately and fairly as possible. However, a direct quotation was not possible as the author could not digitally record the interview because of the ambient noise of the interview location, June 2010.
64. Shepard, "Imam no stranger to controversy," A7.
65. Teotonio, "Toronto 18," 5 July 2010, http://www3.thestar.com/static/toronto18/index.6.html.
66. Interview with former and founding president of the Canadian Islamic Congress (CIC), 30 July 2010. The author has reproduced the interviewee's response to this question from the notes taken during the interview as accurately and fairly as possible. However, a direct quotation was not possible as the author could not digitally record the interview because of the ambient noise of the interview location.
67. For a more elaborate background of Mohamed Robert Heft and his work within the Muslim communities of the Toronto GTA, see: Jacobs, Donna. (Winter, 2010). "Detoxifying Canada's jihadists. How Muhammad Robert Heft work with troubled and radical Muslim youth to rediscover the non-violent instructions of the Koran." *Diplomat & International Canada*, 29–35.
68. Interview with Muhammad Robert Heft, June 2010.
69. Foucault, *Power, Essential Works of Foucault 1954*–1984, 131. According to Michel Foucault, "Each society has its regime of truth, its 'general politics' of truth—that is, the types of discourse it accepts and makes function as true" (131).
70. Special Senate Committee on the *Anti-terrorism Act*, "Fundamental Justice in Extraordinary Times," 22.
71. Author's own notes, 3 April 2013.

CHAPTER 6

A Condition of Transgression: The Group Sphere of Influence

The spectacle of the war *of* terror has produced a social semiology of fear and insecurity that has encoded the popular geopolitical imaginary in North America and Western Europe in such a way that particular cultural symbols, behaviors, practices, and/or activities are interpreted as suspicious, dangerous, and potentially violent. Consequently, as Montague Kern, Marion Just, and Pippa Norris suggest, the ability to disentangle the social construction of reality from the "actual" reality of particular practices and actions has become very difficult to perform for both state and non-state actors, such as elected officials, the media, and the general public.[1] This difficulty in differentiating between the socially constructed and actual reality of particular actions and practices can result in the misapprehension of these same actions and practices. For instance, the wearing of the niqab has become a symbol of Islamic fundamentalism, oppression, and anti-Westernism, and the group formation of Islamitic social actors in specific contexts has become overdetermined as an index of criminal intentionality and extremism. Against these ideological misapprehensions, one should, in the case of the latter, avoid the essentialist tendency to reduce a fortiori these types of group formations to a moment of latent extremist criminality. Although following the events of 11 September 2001 many countries, including Canada, have criminalized specific types of group formations and concomitant actions and practices, these maneuvers of criminological categorization not only reinforce and invite a condemnatory and prosecutorial hermeneutic but construct the presence of Islamitic extremist subjectivities whether or not these subjectivities actually exist. As a result, the role of these specific types of group formations and related actions and practices in the ideological conditioning and political transformation of the Islamitic social actors involved is obfuscated and rendered opaque.

As Louis Althusser argues, ideology manifests in "material actions" which are "inserted into material practices."[2] As Althusser elaborates, [...] "these practices are governed by the *rituals* in which these practices are inscribed, within the *material existence of an ideological apparatus*, be it only a small part of that apparatus: a small mass in a small church, a funeral, a minor match at a sports' club, a school day, a political party meeting, etc." To help illustrate his argument, Althusser refers to Blaise Pascal's defensive dialectic formula for belief: "'Kneel down, move your lips in prayer, and you will believe.'"[3] In effect, in order for an ideology to come into existence, it must find material expression by those who subscribe to the principles and tenets of a particular ideological system. In this sense, performing particular actions and practices becomes a form of ideological conditioning as the performance of these actions and practices not only brings a particular ideology into material existence, but the performance of these actions and practices supports and reinforces the very ideation of the ideological system itself. Therefore, rather than interpreting specific group formations and related actions and practices as being the expressive totality of a previously assimilated ideological system, one should rather interpret them as a series of material articulations of an ideological system that represents the attempt to give what is subjectively confusing an objective coherence. This relationship between ideology and actions and practices is certainly pertinent to developing an understanding of the group sphere of influence in the context of the Toronto 18.

The Actions and Practices of the Group

In the case of the Toronto 18, a number of successive actions and practices contributed to the ideological conditioning and political transformation of the Islamitic social actors involved in the group. However, before discussing the significance of these actions and practices, it is important to not only explicate the interactional geographies of everyday life that facilitated the composition of the group membership but to describe the actions and practices that the group engaged in prior to their arrests. Although the following description does not encapsulate a complete record of the everyday geographies that enabled the formation of the group nor encompass all of the activities and practices of the group members, the following nevertheless describes some of the most salient features of these actions and practices.

In many respects, there is nothing extraordinary about the interactional geographies of everyday life that contributed to the composition and formation of the group. For instance, the two principal figures of the group and one of the adults connected to the bomb plot attended Meadowvale Secondary School located in Mississauga, Ontario. These three individuals were introduced to other members of the group through communal prayer and leisure activities, e.g. playing sports at the Al-Rahman Islamic Center also located in Mississauga. Similarly, other group members came into contact through communal prayer activities at the Salaheddin Islamic Centre located in Scarborough. Furthermore, one of the adult members of the group that attended the Salaheddin Islamic Centre apparently met five of the youths charged with alleged crimes in connection with the group at Stephen Leacock Collegiate Institute, a secondary school located in Scarborough, Ontario. Other spaces of convergence for various members of the group included the Musallah Namira and Abu Huraira prayer/meeting spaces and the Islamic Foundation of Toronto mosque, which are all located in Scarborough. For all intents and purposes, the everyday geographies that brought these social actors into proximity with one another were relatively benign in design and do not represent a deviation from other social relations and patterns.[4] What is extraordinary are the ruptures in the everyday geographies of these social actors as revealed by the anomalous actions and practices that catalyzed the development of the Toronto 18 group formation.

In March 2005, Abid Khan from the UK and Syed Haris Ahmed and Ehsanul Sadequee from Atlanta, Georgia, traveled to the city of Toronto to meet with the principal ideologue and other members of the group. The meeting of these individuals is significant as prior to this meeting these individuals had only interacted and engaged in ideational exchange in a virtual environment. According to Mubin Shaikh, the physical meeting represents a seminal moment in the development of the group as the ideological discussions and ideational exchanges of specific group members shifted from the discursive to the material and actionable.[5] Furthermore, arguably, this moment served as the impetus for the succession of events that followed.

On 27 November 2005, Mubin Shaikh was introduced to the two principal figures of the group (the leader of the Scarborough group and the leader of the Mississauga group) at the Taj Banquet Hall located on Steeles Avenue West in the Greater Toronto Area (GTA). As previously discussed (see Chap. 5), various members of the group, which at the time was at a stage of infancy, were in attendance to observe a presentation on the Canadian security certificate regime. However, in addition to this event serving as a moment of ideological consensus building vis-à-vis institutional violence, the event provided the principal figures with the opportunity to not only engage in the practice of propagation thereby reinforcing their nascent ideological position but advance the development of the group by helping to congeal plans for a subsequent group-building exercise. For example, shortly after the undercover agent, Mubin Shaikh, was introduced to the principal figures, he was asked whether he believed engaging in "jihad" was (*fardh ayn*) an individual or (*fardh kifayah*) a communal obligation. After Mubin Shaikh identified jihad as *fardh ayn*, one of the principal figures began discussing the oppression of Muslims in various jurisdictions around the world. This discussion was followed by the principal figure of the Mississauga group providing Mubin Shaikh with a copy of two texts entitled, *Fundamental Concepts of Jihad* and *The Community of Ibrahim*, and the principal figure of the Scarborough group providing him with a copy of a text entitled, *Blood, Wealth and Honour of Disbelievers*.[6] Furthermore, during this interpersonal exchange, the principal figure of the Mississauga group produced a map identifying possible locations where the current and/or prospective members of the embryonic group could engage in "training" exercises. This same figure intimated to Mubin Shaikh that he could potentially serve a role in the training activities; however, upon learning that he had previously received military training and possessed the requisite license to acquire firearms and ammunition, both of the principal figures agreed to solidify this offer of participation (although the principal figure of the Mississauga group contributed to the initial planning of the "training" camp, it was the principal figure of the Scarborough group that finalized the plan and made all of the arrangements for "training" to commence).[7]

From 18 to 31 December 2005, fourteen individuals traveled two hours north of the GTA to a rural area in Ramara Township close to Washago, Ontario, to participate in what was described by the prosecution, corporate media, and later by the Justices presiding over the trials, as a "training" camp.[8] However, as Mubin Shaikh testified and as Justice Durno outlines in his *Reasons for Sentence* of the principal figure of the Mississauga group, "not everyone who came to the camp realized its purpose. Some were told it had a religious purpose and to learn outdoor skills. Surveillance officers saw a hand written note in the offender's car on December 9 titled, 'Dealing with new recruits.' It said, 'Don't tell them anything, just give them jihadi da'wah, give false name, keep them on down low.'"[9] Moreover, as one of the adult accused indicated during testimony, many of the attendees were unknown to each other prior to meeting at this specific location.[10] Contrary to the stated intent of this winter camping experience, according to testimony provided by Mubin Shaikh, the actual intent of the training camp, which was only known to a small coterie of individuals, was to evaluate and screen potential recruits not only for membership in the embryonic group but to select individuals to attend a more elite camp that was planned for an undetermined future date.[11]

Throughout the training camp, the attendees participated in a variety of activities and practices. For instance, after arriving at the designated location, the principal figure of the Scarborough group and one of the other adults used the topography and natural landscape of the area to design an obstacle course for the other attendees to navigate. Justice Sproat described the obstacle course in the following terms: "It snaked through the woods, at one point it involved crawling under a fallen tree trunk and ended back at the camp with a jump off a two-metre ledge. There was a station at which the participant was supposed to get down on the ground, fire a paintball at a target attached to a tree and then move on to the next station."[12] Over the 12-day period, the attendees also engaged in the following physical activities and practices: jogging in a military-style formation; engaging in combat simulation using paintball equipment, which, according to Mubin Shaikh, was always situated in the context of a conflict zone, such as Chechnya;[13] receiving instruction on how to handle and discharge a 9 mm handgun; and participating in various paramilitary exercises that simulated the taking of designated positions. During one highly choreographed paramilitary exercise, one attendee carried a black flag inscribed with the "Islamic Creed" in white Arabic writing, while the others followed in an arrowhead formation. According to the testimony of Mubin Shaikh, the black flag with white writing in this context possesses a very subtle yet specific connotation and symbolic import: "jihad." However, as Shaikh explained, for someone who isn't informed, the flag would bear little significance and appear completely innocent.[14] In addition to engaging in physical activities and practices, the attendees at the Washago camp also participated in formal discussions or, what were referred to throughout the trials of the various members of the Toronto 18, *halaqat* (gatherings).

Arguably, the apotheosis of the camp occurred on the final evening before the attendees returned to the GTA. On this evening the participants were invited to attend three separate *halaqua* (for the purpose of this argument, only the first two *halaqua* will be described). The first *halaqua* consisted of the principal figure of the Scarborough inviting the participants to listen to a recorded version of the text *Constants on the Path of Jihad*, which was translated into English from Arabic by Anwar al-Awlaki. At the beginning of this *halaqua*, the principal figure in the Scarborough group stated, "listen to this stuff, you need to know, you need to listen."[15] Justice Sproat describes and summarizes the content and subject matter of this recording in the following terms: "This presentation advised that fighting was a religious obligation and that it was not necessary to engage in religious study prior to fighting. The speaker counselled to resist the temptation to peacefully co-exist with disbelievers and indicated that there was an obligation to slay disbelievers wherever they were found."[16] The first *halaqua* was used as a prelude or a primer for the second *halaqua*, which came to be referred to as "The Fall of Rome" speech.[17]

The second *halaqua* was also administered by the principal figure in the Scarborough group. During this *halaqua*, the actual intention of the camp and the aspirations of the nascent group were revealed. The following is an excerpt from the speech:

> So my brothers, the stories we read, they're not fairy tales. They're people that actually put them into implementation. The Prophets, we all know, their stories are in the Qu'ran. The pious people their stories are in the Qu'ran, in the hadith and they're not just meant to look upon and just be like, hmmm, Praise to God no, why can't you be like that. Why can't you bring the message to here. Why can't you be the one to take on the different qualities for example we all know the companions of the Prophet had different qualities. One companion of the Prophet was really soft, one companion of the Prophet was more of an intellectual, one companion of the Prophet was more of a poet. But, you know what, when it came time to go to the battlefield even though they all did their different things, they came back together and they formed a group like a fist and they struck. They struck hard, they struck so hard they destroyed Persia fully and they struck the destructive blows of Rome. [...]
>
> Well, we're here to kick it off man. We're here to get the rewards of everybody that's gonna come after us, God willing, if we don't get a victory,

God willing, our kids will get it. If not them, their kids will get it, if not them the five generations somebody will get it, God willing. This is the promise of Allah. God help and victory is near. It's coming. When it's gonna come doesn't matter man, this is our path we stick to it no matter what the trials are. [...]

Our mission is here. This is where we come back at the end of the day. We all got our missions, which we gotta fulfill. We all know what we gotta do when we go back whether it's like enroll in school and be patient and this and that [...] but this is where the hearts are okay [...]. Our mission's greater, whether we get arrested, whether we get killed, we get tortured, our mission's greater than just individuals. It's not about you or I or this Amir or that Amir, it's not about that. It's about the fact that this has to get done. Rome has to be defeated. And we have to be the one's that do it, no holding back, whether it's one man that survives, you have to do it. This is what the Covenant's all about, you have to do it. And God willing we will do it. God willing, we will get the victory. [...]

Rome, Rome, you guys realize who you're messing with. This is Rome. This is the one empire that has never been defeated. [...] It's like a friggin monster man. You cut off one hand, another one grows here, cut that off, another one grows here, cut that off, another one, another one, another one. Finally, you had to leave Europe because the Muslims are close to their shores. And here they came to North America and they got their fortress, they got their walls, they got their patriot missiles of whatever the heck they call them trying to you know defend their airspace and this and that, but you know what, here we are, we entered your lands, we already started striking you cause you know what this training is striking at them. [...]

And it puts fright in their hearts man, it freaks them out. Imagine we're walking the streets of downtown or even Washington or you're in front of the Whitehouse and you raise the banner of "There is no God except God." Is anybody ever gonna think of facing us. [...]

You know what, this is what the changes are all about. Nobody counts on you and you prove them wrong. And I know you guys don't get involved and you guys haven't been involved for whatever reason, but for the one's that have been, man we've seen the help of Allah. Small or big, we've seen the help of Allah. [...]

And we've seen the help and it will come in bigger and from different forms. It's just, we just gotta stick with it man. If it takes long so be it. We just gotta stick with it because this is our mission. This is our life's mission and Allah has already purchased our lives and our wealth in exchange for heaven. He's already purchased it. We are fulfilling that, living it, alright. [...]

This is our mission. We gotta do it and this is why we're here.[18]

Many of the activities and practices of the attendees at the Washago site were video recorded in order to be used as a recruitment and propaganda tool. Subsequently, copies of the video capturing the actions and practices that transpired at the Washago camp were recovered by law enforcement officials from the homes of several members of the Toronto 18 and were submitted as evidence during the trials of specific members of the group. Following the Washago camp, the ideological conditioning and momentum of the group were sustained by plans to secure a permanent location that would serve both as a safe house and training facility. However, before describing the subsequent actions and practices of the Toronto 18, it is important to comment on the collective actions and practices of the members of the group in attendance at the camp as the articulation of ideology through action and practice needs to be further explicated at this point.

The Actions and Practices of Ideology

As Antonio Gramsci states, "In acquiring one's conception of the world one always belongs to a particular grouping which is that of all the social elements which share the same mode of thinking and acting."[19] However, one's conception of the world is not influenced by a singular social relation or social grouping. Such a conception is instead influenced by a plurality or ensemble of social relations and social groupings.[20] Therefore, just like the paramilitary-style training of any other nascent dissident or insurgent group, the function of the camp was to isolate the actors from outside influences in an attempt to subjugate the attendees to a particular conception of the world. Indeed, the attempt to isolate and seclude these Islamitic social actors from other social relations and outside influences was designed to prevent the ideological position and concomitant geopolitical hermeneutic being presented to the attendees from being undermined or challenged. The principal figure of the Scarborough group was certainly cognizant of these outside influences and attempted to neutralize those influences through two distinctive material and discursive strategies. First, the winter training camp was physically located in a rural area in an attempt to avoid detection by the ubiquitous gaze of law enforcement and security officials in an urban environment and counteract the everyday distractions found in urban settings. Second, the principal figure attempted to rhetorically persuade the attendees that the social grouping of the winter training camp and the related conception of the world propagated in this remote location should always serve as their ideological reference point. Indeed, the awareness of outside influences is clearly demonstrated through the following series of statements made by the principal figure of the Scarborough group during the "Fall of Rome" speech:

> You go home, your wives are gonna start coming with some serious disturbances. Your kids are gonna come with some serious disturbances. Your brothers and sisters and your parents are gonna do some serious disturbance for you. Where'd you go son? What'd you do son? Here's some nice food, here we are eating beans and rice man and thanks to God it tastes so good. [...]
>
> But you know what your minds gotta be on this place. You minds and your hearts have to be here. You go back, you're living with society and you have to put on that face, you know what, we're a bunch of peace lovers, you know what I love all these non-believers, yup I love your wealth, I love your women. [...]
>
> You know what, that's the thing you gotta put on that face but your hearts are here okay. [...]
>
> So although our bodies will be with the non-believers roaming around, going to work, trying to get money, sucking up to your boss and this and that, you know the typical idea of nice uh, do favors with the parents this and that. Our hearts are with the people of heaven, our hearts are with this group right here and everybody else that's given the Covenant for us to be a part of this, who are not here but God willing they are here with their hearts, alright.[21]

In effect, the physical environment becomes a site of inscription for the group and is used to both physically and figuratively locate their collective ideological repositioning within the broader social field. However, the attempt to isolate and subjugate the participants of the winter training camp should not be confused with successfully isolating and subjugating these same actors. Again, the actions and practices of the winter training camp represent one moment in the ideological conditioning of the various members of the group. As such, although the actors involved in the camp participated in the same actions and practices, one should not assume that these collective actions and practices denote a uniform endorsement or acceptance of a particular ideological position. This is evidenced by the fact that several individuals who participated in the winter training camp were not involved in any other activities related to the group following their experience at the location in Washago. Nonetheless, as one Canadian journalist asks: "If a group of young Muslims goes into the woods to don fatigues, fire projectiles and hear speeches, does this amount to a crime?"[22]

Perhaps under different circumstances, one could answer this question in the negative rather than the affirmative. However, in the war *of* terror, where specific group formations comprised of Islamitic social actors have been constructed and designated by the state as the suspect other, unexceptional activity becomes exceptional and is thereby subject to criminal sanction. For example, the several individuals who attended the camp but who also did not engage in any other activity in connection with the group were arrested and detained for terrorism-related offenses, such as knowingly participating in a terrorist group. Conversely, other group formations that engage in similar activities and that are modeled on subversive groups that openly espouse an ideology that directly challenges the authority of the state with the threat of violence are not perceived as exceptional and escape criminal sanction. For instance, the Milice Patriotique Quebecoise (MPQ), a paramilitary group whose *raison d'etre* is to defend an independent Quebec, has posted videos on social media depicting its members dressed in military fatigues, running in a military-style formation, brandishing machetes and other knives, and carrying and shooting various small arms, including handguns, shotguns, and semi-automatic machine guns.[23] Despite these activities, the members of MPQ have not been arrested or forced to face trial for terrorism-related offenses. Although the actions and practices of the participants at the winter training camp in Washago are relatively benign in comparison, how can one account for these types of contradictions? A possible explanation can be found when one considers the complex effects of ideological actions and practices.

As previously argued (see Chap. 5), the state and its law enforcement and security apparatuses are not prediscursive and do not function outside of the terrain of ideology. In the war *of* terror, the Canadian state and its law enforcement and security apparatuses have arguably become subsumed by an Orientalist ideology and geopolitical hermeneutic. As a result, the actions and practices of particular group formations like that of the Toronto 18 become a negative projection of this ideology and are evaluated accordingly. Consequently, group formations that match a particular racial profile are rendered exceptional and by extension are subject to state interdiction. The corollary of this is the ideological victimization of Islamitic social actors as made manifest through the application of associative guilt. For instance, in the case of the Toronto 18, by virtue of the presence of some of the attendees at the winter training camp and their tenuous association with other individuals who continued on a particular trajectory of action and practice, the actions and practices of the attendees whose involvement with the group did not exceed the limits of the training camp were subject to criminal sanction under anti-terrorism laws. Although the charges against these individuals were later stayed or withdrawn by the prosecutors assigned to this case (see epilogue), this form of ideological victimization adversely affects those arrested in very real and embodied ways. For example, an attorney for one of the youth to be released in August 2007 described the impact of the case on his client in the following terms: "The apprehension, arrest and prosecution for terrorism-related offences has had a devastating impact on this young man and his family. [...] This resolution is the first step towards his recovery from the emotional and psychological scars sustained as a result of this ordeal."[24] The attorney of another youth to have charges withdrawn conveyed to the media how his client described the impact of the arrests on himself and his family: "'a nightmare and extremely stressful,' and that it left his family feeling 'isolated and vulnerable.'"[25] However, the ideological manacles of this form of social relation extend beyond the bodies of the victims to the state itself.

As the charges began to be stayed or withdrawn against several of the youth and adult members of the group, it became apparent that the state had wrongfully targeted various individuals for prosecution. As Colin Freeze states, "Some officials now concede Crown lawyers and police may have cast too wide a net in their initial round up, but are quick to add that the core conspiracy remains very serious."[26] However, in making these arrests, the state precipitated its own crisis of legitimacy and undermined its credibility in the various Muslim communities of the GTA. For example, one member of these communities described the implications of the arrest and subsequent release of these individuals in the following terms:

> Yes, there are going to be people that slip through the cracks. However, maybe next time I would say: "look, as much as you guys got that big arrest, now people have gone underground more and you've drawn some skepticism because some of the evidence against them was loose and the associations took a stretch of the imagination to believe. But if you would have arrested five, you would not have gotten the sensational effect of it, but the people in the community would have respected you more and long term it would have generated some more trust.
>
> Instead of arresting 7 extra people arrest one. And the if more evidence come to light arrest more people. However, they cast the net wide and it caused backlash because even myself knowing a lot of information about some of the people I knew that only 3-5 were in big trouble and the rest were borderline.[27]

In effect, in preying on others, the state preys upon itself. As this discussion of the winter training camp demonstrates, the ideological conditioning of Islamitic social actors is a complex process, and actions and practices do not necessarily signify a particular ideological position.

ACTIONS AND PRACTICES OF IDEOLOGY BEYOND THE WINTER TRAINING CAMP

According to testimony provided by Mubin Shaikh, in mid-January of 2006, the principal figure of the Mississauga group began expressing the desire to purchase a property in Northern Ontario to advance the development of the group. On 31 January 2006, Shaikh and the principal figures of the Scarborough and Mississauga groups met at Lake Aquitaine, located in the city of Mississauga, to further discuss the details of purchasing a property in Northern Ontario. Three days after the meeting, Shaikh, the principal figure of the Scarborough group, and two other adult members of the Toronto 18 were tasked with traveling to and evaluating a property identified by the principal figure of the Mississauga group. On 3 February 2006, these four individuals drove approximately ten hours north of the city of Toronto to the township of Opasatika where this property was located.[28] According to the "Agreed Statement of Facts" for one of the adult members of the group who participated in this excursion, while in transit the four individuals listened to recordings including the following: "blow them up, blow them up and defeat them ... for the sake of God and well will revenge for our brothers in Chechnya and in Afghanistan ... and in Palestine and I swear to God ... we will seek revenge from them."[29] After arriving in Opasatika, Ontario, and successfully identifying the location of the real estate they were there to evaluate, Justice Dawson describes in his *Reasons for Sentence* of one of the adult accused who was in attendance on the trip to Opasatika some of the discussions that ensued after viewing the property:

> There was discussion of whether the firing of AK-47 assault rifles nearby would be heard by neighbours, whether the neighbours were too close, about whether the authorities would be able to put surveillance cameras on nearby towers, and about digging a tunnel or putting up barriers to prevent anyone from being able to see the movement of firearms from the garage to the house.[30]

After returning to the city of Toronto on 5 February 2006, Mubin Shaikh, the principal figure of the Scarborough group, and the principal figure of the Mississauga group met to discuss the property they evaluated in Opasatika. The following dialogue was captured by a wiretap:

> Scarborough figure: Okay we either get this place or we get a next place but we gotta get a place. I mean this week, confirmed.
> Mississauga figure: Okay, so what if we don't get this place, what are we gonna do?
> Scarborough figure: Okay, remember, this place is like a last resort, you know what I mean.
> Mississauga figure: Yeah.
> Scarborough figure: If there's nothing else we can find then this place we'll get. Just make it all camouflage. Like okay, it's not a house, it doesn't have running water and heating yes ... but it's insulated and whatever and you're protected in there all that stuff.
> Mubin Shaikh: Fireplace?
> Scarborough figure: Yeah, What specifies a house anyways?
> Mississauga figure: I think just buy it and kill the neighbours.
> Scarborough figure: Is it concrete?
> Mubin Shaikh: I don't know ... I think like building specifications ... but you build anything or residential purposes.
> Mississauga figure: Why don't we just buy the land and kill the neighbours?[31]

Ultimately, the purchase of the property in Opasatika or in any other location did not transpire as a result of the limited monetary resources available to the members of the group.

On the same day as the conversation recorded above, a wiretap intercept captured another exchange between the same three individuals. During this exchange, the principal figure of the Mississauga group informed the other two individuals that he had successfully designed and built a detonation device. As Justice Durno describes in the *Reasons for Sentence* of the principal figure of the Mississauga group, "The offender told the others that he had built the 'first radio frequency detonator'. The problem was that you had to be 30 feet away, which was not good. [The principal figure of the Scarborough group] said you would be blown up so you might as well stay in the car. [The principal figure of the Mississauga group] assured him that it was a step forward. [The other principal figure] said they would do it if it worked at 300 metres."[32] According to materials submitted into evidence and as outlined by Justice Durno, on 15 April 2006 and 3 May 2006, law enforcement officials from the Ontario Division of the Integrated National Security Enforcement Team (INSET) surreptitiously entered the residence of the principal figure of the Mississauga group. On both occasions the law enforcement officials observed the following: electronic devices, packaging for an MK 160 remote control, envelopes of money, and ammunition for a 9 mm handgun. By the end of the month of April, the principal figure of the Mississauga group had constructed a circuit board that, according to this individual, could be signaled from anywhere and initiate the detonation of an explosive device.[33] While the principal figure of the Mississauga group was attempting to design and develop wireless detonation devices, this same figure operating in conjunction with various other group members was also researching the ingredients required to develop explosives and was actively seeking to establish the foundation and resources necessary to acquire these materials.

In the weeks following the trip to Opasatika and the revelation that a relatively unsophisticated detonation mechanism had been developed, the principal figure of the Mississauga group visited the Meadowvale Public Library to utilize their public access computer terminals in order to perform research on the ingredients required to develop explosives using commercially available materials, such as ammonium nitrate, hexamine, and nitric acid. After identifying the materials needed to develop an explosive device, the principal figure of the Mississauga group and one of the adult members to stand trial began maneuvering to physically acquire these materials. However, before describing the actions and practices that ensued after the decision was made to physically acquire these materials, further context is required in order to understand how particular actions and practices were made possible.

In addition to Mubin Shaikh, a second individual, who, similar to Shaikh, first served as an informant for the CSIS and was then later transferred to the RCMP to act as an undercover agent, was tasked with infiltrating the group.[34] Although the decisionmaking calculus of CSIS in approaching this individual to function as an informant is unclear, one can deduce that the decision to use this person as an informant solidified after the CSIS learned that this individual had been contacted by a former acquaintance who happened to be one of the adult members of the group they presumably had under surveillance. The contact of the second agent by one of the adult accused was initiated after this individual learned of the interest of the principal figure in the Mississauga group in obtaining specific fertilizers and other chemical compounds. The reason for initiating contact with the second agent was done primarily because of his formal academic training in agricultural science and the fact that a relative of his owned and operated a business in the chemical industry. However, the actual intent of this adult accused establishing contact with the second agent was not immediately revealed to this agent. Rather, these two individuals met at a variety of different locations, including cafes and restaurants, over approximately a 2-month period of time and would watch, what was referred to during the trial of this adult member of the group as, "jihadi" videos and/or discuss what the "ultimate duty means."[35] Through these various interactions, the adult member of the group who initiated contact with the second agent was attempting to ascertain the position and sentimentality of the agent on this subject area. As Justice Dawson outlines, after determining that the second agent was sufficiently receptive to these materials and related ideas, the second agent was introduced to the principal figure of the Mississauga group on 25 March 2006.[36] It is precisely this introduction that enabled the plan to build explosive devices to be actualized.

During the same period of time as the introduction of the second agent to the principal figure of the Mississauga group, this principal figure consulted with the adult member of the group referenced above regarding his desire to sever linkages with the principal figure of the Scarborough group. This desire was motivated by the belief of the principal figure of the Mississauga group that the principal figure of the Scarborough group lacked the resolve to translate particular forms of thought into a mode of action. In effect, the principal figure of the Mississauga group believed that his counterpart in Scarborough was all talk and no action.[37] Subsequently, on 28 March 2006, the principal figure of the Mississauga group contacted the residence of the principal figure of the Scarborough group and asked his wife to give the principal figure the following message, which was recorded via a wiretap intercept: "everybody in Mississauga, we just quit everything, totally."[38] Consequently, following this decision to sever the linkage between the two principal figures, two factions emerged: the Mississauga faction and the Scarborough faction. Ultimately, both factions oriented themselves on different trajectories of action and practice.

On 7 April 2006, approximately two weeks after being introduced to the second agent, the principal figure of the Mississauga group began discussing with the second agent not only the composition of various fertilizers and other chemical compounds but the logistics of acquiring these fertilizers and chemicals. On 8 April 2006, while meeting in a restaurant, the principal figure of the Mississauga group divulged the formal plan he had developed to detonate explosive devices to the oldest adult member of the group to stand trial and the second agent.[39] According to the "Agreed Statement of Facts" relating to the activities and practices of the principal figure of the Mississauga group, the formal plan involved remotely detonating three separate explosive devices using rented vehicles parked in three different locations throughout the Greater Toronto Area (GTA). The first location was to be the Toronto Stock Exchange (TSE); the second location was to be the CSIS regional office, which is located across the street from the Canadian Broadcasting Corporation (CBC) on Front Street in Toronto; and the third was to be an unspecified Canadian military base. The principal figure of the Mississauga group also indicated at this time that the plan would be executed on 15 November 2006 at approximately 9:00 am.[40] However, during this meeting, there was no discussion of actually moving to procure any of the compounds required to bring this plan to fruition. The actual plan to procure the compounds would evolve over an approximate 8-week period following this meeting.

Over the weeks following the meeting when the plan to detonate explosive devices was divulged, the oldest adult member of the group to stand trial in connection with this plan and the second agent regularly interacted in a variety of locations, including restaurants, coffee shops, and a mosque. During these interactions, the subject of discussion usually revolved around the acquisition of specific chemical compounds, such as nitric acid and ammonium nitrate. On 21 April 2006, the discussion of chemical compounds shifted from the discursive to the material as an order for six liters of nitric acid was submitted to the second agent. During several meetings that were recorded via wiretap intercepts between 25 April and 1 May 2006, the second agent was informed that both the oldest adult to stand trial and the principal figure of the Mississauga group had access to $20,000 CAD not only for the purchase of the chemicals and fertilizer required to build the explosive devices but for the purchase of airline tickets for passage to Pakistan following the detonation of the explosive devices; that the figures involved in the group planned to rent a property where they could both store the chemical compounds that they were seeking to acquire and subsequently assemble the explosive devices; and that the principal figure of the Mississauga group and the oldest adult to stand trial wanted to place an order for six liters of nitric acid and 1.5 tonnes of ammonium nitrate with the relative of the second agent. On 8 May 2006, the second agent was asked by the oldest adult to stand trial to place an order for six liters of nitric acid and twenty kilograms of ammonium nitrate. However, following the placement of this order, the principal figure of the Mississauga group wanted to increase the order to ten liters of nitric acid and two tonnes of ammonium nitrate. On 11 May 2006, the revised order was communicated with news that a rental property would be secured for 1 June 2006. On 12 May 2006, the principal figure of the Mississauga group and the second agent met to discuss delivery of the chemicals. During this exchange, the second agent suggested that rather than renting a house, the individuals could rent an industrial storage unit from an individual that the second agent knew through prior business-related activities. On 19 May 2006, the principal figure of the Mississauga group, the oldest adult member of the group to stand trial, and the second agent met at a restaurant to finalize the details for the delivery of the nitric acid and ammonium nitrate, including the quantity of materials to be ordered and the overall cost of those materials. Following this meeting on 26 May 2006, the principal figure of the Mississauga group met with the second agent at a cafe at which time the principal figure indicated to the second agent that they had secured an address for delivery and that three individuals would be at this address to unload the materials that would be delivered. During this exchange, the second agent communicated to the principal figure that the delivery of the materials would commence on 2 June 2006. Later that day, the second agent met with the oldest adult member of the group and received the address of the house that had been rented. On the evening of 30 May 2006, the oldest adult to stand trial informed the second agent that the delivery address was no longer viable as the two individuals that were sent to rent the property were too young to sign the lease agreement. After being apprised of the situation, the second agent reiterated his offer to contact the individual he previously described to see if an industrial unit was still available for rent. That same evening these two individuals met again at a different location, and the second agent communicated to the oldest adult member to stand trial that the industrial unit was still available for rent and produced a name and a phone number. The following day, the name and number were passed on to one of the figures that had attempted to rent the previous property. This individual later made arrangements to view the industrial unit and make a payment equivalent to two months' rent. Obviously, unbeknown to this figure, the person this figure was speaking with was an undercover law enforcement officer with the RCMP. Subsequent to viewing the industrial unit, the rental transaction was completed.

On 2 June 2006, two individuals that were later charged in connection with the plan to detonate explosive devices at the abovementioned locations arrived at the rented industrial unit to await the delivery of the ammonium nitrate. In an effort to deflect suspicion, both of these individuals were instructed to wear specific T-shirts that were emblazoned with a badge that read the following: "student farmer." While these two individuals waited at the rental unit, the principal figure of the Mississauga group, the oldest adult to stand trial in connection with the Toronto 18, and the second agent made arrangements to meet at a cafe to complete their transactions. During the meeting, the principal figure of the Mississauga group provided the second agent with an envelope containing $4000 CAD to pay the balance owing for the delivery of the ammonium nitrate and nitric acid. At 5:38 pm, a delivery truck driven by an undercover law enforcement official arrived at the location of the industrial unit with one hundred and twenty 25 kg bags of an inert substance labeled "ammonium nitrate" and a box containing what was labeled "nitric acid." Shortly after the delivery, the two individuals began unloading the materials into the industrial unit as instructed. At approximately 6:06 pm, heavily armed law enforcement officers surrounded the industrial unit and arrested the two figures present at the location.[41] In response to the arrests of these two figures, the coordinated arrests of fifteen other individuals associated with either the principal figure of the Mississauga group or the principal figure of the Scarborough group occurred in the GTA for various terrorism-related offenses.

As previously stated, the splitting of the original group into two factions in March 2006 resulted in these two groups orienting themselves on different trajectories of action and practice. Whereas the group located in the city of Mississauga engaged in the actions and practices just described, the group located in the inner suburb of Scarborough pursued actions and practices that were much more benign. Following the rupture of the original group, the principal figure of the Scarborough group resuscitated an earlier plan to hold a second training camp. Although several possible locations were discussed, the decision was made to hold the training camp at the Rockwood Conservation Area, located west of the GTA near Guelph, Ontario. On 20 May 2006, the principal figure of the Scarborough group and nine other individuals composed of both youths and adults traveled to this location for a 2-day period.[42] Similar to the previous training camp in Washago, upon arriving at the Rockwood location, fatigues were distributed to the various attendees to help create the impression that this was a paramilitary exercise. As Justice Sproat indicates in his *Reasons for Judgment* relating to the only youth to stand trial in the context of this case, the attendees engaged in the following activities: hiking, boating, marching. Furthermore, during the evenings, which were spent around a campfire, the principal figure of the Scarborough group would lead political discussions regarding the plight and suffering of Muslims by the USA in spaces of conflict like Afghanistan and Iraq. These political discussions included the principal figure expressing the belief that Muslims were obligated to help other Muslims when being confronted with these types of hostile circumstances.⁴³ During one highly orchestrated discussion that was recorded on a video that was recovered by law enforcement officers from the home of the principal figure of the Scarborough group, the attendees are shown sitting in a circular formation with their individual faces concealed by a *kafiya*. At the center of the circular formation of the attendees hung a black flag with white writing, below which was an unreadable text with machetes positioned above and below the document.⁴⁴ When asked about the purpose of the video and the significance of performing this practice, one of the attendees of the second training camp described the practice in the following terms: "The video was created as a mock to imitate videos that you normally see abroad on CNN and CBC. It was supposed to look like a resistance group's video that they release on the internet, and basically [the principal figure of Scarborough group] was trying to imitate such a scenario."⁴⁵ Certainly, the action and practice of simulating and/or emulating Islamitic groups operating in foreign jurisdictions bear many similarities to the first training camp. Although one would assume that a second training camp would be more focused and would encompass a higher degree of intensity than the first, when asked by the defense counsel of the only youth to face charges in connection with the Toronto 18 if the tone and tenor of the second training camp was the same as the first, Mubin Shaikh answered in the affirmative.⁴⁶ Following the conclusion of the activities at the Rockwood Conservation Area, the formative actions and practices of the Scarborough group dissipated.

The succession of group actions and practices previously described were also punctuated with intermittent and sporadic group meetings in restaurants and cafes throughout the GTA. During these meetings, the group members in attendance would watch various documentaries regarding the atrocities being committed in Afghanistan and Iraq by Western military forces and/or watch Islamitic extremist propaganda that espoused a *clash* narrative and advocated the use of violent action against the perceived enemies of Islam. Furthermore, the principal ideologue of the Scarborough group would assemble these materials and then convert the materials to a CD or DVD format. These CDs or DVDs would then be distributed to various members of the group who would then disseminate these materials to people exiting specific mosques and/or masjids.[47]

CONDITIONING AND TRANSFORMATION THROUGH ACTION AND PRACTICE

Now that the salient actions and practices of the group have been described, an analysis of the significance of these activities with respect to the ideological conditioning and subsequent political transformation of the group can proceed. Although the significance of the meeting and exchange at the Taj Banquet Hall is multidimensional (see Chap. 5), it represents an important moment in the group sphere of influence. If, as Jürgen Habermas argues,[48] a knowing subject comes to know itself through the eyes of others, the ideational dissemination that occurred between the principal figures of the nascent group and Mubin Shaikh serves as a moment of recognition. In effect, the act of disseminating an ideological position and image to others on behalf of a group becomes a practice of group affirmation and group actualization. In other words, through actively projecting a particular ideological image of the group self to others, the group comes to know and recognize itself as the ideological self it projects precisely when identified as such by others. Subsequent to the actions and practices performed at the Taj Banquet Hall, some of the most important ideologically formative actions and practices of the group occurred.

The significance of the first training camp that was held in Washago, Ontario, is twofold. First, during the second *halaqah* that was led by the principal figure of the Scarborough group, in what came to be referred to as the "Fall of Rome" speech, the culminating moment of the training camp was reached as the actual intent of the camp was revealed to all of the attendees. Second, the actions and practices performed at the training camp helped to congeal the individual social actors into a more coherent group form. Whereas the training camp in Washago helped to facilitate the congealment of some of the actors involved, the trip to Opasatika, Ontario, to identify a safe house for continued training as well as for the storage of the fantastical cache of light arms the leader of the Scarborough group claimed to be importing from Mexico solidified what Mubin Shaikh referred to as the "core group," which was very small in numbers.[49] Moreover, the trip to Opasatika helped to facilitate the ideological intensification of the group by giving a sense of operational substance to the actions and practices of the group itself. Similarly, the periodic meetings of the group at various locations throughout the GTA had a similar effect: through repetitiously watching various documentaries portraying the atrocities committed in Afghanistan and Iraq by NATO forces, the ideological intensity of the group was maintained by giving material substance to the Islamitic extremist doctrine that was informing their group action and practice. Arguably, however, the most decisive and significant moment of the group was the splitting of the original group into two factions.

The splitting of the original group into two factions signifies the moment when the original group diverges on to two separate and distinctive trajectories of action and practice. The members of the nascent sub-group from the city of Scarborough continued to follow the trajectory of action and practice of the original group which was characterized by relatively benign and banal activities. Ultimately, this trajectory of action and practice culminated and terminated with the planning and execution of a second training camp. However, the members of the nascent sub-group from the city of Mississauga pursued a trajectory of action and practice that was decidedly different, characterized by activities that were much more bellicose and violent in design. Ultimately, the trajectory of action and practice of members of the sub-group from the city of Mississauga culminated in the plan to not only detonate explosive devices but in acquiring the chemical compounds required to realize these objectives. In effect, the splitting of the original group denotes the ideological shift from the actions and practices of a violent fantasy to the actions and practices of a violent reality.

Cumulatively, the actions and practices of the Toronto 18 represent a series of escalation points that enabled the group to maintain a fragile sense of coherence and move toward a more physically violent mode of ideological expression and ventilation. In this sense, the potential use of physical violence as a mode of ideological ventilation did not induce the formation of the group nor motivate its members to participate in the actions and practices described above. On the contrary, the potential use of physical violence as a mode of ideological ventilation is the outcome of the formation of the group and the collective actions and practices described above. This is evidenced by the disagreements among various group members regarding the interpretation of specific doctrine and the related permissibility of particular strategies and tactics. For instance, as Mubin Shaikh testified in the trial of one of the adults connected to the Scarborough group, this individual often disagreed with the principal figure of this group over the interpretation that all non-believers were considered viable targets.[50] Similarly, the oldest adult member of the group to stand trial in connection with the Mississauga group initially disagreed with the principal figure of this group over the permissibility of targeting Canada.[51] As Justice Dawson outlines in his *Reasons for Sentence* of the oldest adult member of the Toronto 18 to stand trial, when the principal figure of the Mississauga group divulged the details of his plan to the oldest adult accused, the latter initially denounced the plan and questioned whether or not it was "Islamically correct." In response to this denunciation, the principal figure indicated that he was following the justifications of particular Islamic scholars and that on that basis his plan was permissible and would proceed.[52] Therefore, the performance of the actions and practices of the group should be interpreted as a form of ideological conditioning rather than as a sequence of performances resulting from a group of actors already ideologically conditioned.

Although the group sphere of influence was a necessary condition for the transgression of various members of the Toronto 18, it is not a sufficient condition if functioning in the absence of the transnational (Chap. 4) and state (Chap. 5) spheres of influence. Now that all of the spheres of influence relating to the Toronto 18 have been discussed in detail, the argument can proceed to the concluding discussion of how these three spheres of influence conflated and ultimately facilitated the transgression from a dominant discursive formation to a subversive discursive formation in the place-specific context like the Greater Toronto Area (GTA).

Notes

1. Kern, Just & Norris, "The Lessons of Framing Terrorism," 281.
2. Althusser, *On Ideology*, 43.
3. Ibid., 42.
4. Private communication between Mubin Shaikh and the author, 14 February 2014. Although various members of the group came into contact with marginal *amirs* at the Musallah Namira prayer space and Al-Rahman Islamic Center that espoused a particular geopolitical hermeneutic, one should not assume a causal nexus exists between circulating in and through

these spaces and the process of extremization. For instance, according to Raphael Israeli, the *amir* at the Musallah Namira pray space espoused an anti-American political viewpoint (75). (See Israeli, Raphael. (2009). *Muslim Minorities in Modern States: The Challenge of Assimilation*. New Jersey: Transaction Publishers.) However, an anti-American political perspective should not be used to infer an anti-Western or anti-Canadian political or cultural viewpoint. Moreover, one should not reduce the political to a religious moment.
5. Private communication between Mubin Shaikh and the author, 17 October 2012.
6. Justice Sproat, *Reasons for Judgement* (NY), 4–5.
7. R.v. AMD, "Agreed Statement of Facts," 1.
8. See, for example, Roberts, Scott. (2006, June 5). "Rural Field in Ontario said to be training ground." *Globe and Mail*, p. A4 and Blatchford, Christie. (2006, June 8). "Suspects believed they'd be left alone to train at Christmas." *Globe and Mail*, A1, A13, for media-based coverage of this event. As a point of interest, the "training camp" occupied an area that was approximately 275 meters in length and 100 meters in width and was described as an area of mixed topography that had both wooded and cleared sections (Author's notes, 30 May 2008).
9. Author's own notes, 16 June 2010, and Justice Durno, *Reasons for Sentence* (ZA), 5.
10. Author's notes, 18 May 2010.
11. Author's notes, 10 May 2010.
12. Justice Sproat, *Reasons for Judgment*, 8.
13. Author's notes, 10 June 2008.
14. Author's notes, 16 June 2008. During the trial of three of the adult accused, the prosecution questioned one of the adult accused about the flag and its appearance in a variety of documentaries and other Islamitic extremist materials. In the context of this questioning, the prosecution attempted to establish that the use of this flag signifies the "jihadist" orientation of the Washago training camp. Author's notes, 18 May 2010.
15. Justice Sproat, *Reasons for Judgment*, 8.
16. Ibid., 8.
17. Author's notes, 16 June 2008 and 7 June 2010.
18. Transcript of Training Camp Audio, "Fall of Rome Speech," Lines 61–73, Lines 97–103, Lines 194–200, Lines 213–224, Lines 239–243, Lines 256–260, and Line 266.
19. Gramsci, *The Prison Notebooks*, 324.
20. Ibid., 352.
21. Transcript of Training Camp Audio, "Fall of Rome Speech," Lines 110–114, Lines 150–154, Line 160, Lines 172–173, Lines 186–192.
22. Freeze, "Charges stayed against four terrorism suspects," A7.

23. See http://www.youtube.com/watch?v=o0l3E8_FuFc for a video of the activities of this paramilitary group.
24. El Akkad, "Charges stayed for two men in terror case," A6.
25. Teotonio, "Charges stayed for youths in homegrown terror case," A1, A8.
26. Freeze, "Charges stayed against four terrorism suspects," A7.
27. Interview with Muhammad Robert Heft, June 2010.
28. Justice Sproat, *Reasons for Judgment*, 21–22.
29. R.v. AHD, "Agreed State of Facts," 4.
30. Justice Dawson, *Reasons for Sentence* (SC), 19.
31. R.v. AHD, "Agreed Statement of Facts," 10–11.
32. Justice Durno, *Reasons for Sentence*, 5–6.
33. Justice Durno, *Reasons for Sentence*, 8.
34. The second agent and his family were placed in witness protection by the RCMP following the arrests and subsequent trials of the various individuals involved.
35. Author's notes, 15 January 2010.
36. Justice Dawson, *Reasons for Sentence* (SA), 5.
37. Author's notes, 27 May 2008 and 7 August 2008.
38. R.v. SK. "Agreed Statement of Facts," 3.
39. Author's notes, 18 January 2010.
40. R.v. ZA. "Agreed Statement of Facts," 6.
41. R.v. ZA, "Agreed Statement of Facts," 9–24 and R.v. SK, "Agreed Statement of Facts," 15–31.
42. Author's notes, 27 May 2008.
43. Justice Sproat, *Reasons for Judgment*, 35.
44. Author's notes, 27 May 2008.
45. Excerpt of testimony as cited in Justice Sproat, *Reasons for Judgment*, 36.
46. Author's notes, 16 June 2008.
47. R.v. FA, *Reasons for Sentence*, 9, and author's own notes 25 May 2010.
48. See Habermas, Jurgen. (1979). *Communication and the Evolution of Society*. Boston: Beacon Press., and Habermas, Jurgen. (1985). *The Theory of Communicative Action Volume 1: Reason and the Rationalization of Society*. Boston: Beacon Press.
49. Author's notes, July 2011.
50. Author's notes, 10 May 2010.
51. Author's notes, 15 January 2010.
52. Justice Dawson, *Reasons for Sentence* (SA), 7.

Conclusion

In many respects, Islamitic extremism and the process of extremization have effectively become suspended in a sublimated state of mystification. This is due in large measure to the narrow disciplinary spectrum through which this phenomenon is refracted and interpreted. Consequently, material advancements in the collective understanding of this social phenomenon remain anemic. Therefore, to begin the process of demystification requires widening the disciplinary spectrum and modifying the modes of engagement and analysis.

According to Stephen Graham, "contemporary warfare and terror now largely boil down to contests over the spaces, symbols, meanings, support systems and power structures of cities. As has happened throughout the history of war, such struggles are fuelled by dichotomized, Manichean constructions of 'us' and an othered 'them'—the target, the enemy, the hated."[1] Although many individuals like the former Canadian Prime Minister, Stephen Harper, believe that responses to acts of extremism like the shooting on Parliament Hill (October 2014), the conspiracy to derail a Via train (April 2013), the Boston Marathon bombings (April 2013), or the murder of a British soldier in the streets of London (May 2013) should only include harsh condemnation and unequivocal support for counter-terrorism laws and activities to neutralize these types of threats, what is politically expedient does very little to advance serious engagement with the social phenomenon of Domestic Islamitic Extremism. In fact, contrary to Harper's claim that one should not "commit sociology" and by extension enlist other social scientific modes of enquiry to develop a more comprehensive and robust understanding of this social phenomenon, serious rather than propagandistic engagement requires that one actively pursue social scientific modes of inquiry to identify the conditions that not only make bifurcated conceptions of the world possible but which help to animate acts of Domestic Islamitic Extremism. So, how can geography help expand the horizon of inquiry when the discipline "is typically treated as a static backdrop or set of facts that need to be invoked in order to situate something in space"?[2]

Just as the current political geographic/critical geopolitical literature has made significant contributions in analyzing and explaining the multiscalar expressions of state violence engendered by the war *of* terror and the use of popular culture in shaping and propagating specific geopolitical imaginings and hermeneutics, these same geographic sub-disciplines can be harnessed to advance our understanding of the processes of extremization. In effect, this book has attempted to demonstrate how specific geographic concepts and sensibilities can be utilized to deconstruct and illuminate a subject that has to date received very little attention in formal geographical literature. Although political geographic and/or critical geopolitical modes of inquiry may currently be situated on the margins of the analysis of a complex social phenomenon like Domestic Islamitic Extremism, these approaches to this particular subject enable one to identify and evaluate how processes and forces operating simultaneously at multiple scales condense in a place-specific context and implicate the social in very real and material ways. In effect, political geographic and/or critical geopolitical modes of inquiry are able to foreground social relations and structures that are crucial to understanding particular complex social phenomena that may otherwise be relegated to the background or treated as a form of ambient noise in other cognate disciplines. In the context of this argument, by considering the relationship between place, scale, and extremization, the macro-social relations and structures that made the ideological conditioning and political transformation of these Islamitic social actors were identified and analyzed. This bears significance as heretofore macro-social relations and structures have received relatively little attention in the literature that attempts to explain processes of extremization. As a result of identifying and developing an understanding of how these relations and structures can make the development of particular subjectivities probable, the potential to further develop an understanding of the processes of extremization can advance along a more comprehensive analytical trajectory. This trajectory would consider how macro- and micro-social relations and structures dialectically operate in place-specific contexts to generate the conditions through which particular forms of ideological conditioning and political transformations become probable. It is through this type of dialectical analysis that the potential to achieve a more robust understanding of the complex social phenomenon of Domestic Islamitic Extremism can be realized.

In the case of the Toronto 18, three distinct yet interconnected and mutually reinforcing spheres of influence served a vital role in the ideological conditioning and the political transformation of the group: the transnational sphere of influence, the state sphere of influence, and the group sphere of influence. Although each of these spheres was necessary for the ideological conditioning and political transformation of the group, each of these singular spheres of influence was not sufficient to facilitate the transgression from a dominant discursive formation to a subversive discursive formation and its related materialities. However, as these spheres began to conflate, converge, and condense in the place-specific context of the Greater Toronto Area (GTA), the conditions for a transgression by specific Islamitic social actors became probable but not inevitable. So, how did these spheres of influence create the conditions necessary for the political transformation and subsequent transgression of the group to occur?

In conjunction, the transnational, the state, and the group spheres of influence form a network of scales. The significance of this network is twofold: Firstly, it is actively constructed by some of the Islamitic social actors in question to advance a particular ideological position and related trajectory of action and practice. Secondly, it actively constructs these same Islamitic social actors by reinforcing a particular ideological position and related trajectory of action and practice. The outcome of the simultaneity of these Islamitic social actors constructing and being constructed by this particular network of scales and the spheres of influence this network fuses together and concentrates is the production and generation of an ideological closure.

In communication theory, the term ideological closure not only refers to the rhetorical strategies and devices that are utilized in a text to help shape and invite a particular reading of the material under consideration, e.g. the crafting of the angle in a newspaper or magazine article, but refers to the reader's role in the act of interpretation and the production of meaning of textual materials.[3] Though in the context of this argument, ideological closure transcends the textual limits of its application and refers to the fixing of a particular set of social relations and the related centering of a specific conception of the world to the exclusion, marginalization, and repression of other possibilities and perspectives. As it is precisely through this type of ideological closure and the myopia it engenders that the potentiality to violence in its various guises flourishes.[4] However, the phrase "potentiality to violence" bears highlighting, as ideological closure does not guarantee an outcome of violence. Rather, in most cases, the violent outcome of ideological closure is the exception and not the rule. Moreover, the production and generation of ideological closure are not immediate but involve a complex process of ideological conditioning that transpires over a period of time.

A corollary of the ideological conditioning process that is integral to catalyzing ideological closure is what I refer to as *spatial agony*. Currently, the spatial agony construct is impressionistic, and its deployment is unstable as its introduction here is the first step toward developing a more comprehensive treatment of this analytical tool. Nonetheless, the construct of spatial agony is conceptualized as follows: as the process of ideological conditioning escalates and the Islamitic social actors undergoing this process begin to approach ideological closure, the use of a non-violent modality of action and practice to communicate and achieve political objectives becomes less and less tenable and defensible as the material conditions of existence mediated by a particular ideology appear ontologically real. As a consequence, if a point of ideological closure is reached, the use of a violent modality of action and practice to communicate and achieve political objectives becomes more and more probable as the use of non-violence is rendered virtually untenable and indefensible as particular oppositional and antagonistic material conditions of existence are concretized. In effect, the ideological conditioning process and the spatial agony it engenders are directly proportional: as the ideological conditioning of an actor/group intensifies the acuteness of the spatial agony experienced by the actor/group increases and can incrementally lead to ideological closure and the potentiality to violence. Although in the context of this argument, the conceptualization of the construct of spatial agony applies to Domestic Islamitic Extremism, it can also be applied to other forms of political activity that resort to the use of violent methods to realize their respective political agenda, such as Islamitic nationalist, secessionist, irredentist, and transnational groups. However, the use of spatial agony as an analytical tool is not meant to be universally applied to all forms of political activity. Instead, the construct of spatial agony is designed to help further explain the processes inherent to particular forms of activity in specific time-space conjunctures.

In the case of the Toronto 18, the network of scales encapsulated by the transnational, state, and group spheres of influence collectively created the conditions for the ideological conditioning and political transformation of the group by fixing the social relations, centering a specific conception of the world, and concretizing the material conditions of existence embodied by Samuel Huntington's *clash of civilizations* paradigm. In effect, the conflation, convergence, and condensing of these spheres in this specific time-space conjuncture made Huntington's *clash* both a subjective truth and an objective reality, thereby producing the ideological closure and generating the spatial agony necessary to not only facilitate the transgression from a dominant to a subversive discursive formation but motivate various members of the group to pursue a trajectory of violent action and practice to achieve their primary political objective: to harm the Canadian nation-state and ultimately change Canadian foreign policy vis-à-vis Afghanistan. However, despite these collective spheres of influence acting upon the group in this place-specific context, and despite the use of undercover agents, only a small number of the individuals—some of those in connection with the Mississauga group—actually conspired to commit an act of violence. The fact that only a small number of the individuals involved in the Toronto 18 were actually committed to using violence to achieve their political objective is significant as it not only illuminates the inherent complexity of Domestic Islamic Extremism but illustrates how marginal the potentiality to violence is by Islamic social actors even when confronted with conditions that make the ideological conditioning and political transformation of these actors probable. Furthermore, the dominant neo-Orientalist narrative that frames the actions and practices of Domestic Islamic Extremism as being motivated by an abstract anti-Westernism is fallacious as evidenced by an address the oldest member of the group to stand trial delivered to the court before receiving his sentence:

> [...] I would like to say a word to all Canadians. I want to say that Canadians are individual and the society are truly wonderful people. In my 25 years living amongst them I've never been discriminated against because of my colour, religion or anything else. I have never had trouble getting work, living in a specific place, or buying cars or clothes or eating at specific places, as a matter of on the contrary, I was treated as an equal and on occasion even better than an equal on every level. I have lived a very comfortable life, drove a nice car, at the best food, and enjoyed all the creature comforts that everyone else enjoys. Individuals in this society should be proud of

themselves as I am proud of them, for achieving a truly—a true egalitarian society. But this Your Honour is the individuals. I feel otherwise from the system. Not the justice system but the system at large [.]

Instead, as the aforementioned statement alludes, the actions and practices of the actors involved in Domestic Islamitic Extremism are motivated by state violence in its various forms. This is obliquely explicated by the same member of the group referenced above:

> Sir, on the 2nd day of July, 2010, a group operating out of Quebec managed to blow up three different sites on Canadian soil. They confessed to their crime. They said, and I quote, "We did it to protest the occupation of Afghanistan." This was in their letter that they wrote in admission. They called the soldiers serving, Canadian soldiers serving in Afghanistan as traitors. However, it was buried in all the newspapers on page 15 sometimes. The Sun had a small article on page 15. The government officials in addressing the media with regards to the bombing have described this on national television, the perpetrators of these bombs are extremist, not terrorists. They simply took their protesting right to an extreme. [...]

> These extremists have bombed three different locations. The only difference between me and them is my loose affiliation, I'm not very religious, with Islam. The method, the motive and the misguided means of achieving a goal and the mitigating circumstances are all the same. They are non-Muslim, probably Caucasian of European descent. However, I am a brown Muslim. So I become a terrorist and they become extremists who took their protesting rights to an extreme. [...]

> It is pure discrimination against Muslims in the 21st Century. In the 21st Century discrimination is no longer based on colour but on creed and Muslims and Islam are the targets.[5]

The correlation between Domestic Islamitic Extremism and state violence is further evinced by the Boston Marathon bombings and the attack on a British soldier in Woolwich, London. In the case of the Boston bombings, while one of the suspects in the bombings was attempting to evade capture, this individual drafted a note that outlined the motivations for the attack: retaliation for the US wars in Afghanistan and Iraq. Similarly, the individuals responsible for the knife attack on the British soldier in

London were apparently motivated by British involvement in various conflicts in Muslim-majority countries. As long as the Canadian state, the US state, the British state, and others continue to engage in actions and practices that consciously or unconsciously reify and reinforce the *clash* paradigm with violent materialities, under place-specific conditions, the ideological conditioning, political transformation, transgression, and potentiality to violence of a small number of Islamitic social actors will persist. Indeed, to ignore, dismiss, or deny the organic linkage between Domestic Islamitic Extremism and state violence in its various forms is to engage in conceptual and analytical folly, is to suffer from what Edward Said describes as a "negative hallucination,"[6] and is to confuse illusion with reality. As William Shakespeare's *Macbeth* states:

> Is this a dagger I see before me, / The handle toward my hand? / Come let me clutch thee. / I have thee not, and yet I see thee still. / Art thou not, fatal vision, sensible / To feeling as to sight or art thou but / A dagger of the mind, a false creation / Proceeding from the heat-oppressed brain? / I see thee yet, in form as palpable / As this which now I draw. / Thou marshals't me the way that I was going; / And such an instrument I was to use. / Mine eyes are made the fools o' th' other senses, / Or else worth all the rest. / I see thee still; / And on thy blade and dudgeon gouts of blood, / Which was not so before. / There's no such thing. / It is the bloody business which informs / Thus to mine eyes.[7]

Over a decade following the events of 11 September 2001, the large amount of material that has been produced to evaluate, assess, and explain the various incarnations of Islamitic extremism in general and the political transformation and extremization of Islamitic social actors in particular has done very little to actually advance the collective understanding of this phenomenon. In actuality, despite the enormity of material that has been produced, this area of inquiry is courting analytical ossification. As such, a conceptual shift is required to broaden the spectrum of analysis and introduce other vantage points that offer a more multilayered and nuanced perspective of this phenomenon. The need for a conceptual shift is becoming even more pronounced as the securitized gaze of Canada, the USA, and various Western European states is increasingly focused inward as the supposed threat environment of Islamitic extremism has changed from a predominantly external source of danger and fear to a predominantly internal source of danger and fear. As a consequence, the internalization of the war *of* terror has many implications for communities perceived as vulnerable or susceptible to a particular ideological system and for Islamitic social actors who engage in activities that appear to countenance the acceptance of a specific ideological position and related modality of action and practice. This book provides a critical intervention that is designed to help contribute to the conceptual shift referred to above.

By deconstructing the phenomenon of Domestic Islamitic Extremism as expressed through the case of the Toronto 18, this book has attempted to elucidate the complex social processes and forces that make the emergence of these types of actors probable in the place-specific context of the Greater Toronto Area (GTA). In developing an appreciation for the complexities of this phenomenon, it is hoped that a greater degree of clarity will be afforded to elite opinionmakers and other policymakers when informing and crafting anti-terrorism policies. Ultimately, greater conceptual clarity is needed if the policies enacted and pursued by the Canadian state and others are to be productive rather than potentially counter-productive and are to contribute to the deepening of democracy rather than contribute to the erosion of democracy vis-à-vis specific "suspect communities."

Although one could dismiss this analysis as a single case study and therefore construe it as not being useful in helping to inform state policy, the events of 11 September 2001 was one case that occurred outside Canada but which was evidence enough to transform Canada into a national security state that has allocated an additional $92 billion CAD to security and defense apparatuses and programs following 11 September 2001.[8] In actuality, it is precisely these types of case studies that enable one to more accurately evaluate this type of social phenomenon because one is given the opportunity to assess these actors at an organic level. The case of the Toronto 18 has presented the research community with a rich empirical manifold that illuminates the dynamics of these types of group formations. As a result, this case has the potential to advance a multidimensional appreciation for, and understanding of, the conditions that make Domestic Islamitic Extremism probable even though it requires that one confront the haunting specter of Orientalist rationalities and the different forms of violence it makes possible.

The same in-depth, vertical approach utilized to analyze and evaluate the case of the Toronto 18 should be applied to other related events and/or cases, e.g. the Copenhagen shooting (2015), the Charlie Hebdo attack (2015), the Canadian Parliament Hill shooting (2014), the Canadian Via train derailment plot (2013), the Boston Marathon bombings (2013), the

London transit bombings (2005), and the case of the so-called Asparagus 18 in Belgium (2005). It is only after a comprehensive analysis of each individual case has been conducted that proper comparative analyses can be completed in order to identify the similarities and differences between various events and cases. To engage prematurely in a horizontal (comparative) approach can lead to reductionist conclusions and essentializing generalizations and simplifications that fallaciously reduce these events to a religious and/or cultural moment. The corollary being that Islam becomes a tautological explanatory framework used to interpret the development of extremist subjectivities, thereby perpetuating the mystification rather than contributing to the demystification of this social phenomenon.

Prosecuting Terrorism: (Cross) Examining the Courtroom as a Research Space

The judicial prosecution of the so-called Toronto 18 provided the academic research community with a significant opportunity: to act as a participant observer in what Marc Sageman characterizes as "one of the largest international terrorism cases of its kind."[9] On 1 April 2008, approximately twenty-two months after the Canadian public and international community learned of the concerted arrest and detention in the Greater Toronto Area (GTA) of seventeen[10] individuals alleged to be members of an al-Qaeda-inspired terrorist group, I entered a courtroom in the Superior Court of Justice located in Brampton, Ontario (a city situated within the GTA). In this courtroom, the pretrial motions were being presented and argued for not only the first member of the group to face trial but for the only remaining youth to be charged with terrorism-related offenses connected to this case. My decision to enter the courtroom was methodologically motivated as the courtroom provided me with an opportunity to situate myself as a participant observer. According to Robin Kearns, "participant observation for a geographer involves strategically placing oneself in situations in which systematic understandings of place are most likely to arise."[11] Through situating myself in the courtroom, I was presented with the opportunity to develop multiple understandings of place: the courtroom as a place of research, the courtroom as a place of state power, and the courtroom as a place through which one can ascertain how particular actors involved in the case socio-ideologically constructed place. However, as Richard Phillips and Jennifer Johns indicate, "Participant observation takes many different forms and involves different degrees of participation."[12]

For instance, as Phillips and Johns continue, "Distinctions have been drawn between the participant-as-observer, who gets more involved, and the observer-as-participant, who tends to stand back from situations and play a less active role."[13] In effect, as Kearns suggests, every participant observation situation is unique.[14] As such, "success of the approach depends less on the strict application of rules and more upon introspection on the part of the researcher with respect to his or her relationship to what is to be (and is being) researched."[15] My experiences as an observer-as-participant—an approach necessitated by the dynamics associated with a courtroom environment—in this court case, as well as the other cases related to the "Toronto 18" that reached trial, has illuminated not only the value of the courtroom as a research space but also, and perhaps more importantly, the obstacles that researchers may encounter and the ethical imperative researchers must be cognizant of when performing terrorism-related research in a courtroom setting.

Although the challenges associated with terrorism research are manifold,[16] one of the most salient obstacles is actually gaining access to the actors engaged in this modality of political violence. As Andrew Silke states, "the first problem is that terrorism quite simply is not a topic that is easily researched. Or at least, it does not give that impression on first inspection. The central actors involved in the phenomenon are difficult to access—and extremely difficult to access in a systemic manner."[17] Given the obvious importance of accessing the actors involved in this social phenomenon to expand the empirical corpus of information necessary to advance a more comprehensive understanding of the processes, forces, and dynamics associated with this area of research, identifying research spaces that facilitate accessibility to these actors is paramount. One such research space is the courtroom.

The value of performing participant observation in a courtroom setting derives from the ability of the researcher to:

1. Identify and establish contact with potential high-value research participants by meeting and interacting with a variety of actors involved in the prosecutorial process related to terrorism, e.g. law enforcement and security officials, prosecutors and defense attorneys, interested community leaders, journalists, etc.
2. Observe how the prosecution and defense actively construct the interpretive lenses through which they invite the judge and/or jury to evaluate the evidence presented. The ability to observe these con-

structions enables the researcher to develop an understanding of the performative character of the prosecutorial process vis-à-vis the production of guilt and/or innocence. For instance, the prosecutors presented the seemingly banal activities of the supposed winter training camp, e.g. running an obstacle course, playing paintball, and the videotaping of the carrying of a particular flag while in an arrowhead formation, as evidence of the existence of a nefarious terrorist group, whereas defense attorneys presented the same activities as the enactment of a fantasy. An appreciation for and awareness of the performative character of the juridical space enables one to develop a nuanced understanding of these types of group formations and their related activities and to recognize the strength of terrorism-related laws as a social relation of power through their ability to selectively render prosaic and facile gestures criminally malignant.
3. Observe testimony and access court documents, including transcripts of witness testimony, wiretap evidence, and various materials retrieved from the computer(s) of the suspect(s). Access to these materials can help illuminate not only the internal dynamics of the state security and law enforcement apparatuses and the group being investigated but can be used by the researcher to help construct and establish the ideological framework and discursive formation the actors involved in the arrests occupied.

However, as the author discovered, utilizing the courtroom as a research space and being granted access to the evidentiary material submitted to the court can be an invasive and cumbersome process that requires both a willingness to subject oneself to (in)direct scrutiny by various state apparatuses and, above all, patience.

Although the courtroom is not what Linda Fuller has characterized as a forbidden research terrain, which she describes as "whole areas of possible investigation, which may be geographically, intellectually, or institutionally defined, where social scientists are strongly discouraged from pursuing research,"[18] the political and judicial sensitivities associated with the prosecution of terrorism-related offenses do significantly shape the courtroom as a research space. In the context of terrorism-related research and its related sensitivities, the courtroom can be characterized as a restricted research terrain or as an interdictory research space where access is highly regulated and controlled. For example, in the trial of the only youth to face charges in connection with the Toronto 18, I was approached by officers of the court as well as by law enforcement officials inquiring as to who I was and why I was there. These initial inquiries lead to a more invasive background check, including a review of my Geography MA thesis. This was indirectly divulged to me during a brief conversation I had with a law enforcement officer while waiting for the proceedings to begin. During this brief encounter, the law enforcement officer asked me the following questions: "why do you define terrorism the way you do?" For me it became clear that the officer was alluding to my aforementioned Geography MA thesis, which is readily available online and the only published document where I clearly include a definition of terrorism.[19] Shortly after this question was posed to me, the law enforcement official informed me that I had "wandered into a very sensitive area." Moreover, the courtroom as a restricted research terrain or as an interdictory research space is perhaps best illustrated through the process required to gain access to the exhibits and evidentiary materials submitted to the court.

In the context of the courtroom proceedings of the Toronto 18, procedurally all requests for copies of or access to the exhibits and evidentiary materials were to be submitted to the court via the courtroom registrar. Upon requesting specific materials after several days of court proceedings, I was asked to produce media credentials. After I explained who I was and why I was there—an academic observer conducting field research for a doctoral dissertation—my request was submitted to the judge presiding over the trial. My request was then introduced to the court via the judge, and the prosecution and defense counsels were asked to consider the request. Although, ultimately, neither the counsel for the prosecution nor counsel for the defense objected to my request for access to the court documents, the counsel for the prosecution requested that I submit a sworn affidavit outlining who I am, the nature of my research, and why I wanted access to the court documents beyond what I could record while observing the proceedings. This request necessitated the securing of the services of a lawyer to not only notarize the affidavit but attend court with me on the day that the affidavit was officially submitted to the court. Furthermore, upon submission of the affidavit, I was subjected to an official examination by the lead prosecutor during which I was asked a series of questions pertaining to the research. After the formal submission of the sworn affidavit, the judge then considered my request and issued a formal ruling a couple of weeks later concluding that I was a class of person with legitimate interest in the materials and was, therefore, granted access to the materials similar to that of the media. However, the ruling in this case did not guarantee nor provide universal access to the exhibits and evidentiary materials in the other court cases pertaining to the Toronto 18 that I attended. In effect, receiving permission to access court documents in other proceedings was subject to a process of renegotiation that was always suffused with the rules of accessibility outlined by each individual judge presiding over each proceeding. Indeed, these changing environments of regulation and control in the courtroom can frustrate research initiatives and objectives; however, anticipating these encumbrances will enable researchers to adapt to and successfully negotiate the obstacles they may confront with when performing research in a courtroom setting (the encumbrances a researcher may confront are, however, contingent upon the country and jurisdiction in which they are operating).

The courtroom is an environment rarely experienced by a large segment of society in general let alone the academic community. As such, a small amount of people outside of those standing in the dock are rarely afforded the opportunity to encounter the power relations embedded within judicial spaces in general and judicial spaces where criminal offenses related to terrorism are involved in particular. As the judiciary is a component of the security apparatus of the state, to encounter the power relations embedded within judicial spaces is to encounter the repression of the state. One of the clearest expressions of these repressive power relations is the prerogative of the state to interpolate and evaluate. In this sense, the courtroom as an interdictory space is designed to intimidate and undermine the confidence even of those standing outside the dock. However, this interdiction has implications not only for the researcher but for the researched.

Another important dimension of performing terrorism-related research in a courtroom environment is the power asymmetries that exist not only between the state and the researcher but between researcher and the researched, including the families, friends, and community of the accused. As Raymond Lee states, "while the threat posed by research most obviously affects research participants it may also have an impact on others. These include the researcher, but also the family members and associates of those studied, the social groups to which they belong, the wider community, research institutions and society at large."[20] These potential threats are especially apparent when conducting terrorism-related research not only because of the politically, socially, morally, and emotionally sensitive nature of terrorism in general but because of how highly sensationalized terrorism cases often become. In effect, the courtroom environment possesses a centripetal affectivity that extends far beyond this research space. For example, in the case of the Toronto 18, a journalist from one of Canada's largest daily newspapers described the arraignment of the terrorism suspects in the following terms: "a media circus overwhelmed a Brampton courthouse yesterday as more than 100 journalists from across the country, the United States and abroad clamoured for coverage of Canada's biggest terror-related bust." The journalist went on to state that, "the family members and friends of the 12 men and five youths accused of planning terrorist attacks in Ontario were swarmed by journalists as soon as they arrived. The bodies of media personnel would surround them and move together in a moss of clicking shutters, flashing lights and bobbing boom microphones.[21]" In a separate newspaper article, a senior member of the Muslim Canadian Congress in attendance of the arraignment was quoted as asserting, "these are not the accused. It is unethical to harass the families. Look at them, they're teary-eyed [...]. This is racial profiling. It is the people that appear to look like Muslims who are the ones being questioned about their families."[22] Furthermore, the "spectacle of terrorism"[23] can isolate and alienate the families and friends of the accused within their own social spheres: "on the surface, ostracism would seem the inevitable fate of the families of anyone accused of a high-profile crime. But within the Muslim community, avoiding any of the suspects' friends, families, and hangouts is often seen as a method of survival: If you're caught talking to a suspect, the thinking goes, you're also a suspect."[24] Therefore, given the affectivities that manifest both within and beyond the courtroom environment, it is incumbent upon the researcher to be cognizant of these affectivities and to actively ensure that his or her activities of the researcher do not contribute to or magnify the threats confronting families and/or communities.

To effectively mitigate the threats to the families and/or communities posed by performing terrorism-related research in a courtroom environment requires the researcher to be self-reflexively aware of their own positionality as a potential agent of affectivity. An integral component of this positionality is the awareness of the ramifications the researcher's work may have on those that are peripheral to the research but are nonetheless implicated by it. As the aforementioned examples reveal, the affective character of the courtroom environment does impact the families and/or communities in very real and embodied ways. Therefore, it is the ethical imperative of the researcher operating as a participant observer in a courtroom environment to mitigate these affectivities within the obvious limits of the researcher's sphere of influence. One mitigation strategy is to ensure that the identity or identities of the accused never appear in their own work. Certainly, the identities of the accused may be readily attained through cursory archival research of the local and national media covering a particular terrorism-related case; however, that information should not be divulged by an academic researcher. Although the identification of the actors involved in a particular case may possess organizational value when crafting research in written form, there is very little if any inherent analytical value in disclosing the names of the actors involved in a particular case like that of the Toronto 18. For instance, under provisions contained within the Canadian Youth Criminal Justice Act, the names of youth cannot be used in order to protect their identity and the identity of their family. Indeed, in the case of the Toronto 18, the identity of the only youth to stand trial was subject to a publication ban as per the Youth Criminal Justice Act. This publication ban did not inhibit the media from describing the proceedings of the trial nor did it complicate the analysis of the case. However, more importantly, due to the frenzied and racialized sensationalism that accompanies particular criminal acts, the practice of avoiding the identification of the actors involved should extend to all of the actors irrespective of age. The need for this type of voluntary self-censure is demonstrated by the more recent events surrounding the Boston Marathon bombings. In relying upon what is considered common sense in the war *of* terror, various corporate media irresponsibly began identifying suspects using a specific racial profile as evidence of guilt. In one instance, a Saudi national was wrongfully identified as a suspect for his erratic behavior in the immediate aftermath of the explosions: he was seen hurriedly running from the blast zone. In another instance, a high school student of Moroccan descent was falsely implicated as a suspect by virtue of his presence in the area of the explosion. As these examples illustrate, the decision to identify particular actors can have devastating consequences on the broader community. The researcher must be cognizant of the fact that the in situ observation of terrorism-related cases and its concomitant proceedings do not exist in a vacuum. The courtroom as a research space is an affective environment that is materially entangled with individuals, families, groups, and society as a whole, and these entanglements, however complex, must inform the actions of the researcher both inside and outside the courtroom.

Epilogue

In February 2007, approximately eighteen months after a carefully choreographed news conference held at the Toronto Congress Centre by Canadian law enforcement and security officials regarding the arrests of seventeen terrorist suspects (the eighteenth was arrested one month later), one of the youth arrested in connection with the Toronto 18 had his charges stayed and was subsequently released. Similarly, in July of that same year, prosecutors issued a stay of proceedings against two more youth who were detained for participating in what reporters for the *National Post* described as, "a homegrown terror cell."[25] Following the release of three of the youth involved in the case in April 2008, the prosecution filed a stay of proceedings and effectively dismissed the charges against four adult members of the group. Consequently, a disjuncture began to emerge between the performance of the arrests and the actual character of the group. As James Stribopoulos, a professor at Osgoode Hall Law School, was quoted as stating in the *National Post*: "the threat was not as strong as it was initially made out to be, especially in light of strong pronouncements of law enforcement at the time of the arrests in June 2006."[26] Stribopoulos goes on to state that "the latest developments indicated a weakness in the evidence that was alarming for public confidence and individual rights, considering many of the suspects had been in prison for almost two years."[27] As a result of the stay of proceedings against these individuals, the Toronto 18 was reduced to the Toronto 11, which was comprised of ten adults and one youth.

On 30 May 2008, the trial for the only remaining youth to face charges in connection with this case began. Given the obstacles that the Public Prosecution Service of Canada had confronted leading up to this point in the prosecution of the group, the gravity of this trial was enormous. Its outcome would have serious implications for the cases against the remaining ten adult members facing charges in connection with the Toronto 18. On 25 September 2008, the youth was found guilty of knowingly participating in a terrorist group and became the first person in Canada to be successfully prosecuted under the anti-terrorism legislation that was enacted in the wake of 11 September 2001. The significance of this verdict was that it vindicated the state and clearly demonstrated the strength of Canada's anti-terrorism laws. As Thomas Walkom states:

> The first conviction in the Toronto 18 terror case is a signal victory for Ottawa and its national security agencies. It also demonstrates the remarkable reach of Canada's new anti-terrorism laws. To a layman, the Crown's case against the young Toronto man convicted yesterday (he cannot be named because he was 17 at the time of the offence) might have seemed weak. He did not make bombs or buy guns. Nor did he advocate doing so. He did not threaten to kill anyone, did not call of holy war, did not pledge allegiance to Osama bin Laden. He did not even badmouth Canada's military efforts in Afghanistan. [...] More to the point, yesterday's verdict indicates that under anti-terror laws, the government need not supply incontrovertible, direct evidence of a person's guilt.[28]

In other words, as experts interviewed by Colin Freeze state, "the weaknesses in the case illustrate how strong the law is."[29] On 22 May 2009, the youth was sentenced to time served or the equivalent of 2.5 years in custody and released.

Unsurprisingly, following the trial and conviction of the youth, a succession of guilty pleas were submitted to the prosecution by various adult members of the Toronto 18. Within a week of the guilty verdict of the youth, one of the adult accused from the Mississauga group pleaded guilty to charges in connection with the plot to detonate explosives at the Canadian Security Intelligence Service (CSIS office in downtown Toronto), the Toronto Stock Exchange (TSX), and an undisclosed military base located between Toronto and Ottawa. This individual was sentenced in September 2009 and received a 14-year sentence with 7-year credit for time already served in pretrial custody. A second adult accused of the Mississauga group pleaded guilty in September 2009 to charges in connection with the same plan. This individual was sentenced in January 2010 and received a 12-year sentence with 7-year credit for time already served. However, in both of these cases, the prosecution filed an appeal for the sentences. On 17 December 2010, the Court of Appeal for Ontario overturned the original sentences these individuals received given the supposed extraordinary and exceptional character of terrorism-related crimes. As a result, the first individual had his sentence increased from 14 to 20 years and the second individual had his sentence increased from 12 to 18 years.[30] In October 2009 the principal figure of the Mississauga group pleaded guilty and was sentenced to life in prison. The lawyer for this individual and the lawyers for the other two members of the Mississauga group to be sentenced filed appeals to the Supreme Court of Canada in an effort to have their sentences reduced. In February 2013 the Supreme Court of Canada ruled that it would not hear the appeals.

In September 2009 a member of the Scarborough group entered a plea of guilt for two offenses: participating in a terrorist group and to importing firearms for a terrorist group. This individual was sentenced in October 2009 to 7 years of imprisonment with 5 years of credit for his pretrial custody. In January 2009 a second individual charged with an offense in connection with the Scarborough group submitted a plea of guilt for participating in a terrorist group. Subsequent to entering a plea of guilt, this individual was sentenced to seven and a half years in prison with the same amount of time credited to him for pretrial custody. As a result, this individual was released almost immediately after pleading guilty to his offense. In February 2009 a third individual charged with an offense in connection with the Scarborough group submitted a plea of guilt for traveling abroad to receive paramilitary training in support of a terrorist group. Subsequent to this individual pleading guilty to his offense, he was sentenced to a 7-year term in prison, was credited with time already served in pretrial custody, and was immediately released.

With the pleas of guilt submitted by three adults charged in connection with the Mississauga group and the pleas of guilt entered by three adults charged in connection with the Scarborough group, the offenses against four adult members of the Toronto 18 remained. The first adult to stand trial in connection with the Toronto 18 commenced on 11 January 2010. This individual selected a judge-only trial and was found guilty of participating in a terrorist group and intending to cause an explosion for the benefit of a terrorist group approximately 10 days after his trial began. However, a conviction was not registered as the counsel for this individual filed a notice for a stay of proceedings on the basis of entrapment. On 16 February 2010 the judge presiding over the trial dismissed the allegation of entrapment and found that this individual was a willing participant in advancing the activities of the Mississauga group. Finally, on 4 March 2011, this individual was sentenced to life in prison for his offenses.

The trial for the final three adults charged in connection with the Toronto 18 began on 12 April 2010. Whereas the trials of the youth and an adult charged in connection with the Toronto 18 were conducted as judge-only trials, the trial of the final three adults was conducted in the presence of a jury. After approximately 2 weeks of evidence being introduced to the jury, one of the three adults, who, incidentally, was the principal figure of the Scarborough group, entered a change of plea. As a consequence, this individual plead guilty to participating in a terrorist group, importing firearms into Canada for the benefit of a terrorist group, and knowingly instructing others to carry out an activity for the benefit of a terrorist group. Subsequently, on 25 October 2010, this individual was sentenced to 16 years of imprisonment with 8 years and 9 months credited for time already served in pretrial custody. The trial for the other two adults continued after the principal figure of the Scarborough group filed a change of plea. On 23 June 2010, the jury found the last two adults charged in connection with the Toronto 18 guilty. Following the conviction by the jury, on 25 October 2010, the first of these two adults was sentenced to approximately 6 and a half years in prison with 6 years and 5 months credit for time served in pretrial custody. As a result, the judge in this case ordered that this individual be released after spending one more additional day in prison. On 26 November 2010, the second of these two adults was sentenced to 10 years in prison with 9 years, 2 months, and 20 days credited for time served in pretrial custody. As such, this individual was required to serve an additional 6 and a half months before his release.

Following the conclusion of the prosecution of the last two members of the so-called Toronto 18, Canadians were quickly reminded of the omnipresent and existential threat of Domestic Islamitic Extremism. As Isabel Teotonio reports, "experts warn there is no end to the threat of homegrown religious extremism among Muslim youth."[31] Indeed, this warning has been bolstered by two Islamitic social actors traveling from London,

Ontario, to Algeria to engage in hostilities (2013), the arrest of two men engaged in a purported al-Qaeda-inspired plot to attack a Via train somewhere between the city of Toronto and the American border (2013), the shooting on Parliament Hill (2014), the traveling of "foreign fighters" to Syria and Iraq to join ISIS, and the coordinated assaults in Paris by Islamitic extremists purportedly connected to the Islamic State. However, if the level of threat propounded by the "experts" is real, then the need for greater critical reflection on the subject is equally real.

NOTES

1. Graham, *Cities Under Siege*, 36.
2. Murphy, "Enhancing Geography's Role in Public Debate," 2.
3. Cooke, "Closure/dis-closure," 523.
4. Zulaika and Douglas, *terror and taboo*, 125–126.
5. R.v. SA. Excerpts from the transcript of the address SA delivered to Justice Dawson on 4 March 2011.
6. Said, *Freud and the Non-European*, 6.
7. Shakespeare, *Macbeth*, II.i.32-49.
8. Macdonald, "The Cost of 9/11: Tracking the Creation of a National Security Establishment in Canada," 3.
9. Sageman, *Leaderless Jihad*, 110.
10. Seventeen actors were initially arrested; however, on 3 August 2006 an additional actor was arrested in related to the group. It is shortly after the arrest of this individual that the group became codified in the corporate media as the "Toronto 18."
11. Kearns, *Qualitative Research Methods in Human Geography*, 196.
12. Phillips and Johns, *Fieldwork for Human Geographers*, 177.
13. Ibid., 177.
14. Kearns, *Qualitative Research Methods in Human Geography*, 195.
15. Ibid., 195–196.
16. For a discussion of some of these problematics, see, for example, Schmidt & Longman (1988), *Political Terrorism*; Gordon (1999), "Terrorism Dissertations and the Evolution of a Specialty"; White (2000), "Issues in the Study of Political Violence"; Silke (2004), *Research on Terrorism*; and Horgan (2005), *The Psychology of Terrorism*.
17. Silke, "The Devil You Know: Continuing Problems with Research on Terrorism," 2.
18. Fuller quoted in Lee, *doing research on sensitive topics*, 21.

19. The author's Geography MA thesis can be accessed through a variety of web-based sources. The following is one access point: http://uwspace.uwaterloo.ca/bitstream/10012/980/1/jdkowals2005.pdf.
20. Lee, *doing research on sensitive topics*, 5.
21. Leong, "World's media descend on Brampton Court," A3.
22. Bhattacharya, "Relatives overwhelmed by intense media crush," A1, A8.
23. Giroux, "Beyond the Spectacle of Terrorism," 1.
24. El Akkad, "Suspects families suddenly become pariahs within the Muslim Community," A1, A8.
25. Leong & Kim, "Two terror cell accused won't face charges," A13.
26. Hanes, "Prosecutors face balancing act: security expert," A12
27. Ibid., A12. For other media coverage of the staying of charges against the four adult members of the Toronto 18, see: Teotonio, Isabel. (2008, April 16). "So-called terror zealot vindicated." *Toronto Star*, A1, A11; and Wente, Margaret. (2008, April 17). "Awaiting Toronto 11 answers." *Globe and Mail*, A19.
28. Walkom, "Terror verdict bad news for rest of Toronto 18," A6.
29. Freeze, "Terrorism laws pass their first test as youth convicted in home-grown plot," A1, A7. For other media coverage of the conviction of the youth connected to the Toronto 18, see: Dimanno, Rosie. (2008, September 26). "Inept or not, he wanted to be a terrorist." *Toronto Star*, A7; Leong, Melissa. (2008, September 26). "Toronto 18 Youth. 'Overwhelming' evidence against first suspect to face trial: judge." *National Post*, A1, A6; Teotonio, Isabel. (2008, September 26). "Youth becomes Canada's first convicted terrorist." *Toronto Star*, A1, A6; and Teotonio, Isabel. (2008, September 27). "Convicted youth excelled at training camp." *Toronto Star*, A1, A23.
30. R.v. SK, 2010 ONCA 861 and R.v. SG, 2010 ONCA 860.
31. Teotonio, "Terror trial ends, threat of extremism still growing," A1, A21.

BIBLIOGRAPHY

SECONDARY SOURCES

Aaronson, T. (2013). *The terror factory: Inside the FBI's War on terrorism.* Brooklyn: Ig Publishing.

Abou El Fadl, K. (2005). *The great theft: Wrestling Islam from the extremists.* New York: Harper One.

Abrahamian, E. (2003). The US media, Huntington, and September 11. *Third World Quarterly, 24*(3), 529–544.

Adelman, H. (2004). Governance, immigration policy, and security: Canada and the United States post-9/11. In J. Tirman (Ed.), *The maze of fear: Security and migration after 9/11.* New York: The New Press.

Ahmad as-Salim, b. M. *39 Ways to Serve and Participate in the Jihad* (trans: Anonymous.). London: At-Tibyan Publications.

Alansseri, S. (2011). Imperialism and the social question in (semi)-peripheries: The case for a Neo-National Bourgeoise. *Global Discourse, 2*(11), 1–25. http://globaldiscourse.files.wordpress.com/2011/12/alnasseri1.pdf.

Al-Azmeh, A. (1984). The articulation of orientalism. In A. Hussain, R. Olson, & J. Qureshi (Eds.), *Orientalism, Islam, and Islamists* (pp. 89–124). Brattleboro: Amana Books.

Al-Azmeh, A. (1996). *Islams and modernities.* London: Verso.

Albo, G. (2013). Fewer illusions: Canadian Foreign Policy since 2001. In J. Klassen & G. Albo (Eds.), *Empire's Ally: Canada and the war in Afghanistan.* Toronto: University of Toronto Press.

Al-Maqdisi, A. M. A. *Millat Ibrahim* (trans: Anonymous). London: At-Tibyan Publications.

Alnasseri, S. (2004). Die Konstruktion der orientalischen Feinbilder. In S. Alnasseri (Ed.), *Politik jenseits der Kreuzzuge. Zur aktuellen politischen der Mittleren und Nahen Osten* (pp. 184–197). Munster: Westfalisches Dampfboot.

Al-Rasheed, M. (2009). The local and the global in Saudi Salafi discourse. In R. Meijer (Ed.), *Global Salafism*. New York: Columbia UP.

Althusser, L. (2008). *On ideology*. London: Verso.

Amery, Z. (2013). The securitization and racialization of Arabs in Canada's immigration and citizenship policies. In J. Hennebry & B. Momani (Eds.), *Targeted transnationals: The state, the media, and Arab Canadians*. Vancouver: UBC Press.

Appadurai, A. (2006). *Fear of small numbers*. Durham: Duke University Press.

Arat-Koc, S. (2005). The disciplinary boundaries of Canadian identity after September 11: Civilizational identity, multiculturalism, and the challenge of anti-imperialist feminism. *Social Justice, 32*(4), 32–49.

Arkoun, M. (1994). *Rethinking Islam*. (trans: Lee, R.D.). Colorado: Westview Press.

Arquilla, J., Ronfeldt, D., & Zanini, M. (2000). Information-age terrorism. *Current History, 99*(636), 179–185.

Ayoob, M. (2008). *The many faces of political Islam*. Michigan: University of Michigan Press.

Aysha, E. E.-D. (2003). Samuel Huntington and the geopolitics of American identity: The function of foreign policy in America's domestic clash of civilizations. *International Relations, 17*(4), 429–452.

Ayubi, N. (1991). *Political Islam: Religion and politics in the Arab World*. New York: Routledge.

Bakht, N. (2008). Introduction. In N. Bakht (Ed.), *Belonging and banishment: Being Muslim in Canada*. Toronto: TSAR Publications.

Barnes, T., & Farish, M. (2006). Between regions: Science, militarism, and American geography from World War to Cold War. *Annals of Association of American Geographers, 96*(4), 807–826.

Barthes, R. (1975). *The Pleasure of the Text* (trans: Miller, R.). New York: Hill and Wang.

Bartolucci, V. (2010). Analysing elite discourse on terrorism and its implications: The case of Morocco. *Critical Studies on Terrorism, 3*(1), 119–135.

Bassin, M. (2007). Civilizations and their discontents: Political geography and geopolitics in the Huntington Thesis. *Geopolitics, 12*(7), 351–374.

Bauder, H., & Sharpe, B. (2002). Residential segregation of visible minorities in Canada's gateway cities. *The Canadian Geographer, 46*(3), 204–222.

Benmelech, E., & Berrebi, C. (2007). Human capital and the productivity of suicide bombers. *Journal of Economic Perspectives, 21*(3), 223–238.

Bernazzoli, R., & Flint, C. (2010). Embodying the Garrison State? Everyday geographies of militarization in American society. *Political Geography, 29*(3), 157–166.

Bjelopera, J. (2013). American Jihadist terrorism: Combating a complex threat. Congressional Research Service. http://fpc.state.gov/documents/organization/203728.pdf

Blaire, G., et al. (2012). Poverty and support for militant politics: Evidence from Pakistan. *American Journal of Political Science*. doi:10.1111/j.1540-5907.2012.00604.x.

Bonney, R. (2008). *False Prophets: The 'clash of civilizations' and the global war on terror*. Oxford: Peter Lang Ltd.

Boroumand, L., & Boroumand, R. (2002). Terror, Islam, and democracy. *Journal of Democracy, 13*(2), 5–20.

Borum, R. (2011). Understanding terrorist psychology. In A. Silke (Ed.), *The psychology of counter-terrorism*. New York: Routledge.

Botwinick, J. (1961). My husband and father-in-law: A reversible figure. *American Journal of Psychology, 74*(2), 312–313.

Burke, J. (2003). *Al Qaeda: The true story of radical Islam*. London: I.B. Tauris.

Burke, K., Hyman, S., & Karmiller, B. (Eds.). (1964). *Perspectives by incongruity*. Bloomington: Indiana University Press.

Byles, J. M. (2003). Psychoanalysis and war: The superego and projective identification. *Journal for the Psychoanalysis of Culture and Society, 8*(2), 208–213.

Campbell, D. (1998). *Writing security: United States Foreign Policy and the politics of identity*. Minneapolis: University of Minnesota Press.

Canetti, E. (1998). *Crowds and power*. New York: The Noonday Press.

Carter, S., & Dodds, K. (2011). Hollywood and the 'war on terror': Genre-geopolitics and 'Jacksonianism' in *The Kingdom*. *Environment and Planning D: Society and Space, 29*, 98–113.

Carter, S., & McCormack, D. (2006). Film, geopolitics and the affective logics of intervention. *Political Geography, 25*, 228–245.

Chomsky, N. (1988). *The culture of terrorism*. New York: Black Rose Books.

Chomsky, N. (1989). *Necessary illusions: Thought control in democratic societies*. Toronto: Anasi Press.

Chomsky, N. (2010). *Hopes and prospects*. Chicago: Haymarket Books.

Cook, N. (1993). Closure/dis-closure. In I. Makaryk (Ed.), *Encyclopedia of contemporary literary theory*. Toronto: University of Toronto Press.

Cox, R. (1981). Social forces, states and world orders: Beyond international relations theory. *Millennium—Journal of International Studies, 10*(2), 126–155.

Cox, K. (1998). Spaces of dependence, spaces of engagement and the politics of scale, or: Looking for local politics. *Political Geography, 17*(1), 1–23.

Crawford, N. (2011). Civilian death and injury in Afghanistan, 2001–2011. http://costsofwar.org/sites/default/files/articles/14/attachments/Crawford%20Afghanistan%20Casualties.pdf

Cresswell, T. (1996). *In place/out of place: Geography, ideology, and transgression*. Minneapolis: University of Minnesota Press.

D'Addario, S., et al. (2008). Finding home: Exploring Muslim settlement in the Toronto CMA. *CERIS Working Paper*, No. 68.

Dalby, S. (2008). Warrior geopolitics: Gladiator, Black Hawk Down and the Kingdom Heaven. *Political Geography, 27*(4), 439–455.

Davies, J.-A. (2008). Clashing civilizations or conflicting interests?". *Geopolitics, 13,* 757–760.

Der Darian, J. (2005). Imaging terror: Logos, pathos, ethos. *Third World Quarterly, 26*(1), 23–37.

Diab, R. (2008). *Guantanamo North: Terrorism and the administration of justice in Canada.* Halifax: Fernwood Publishing.

Dikec, M. (2007). *Badlands of the republic: Space, politics, and urban policy.* Oxford: Blackwell Publishing.

Dittmer, J. (2010). *Popular culture, geopolitics & identity.* New York: Rowman & Littlefield Publishers, Inc.

Dittmer, J. (2011). American exceptionalism, visual effects, and the post-9/11 cinematic superhero boom. *Environment and Planning D: Society and Space, 29,* 114–130.

Dodds, K. (2008). Screening terror: Hollywood, the United States and the construction of danger. *Critical Studies on Terrorism, 1*(2), 227–243.

Dodge, M., & Kitchin, R. (2001). *Mapping cyberspace.* New York: Routledge.

Drakulic, S. (1993). *The Balkan express: Fragments from the other side of the war.* New York: W.W. Norton and Company.

Eid, P. (2007). *Being Arab: Ethnic and religious identity building among second generation youth in Montreal.* Montreal: McGill-Queen's University Press.

Engler, Y. (2012). *The ugly Canadian: Stephen Harper's Foreign Policy.* Winnipeg: Fernwood Publishing.

Euben, R. (2001). *Enemy in the mirror: Islamic fundamentalism and the limits of modern rationalism.* Karachi: Oxford University Press.

Fanon, F. (2004). *The Wretched of the Earth.* New York: Grove.

Flatt, J. (2012). The security certificate exception. In J. Zine (Ed.), *Islam in the Hinterlands: Muslim cultural politics in Canada.* Vancouver: University of British Columbia Press.

Flint, C. (2003). Terrorism and counterterrorism: Geographic research questions and agendas. *The Professional Geographer, 55*(2), 162–169.

Flint, C. (2007). Netwar, the modern geographical imagination, and the death of the civilian. In M. Innes (Ed.), *Denial of sanctuary* (pp. 34–48). London: Praeger Security International.

Foucault, M. (2000). J. Faubion (Ed.), *Power: Essential works of Foucault 1954–1984*(Vol. 3). London: Penguin.

Fukuyama, F. (2006). *The end of history and the last man.* New York: Free Press.

Funk, N., & Said, A. A. (2004). Islam and the West: Narratives of conflict and conflict transformation. *International Journal of Peace Studies, 9*(1), 1–28.

George, A. (1991). The discipline of terrology. In A. George (Ed.), *Western State terrorism*. Cambridge, UK: Polity Press.

Gerges, F. (1999). *America and political Islam*. New York: Cambridge University Press.

Gilbert, L. (2007). Legitimizing neoliberalism rather than equality: Canadian multiculturalism in the current reality of North America. *Norteamérica Revista Académica del CISAN-UNAM, 2*(1), 11–35.

Giroux, H. (2006). *Beyond the spectacle of terrorism: Global uncertainly and the challenge of the new media*. London: Paradigm Publishers.

Giroux, H. (2010). *Hearts of darkness: Torturing children in the war on terror*. London: Paradigm Publishers.

Gordon, A. (1999). Terrorism dissertations and the evolution of a specialty: An analysis of meta-information. *Terrorism and Political Violence, 11*(2), 141–150.

Gottschalk, P., & Greenberg, G. (2008). *Islamophobia: Making Muslims the enemy*. Lanham: Rowman & Littlefield Publishers, Inc.

Graham, S. (2004). "Introduction: Cities, warfare, and states of emergency. In S. Graham (Ed.), *Cities, war and terrorism: Towards an urban geopolitics*. Oxford: Blackwell Publishing.

Graham, S. (2006). Cities and the 'war on terror'. *International Journal of Urban and Regional Research, 30*(2), 255–276.

Graham, S. (2010). *Cities under siege*. London: Verso.

Gramsci, A. (1971). In Q. Hoare & G. Smith (Eds.), *Prison Notebooks*. New York: International Publishers.

Gray, M., & Wyly, E. (2007). The terror city hypothesis. In D. Gregory & A. Pred (Eds.), *Violent geographies: Fear, terror, and political violence* (pp. 329–348). New York: Routledge.

Gregory, D., & Pred, A. (2007). Introduction. In D. Gregory & A. Pred (Eds.), *Violent geographies: Fear, terror, and political violence* (pp. 1–6). New York: Routledge.

Gunning, J. (2007). A case for critical terrorism studies. *Government and Opposition, 42*(3), 363–393.

Hall, S. (1996a). Who needs 'identity'? In S. Hall & P. du Gay (Eds.), *Questions of cultural identity*. London: Sage Publications.

Halliday, F. (2003). *Islam & the myth of confrontation*. London: I.B. Tauris.

Halverson, J., Goodall, H. L., & Corman, S. (2011). *Master narratives of Islamist extremism*. New York: Palgrave Macmillan.

Hannah, M. (2006). Torture and the ticking bomb: The war on terrorism as a geographical imagination of power/knowledge. *Annals of the Association of American Geographers, 96*(3), 622–640.

Haraway, D. (1991). *Simians, cyborgs, and women: The reinvention of nature*. New York: Routledge.

Harvey, D. (1996). *Justice, nature and the geography of difference*. Cambridge, MA: Blackwell Publishers.
Hassan-Yari, H., & Ousman, A. (2005). Incremental changes in Canada's defense and security policy Since September 11, 2001." In A. Netherton, A. Seager, & K. Froschauer (Eds.), *IN/SECURITY: Canada in the post-9/11 world*. Burnaby, B.C.: Centre for Canadian Studies.
Hellmich, C. (2011). *Al-Qaeda: From global network to local franchise*. London: Zed Books Ltd.
Hillyard, P. (1993). *Suspect community*. London: Pluto Press.
Horgan, J. (2005). *The psychology of terrorism*. New York: Routledge.
Hourani, A. (1991). *Islam in European thought*. New York: Cambridge University Press.
Hunter, S. (1998). *The future of Islam and the West: Clash of civilizations or coexistence*. West Port: Praeger Publishers.
Huntington, S. (2003). *The clash of civilizations and the remaking of world order*. New York: Simon & Schuster Paperbacks.
Huntington, S. (2006). *Political order in changing societies*. New Haven: Yale University Press.
Hussain, A. (1984). The ideology of orientalism. In A. Huassain, R. Olson, & J. Quereshi (Eds.), *Orientalism, Islam, and Islamists*. Vermont: Amana Books.
Ibn Abdul-Aziz, A-Q. *Fundamental Concepts Regarding Al-Jihad* (trans: Anonymous.). London: At-Tibyan Publications.
Inge, J., & Findley, E. (2006). North American defense and security after 9/11. *Joint Force Quarterly, 40*, 23–28. www.dtic.mil/cgibin/GetTRDoc?AD=ADA521750.
Ingram, A., & Dodds, K. (2009). Spaces of security and insecurity: Geographies of the war on terror. In A. Ingram & K. Dodds (Eds.), *Spaces of security and insecurity: Geographies of the war on terror* (pp. 1–20). Surrey: Ashgate Publishing Limited.
Ismail, S. (2006). *Rethinking Islamist politics: Culture, the state and Islamism*. London: I.B. Tauris.
Jabri, V. (2009). Security, multiculturalism, and the cosmopolis. In A. C. Stephens & N. Vaughan-Williams (Eds.), *Terrorism and the politics of response*. New York: Routledge.
Jackson, R. (2007). Constructing enemies: 'Islamic Terrorism' in political and academic discourse. *Government and Opposition, 42*(3), 394–426.
Jackson, R. (2012). The study of terrorism 10 years after 9/11: Successes, issues, challenges. *International Affairs, 8*(32), 1–16.
James, C. (2005). Introduction: Perspectives on multiculturalism in Canada. In C. James (Ed.), *Possibilities and limitations: Multicultural polices and programs in Canada*. Halifax: Fernwood Publishing.
Johnson, I. (2010). *A Mosque in Munich: Nazis, the CIA, and the rise of the Muslim brotherhood in the West*. New York: Houghton Mifflin Harcourt Publishing Company.

Juergensmeyer, M. (2000). Understanding the new terrorism. *Current History*, *99*, 158–163.
Junning, J. (2007). A case for critical terrorism studies. *Government and Opposition*, *42*(3), 363–393.
Kearns, R. (2005). Knowing seeing? Undertaking observational research. In L. Hay (Ed.), *Qualitative research methods in human geography* (2nd ed., pp. 192–206). New York: Oxford University Press.
Kern, M., Just, M., & Norris, P. (2003). The lessons of framing terrorism. In P. Norris, M. Kern, & M. Just (Eds.), *Framing terrorism: The news media, the government, and the public*. New York: Routledge.
Klassen, J. (2013). Introduction: Empire, Afghanistan, and Canadian Foreign Policy. In J. Klassen & G. Albo (Eds.), *Empire's Ally: Canada and the war in Afghanistan*. Toronto: University of Toronto Press.
Kress, G., & Van Leeuwen, T. (2001). *Multimodal discourse: The modes and media of contemporary communication*. London: Arnold.
Lacan, J., & Miller, J-A. (Eds.). (2007). *The Other Side of Psychoanalysis* (trans: Grigg, R.). New York: W.W. Norton & Company.
Lee, R. (1993). *Doing research on sensitive topics*. London: Sage Publications.
Lewis, B. (1990). The roots of Muslim rage. *The Atlantic Monthly*, *266*(3), 47–60.
Lia, B. (2009). Destructive Doctrinarians: Abu Mus' ab al-Suri's critique of the Salafis in the Jihadi current. In R. Meijer (Ed.), *Global Salafism*. New York: Columbia UP.
Lockman, Z. (2004). *Contending visions of the Middle East: The history and politics of orientalism*. New York: Cambridge University Press.
Luke, T. (2004). Everyday technics as extraordinary threats: Urban technostructures and non-places in terrorist actions. In S. Graham (Ed.), *Cities, war, and terrorism: Towards an urban geopolitics*. Oxford: Blackwell Publishing.
Macdonald, D. (2011). *The cost of 9/11: Tracking the creation of a national security establishment in Canada*. Ottawa: The Rideau Institute.
Mamdani, M. (2002). Good Muslim, bad Muslim: A political perspective on culture and terrorism. *American Anthropologist*, *104*(3), 766–775.
Mamdani, M. (2004). *Good Muslim, bad Muslim: America, the Cold War, and the roots of terror*. New York: Pantheon Books.
Marcuse, P. (2004). The "War on terrorism" and life in cities after September 11, 2001. In S. Graham (Ed.), *Cities, war and terrorism: Towards an urban geopolitics*. Oxford: Blackwell Publishing.
Marx, K. (1969). *Theses on Feuerbach*. Moscow: Progress Publishers. http://www.marxists.org/archive/marx/works/1845/theses/theses.htm.
Massey, D. (2005). *For space*. London: Sage Publications.
Mathur, S. (2006). Surviving the dragnet: 'Special interest' detainees in the US after 9/11. *Race & Class*, *47*(3), 31–46.
Miniter, R. (2011). *Mastermind: The many faces of the 9/11 architect, Khalid Shaikh Mohammed*. New York: Sentinel.

Mitchell, R. (1993). *The society of the Muslim brothers*. New York: Oxford University Press.
Mitchell, K. (2011). Zero tolerance, imperialism, dispossession. *Acme, 10*(2), 293–312.
Moore, D. (1997). Remapping resistance: 'Ground for struggle' and the politics of place. In S. Pile & M. Keith (Eds.), *Geographies of resistance*. New York: Routledge.
Morton, D. (2005). Canada's asymmetrical war. In A. Netherton, A. Seager, & K. Froschauer (Eds.), *IN/SECURITY: Canada in the post-9/11 world*. Burnaby, B.C.: Centre for Canadian Studies.
Murphy, A. (2003). The space of terror. In S. Cutter et al. (Eds.), *The geographical dimensions of terrorism* (pp. 47–52). New York: Routledge.
Murphy, A. (2006). Enhancing geography's role in public debate. *Annals of the Association of American Geographers, 96*(1), 1–13.
Netherton, A., & Seager, A. (2005). Introduction: Framing In/Security. In A. Netherton, A. Seager, & K. Froschauer (Eds.), *IN/SECURITY: Canada in the post-9/11 world*. Burnaby, B.C.: Centre for Canadian Studies.
Oriola, T. (2009). Counter-terrorism and alien justice: The case of security certificates in Canada. *Critical Studies on Terrorism, 2*(2), 257–274.
Pain, R., & Smith, S. (2008). Fear: Critical geopolitics in everyday life. In R. Pain & S. Smith (Eds.), *Fear: Critical geopolitics in everyday life* (pp. 1–24). Surrey: Ashgate Publishing Limited.
Parker, T. (2007). Fighting an Antaean enemy: How democratic states unintentionally sustain the terrorist movements they oppose. *Terrorism and Political Violence, 19*, 155–179.
Patel, S. (2012). The Anti-terrorism Act and national security: Safeguarding the nation against the uncivilized Muslims. In J. Zine (Ed.), *Islam in the Hinterlands: Muslim cultural politics in Canada*. Vancouver: University of British Columbia Press.
Peach, C. (2006). Islam, ethnicity, and South Asian religions in the London 2001 Census. *Transactions of the Institute of British Geographers, 31*(3), 353–370.
Perdue, W. (1989). *Terrorism and the state: A critique of domination through fear*. West Port: Praeger Publishers.
Phillips, R., & Jones, J. (2012). *Fieldwork for human geographers*. London: Sage.
Poulantzas, N. (1978). *State, power, socialism*. London: Verso.
Poynting, S., & Whyte, D. (2012). Introduction: Counter-terrorism and the terrorist state. In S. Poynting & D. Whyte (Eds.), *Counter-terrorism and state political violence*. London: Routledge.
Preston, V., Kobayashi, A., & Siemiatycki, M. (2005). Transnational urbanism: Toronto at a crossroads. In V. Satzewich & L. Wong (Eds.), *Transnational identities and practices in Canada*. Vancouver: UBC Press.
Pruett, G. (1984). Islam' and orientalism. In A. Huassain, R. Olson, & J. Quereshi (Eds.), *Orientalism, Islam, and Islamists*. Vermont: Amana Books.

Rapoport, D. (2001). The fourth wave: September 11 in the history of terrorism. *Current History, 100,* 419–424.
Reitz, J., et al. (2009). Race, religion, and social integration of new immigrants in Canada. *International Migration Review, 43*(4), 695–726.
Roach, K. (2006). National security, multiculturalism and Muslim minorities. *Singapore Journal of Legal Studies,* 405–438.
Rodinson, M. (2002). *Europe and the Mystique of Islam.* London: I.B. Tauris.
Rogers, B. (2011). The psychology of violent radicalization. In A. Silke (Ed.), *The psychology of counter-terrorism.* New York: Routledge.
Roy, O. (2004). *Globalized Islam: The search for a New Ummah.* New York: Columbia University Press.
Sageman, M. (2008). *Leaderless Jihad.* Philadelphia: University of Pennsylvania Press.
Said, E. (1979). *Orientalism.* New York: Vintage Books.
Said, E. (1997). *Covering Islam: How the media and the experts determine How We See the rest of the world.* New York: Vintage Books.
Said, E. (2003). The clash of definitions. In E. Qureshi & M. Sells (Eds.), *The new crusades: Constructing the Muslim enemy.* New York: Columbia UP.
Salvatore, A. (1997). *Islam and the political discourse of modernity.* Reading: Ithaca Press.
Sayer, A. (1992). *Method is social science: A realist approach* (2nd ed.). New York: Routledge.
Sayyid, S. (2003). *A fundamental fear: Eurocentrism and the emergence of Islamism.* London: Zed Books Ltd.
Schmid, A., & Jongman, A. (1988). *Political terrorism.* London: Transaction Publishers.
Shakespeare, W. (1963). S. Barnet (Ed.), *Macbeth.* New York: The New American Library.
Shakespeare, W. (1964). J. A. Bryant (Ed.), *Romeo and Juliet.* New York: The New American Library.
Shanahan, T. (2010). Betraying a certain corruption of mind: How (and how not) to define 'terrorism. *Critical Studies on Terrorism, 3*(2), 173–190.
Sharify-Funk, M. (2010). Muslims and the politics of "reasonable accommodation": Analyzing the Bouchard-Taylor report and its impact on the Canadian Province of Quebec. *Journal of Muslim Minority Affairs, 30*(4), 535–553.
Sharp, J. (2000). Refiguring geopolitics: The *Reader's digest* and popular geographies of danger at the end of the Cold War. In K. Dodds & D. Atkinson (Eds.), *Geopolitical traditions: A century of geopolitical thought* (pp. 332–352). New York: Routledge.
Shepard, W. (1987). Islam and ideology: Towards a typology. *International Journal of Middle East Studies, 19,* 307–336.
Shklovsky, V. (1994). Art as technique. In *Contemporary literary criticism* (3rd ed.). London: Longman.

Siddiqui, H. (2008). Muslims and the rule of law. In N. Bakht (Ed.), *Belonging and banishment: Being Muslim in Canada*. Toronto: TSAR Books.

Silke, A. (2004). An introduction to terrorism research. In A. Silke (Ed.), *Research on terrorism: Trends, achievements and failures*. London: Frank Cass.

Silke, A. (2008). Holy Warriors: Exploring the psychological processes of Jihadi radicalization. *European Journal of Criminology, 5*(1), 99–123.

Slater, D. (1997). Spatial politics/social movements: Questions of (b)orders and resistance in global times. In S. Pile & M. Keith (Eds.), *Geographies of resistance*. New York: Routledge.

Smith, N. (2001). Scales of terror and the resort to geography: September 11, October 7. *Environment and Planning D: Society and Space, 19*, 631–637.

Springer, S. (2011). Violence sits in places? Cultural practice, neoliberal rationalism, and virulent imaginative geographies. *Political Geography, 30*, 90–98.

Staeheli, L. (2008). Migration, civilizational thinking, and the possibility of democracy. *Geopolitics, 13*, 749–752.

Swyngedouw, E. (1997). Neither global or local: "Globalization" and the politics of scale. In K. Cox (Ed.), *Spaces of globalization: Reasserting the power of the local*. New York: Guildford Publications.

Taylor, J., & Jasparo, C. (2003). "Editorials and geopolitical explanations for 11 September. *Geopolitics, 8*(3), 217–252.

Thorton, W. H. (2003). Cold War II: Islamic terrorism as power politics. *Antipode, 35*(2), 205–211.

Tibi, B. (2000). Post-bipolar order in crisis: The challenge of politicized Islam. *Millenium Journal of International Relations, 29*(3), 843–859.

Trumpbour, J. (2003). The clash of civilizations: Samuel P. Huntington, Bernard Lewis, and the remaking of the post-Cold War world order. In E. Qureshi & M. Sells (Eds.), *The New crusades: Constructing the Muslim enemy*. New York: Columbia UP.

Tuan, Y.-F. (1979). *Landscapes of fear*. New York: Pantheon Books.

Turner, B. (1994). *Orientalism, postmodernism & globalism*. New York: Routledge.

Turner, B. (2007). Religious authority and the new media. *Theory, Culture & Society, 24*(2), 117–134.

Volpi, F. (2007). Constructing the 'Ummah' in European security: Between exit, voice and loyalty. *Government and Opposition, 42*(3), 451–470.

Wagemakers, J. (2009). The transformation of a radical concept: *al-wala' wa-l-bara'* in the ideology of Abu Muhammad al-Maqdisi. In R. Meijer (Ed.), *Global salafism*. New York: Columbia University Press.

Watts, M. (2007). Revolutionary Islam. In D. Gregory & A. Pred (Eds.), *Violent geographies: Fear, terror, and political violence* (pp. 329–348). New York: Routledge.

Waxman, M. (2011). Terrorism: Why categories matter. *Terrorism and Political Violence, 23*, 19–22.

Weimann, G. (2006). *Terror on the Internet*. Washington, D.C.: United States Institute of Peace Press.
Žižek, S. (2008). *The sublime object of ideology*. London: Verso.
Zulaika, J., & Douglass, W. (1996). *Terror and taboo: The follies, fables, and faces of terrorism*. New York: Routledge.

Newspaper/Corporate Media Sources

Afaq Moin, S. (1997, January 6). Muslim fundamentalists not the same as terrorists. *Toronto Star*, A14.

Appleby, T., & Freeze, C. (2006, June 5). Complex operation leading to arrests of alleged terrorists shrouded in secrecy. *Globe and Mail*, A1, A4.

Bell, S. (2006, June 3). Never mind foreign terrorists, why is Canada growing it own extremists? *National Post*, A8.

Bhattacharya, S. (2006, June 7). Relatives overwhelmed by intense media crush. *Toronto Star*, A1, A8.

Blatchford, C. (2006, June 5). Ignoring the biggest elephant in the room. *Globe and Mail*, A1, A6.

Blatchford, C. (2008, September 26). A judgment drenched in common sense. *Globe and Mail*, A7.

Chaudhary, M. (1990, June 14). Don't link terrorists with Muslims' beliefs. *Toronto Star*, A26.

Cowell, A., & Van Natta, D. (2005, July 24). Britain says man killed had no tie to bombing. *New York Times*. www.nytimes.com/2005/07/24/international/24london.html

El Akkad, O. (2006, June 7). Suspects families suddenly become pariahs within the Muslim Community. *Toronto Star*, A1, A8.

El Akkad, O. (2007, August 1). Charges stayed for two men in terror case. *Toronto Star*, A6.

Freeze, C. (2008, September 26). Terrorism laws pass their first test as youth convicted in homegrown plot. *Globe and Mail*, A1, A7.

Freeze, C. (2008, April 16). Charges stayed against four terrorism suspects. *Globe and Mail*, A7.

Freeze, C. (2009, September 3). How a police agent cracked a terror cell. *Globe and Mail*, A4.

Freeze, C., & Hammer, K. (2012, June 18). Mounties ask to be allowed in schools—to teach, not spy. *Globe and Mail*. http://m.theglobeandmail.com/news/toronto/mounties-ask-to-be-allowed-into-schools---to-teach-not-spy/article4106476/?service=mobile

Gable, B. (2006, June 8). In other news today. *Globe and Mail*, A18.

Goraya, N. (1997, May 8). Media make life difficult for Muslims. *Toronto Star*, A32.

Gwyn, R. (2006, June 9). How do you fight a moral sickness? *Toronto Star*, A21.
Hall, J. (1996, October 13). Muslims misunderstood, conference told stereotyped as terrorist, scholar says. *Toronto Star*, A3.
Hanes, A. (2008, April 16). Prosecutors face balancing act: Security expert. *National Post*, A12.
Jamal, T. (2008, June 8). I'm the one who defines myself as a Muslim. *Globe and Mail*, A20.
Jenkins, A. (2006, June 10). South Toronto Maple Leafs. *Globe and Mail*, A22.
Kay, J. (2006, June 6). Terror and tolerance. *National Post*, A17.
Lacina, A-S. (1992, March 24). Why is Islam treated like a foreign faith? *Toronto Star*, A18.
Lacina, A-S. (1992, August 22). Violence is extremely rare in Islamic revival. *Toronto Star*, D3.
Laidlaw, K. (2009, June 22). Details of alleged Toronto 18 bomb plot revealed. *National Post*. On-line edition: last accessed on 21 March 2010.
Leong, M. (2006, June 7). World's media descend on Brampton Courtroom. *National Post*, A3.
Leong, M., & Kim, G. (2007, August 1). Two terror cell accused won't face charges. *National Post*, A13.
Mansbridge, P. (2011, September 8). [Interview with Stephen Harper]. *The National*. http://www.cbc.ca/news/politics/transcript-of-peter-mansbridge-s-interview-with-pm-stephen-harper-1.985393
McArthur, G., & Friesen, J. (2006, June 10). From soccer field to schism to arrests. *Globe and Mail*, A7.
Rabbani, F. (1993, December 13). Pious Muslims are not violent or dangerous. *Toronto Star*, A16.
Saunders, D. (2013, February 9). We're looking for terrorists in all the wrong places. *Globe and Mail*, F2.
Shepard, M. (2006, June 3). Threat on the home front: How Internet monitoring sparked a CSIS investigation into what authorities allege is a homegrown Canadian terror cell. *Toronto Star*, A1, A14.
Shephard, M. (2006, June 7). Imam no stranger to controversy. *Toronto Star*, A7.
Shephard, M., Bhattacharya, S., & Josey, S. (2006, June 6). Men attended 'training camps': Sources. *Toronto Star*, A1.
Teotonio, I. (2007, August 1). Charges stayed for youths in homegrown terror case. *Toronto Star*, A1, A8.
Teotonio, I. (2010, June 24). Terror trial ends, threat of extremism still growing. *Toronto Star*, A1, A21.
Teotonio, I., & Leeder, J. (2006, June 10). Jihadist generation: In search of roots. *Toronto Star*.
Turnbull, B. (1998, September 24). Media biased against Muslims. *Toronto Star*, A28.

Walkom, T. (2008, April 16). The incredible shrinking terror case. *Toronto Star*, AA8.
Walkom, T. (2008, September 26). Terror verdict bad news for rest of Toronto 18. *Toronto Star*, A6.
Wark, W. (2006, June 6). Knowing the enemy within. *Globe and Mail*, A17.
Wente, M. (2006, June 6). Generation jihad: Angry, young, born-again believers. *Globe and Mail*. http://www.theglobeandmail.com/globe-debate/generation-jihad-angry-young-born-again-believers/article1100587
Woods, M. (2011, July 25). It is better to kill too many than not enough. *Toronto Star*, A10.

GOVERNMENT DOCUMENTS AND REPORTS

Canadian Security Intelligence Service. (1999). *Trends in terrorism*, Report No. 2000/1. Ottawa. https://www.csis.gc.ca/pblctns/prspctvs/200001-eng.asp
Canadian Security Intelligence Service. (2000a). *International terrorism: The threat to Canada*, Report No. 2000/04. Ottawa. https://www.csis.gc.ca/pblctns/prspctvs/200004-eng.asp
Canadian Security Intelligence Service. (2000b). *2000 Public Report*. Ottawa. https://www.csis.gc.ca/pblctns/nnlrprt/2000/rprt2000-eng.asp
Clerk of the Privy Council and Secretary to the Cabinet. (2006). *Intelligence briefing on radicalization and Jihad in the West*. Ottawa: Canadian Security Intelligence Service.
Millward, W. (1993a). The rising tide of Islamic fundamentalism (I). *CSIS Commentary No. 30*. Ottawa. https://www.csis.gc.ca/pblctns/cmmntr/cm30-eng.asp
Millward, W. (1993b). The rising tide of Islamic fundamentalism (II). *CSIS Commentary No. 31*. Ottawa. https://www.csis.gc.ca/pblctns/cmmntr/cm31-eng.asp
Public Safety Canada. (2013). *Building Resilience Against Terrorism*. Ottawa: Government of Canada.
R.v. AHD. Agreed Statement of Facts.
R.v. SK. Statement of Uncontested Facts.
R.v. ZA. Agreed Statement of Facts.
R.v. AA, 2010 ONSC 5455. Reasons for Sentence.
R.v. FA, 2010 ONSC 5874. Reasons for Sentence.
R.v. NY, CRIMJ(F)1587/07. Agreed Statement of Facts.
R.v. SA, 2011 ONSC 1428. Reasons for Sentence.
R.v. SA, CR-07-2025. Excerpt of Sentencing.
R.v. SC, 2010 ONSC 6538. Reasons for Sentence.
R.v. SG, 2010 ONSC 434. Reasons for Sentence.
R.v. SG, DR (F)2541/08. Reasons for Judgment.
R.v. ZA, 2010 ONSC 441. Reasons for Sentence.

Senate Committee on National Security and Defence. (2002). *Defence of North America: A Canadian responsibility.* Ottawa: Colin Kenney & Michael Forrestall.

Special Senate Committee on the *Anti-Terrorism Act.* (2007). *Fundamental justice in extraordinary times: Main report of the special Senate Committee on the Anti-Terrorism Act.* Ottawa: The Senate of Canada.

Statistics Canada. (2007a). *The West Asian Community in Canada.* Statistics Canada Catalogue No. 89-621-XIE—No. 3. Ottawa: Colin Lindsay.

Statistics Canada. (2007b). *The South Asian Community in Canada.* Statistics Canada Catalogue No. 89-621-XIE—No. 6. Ottawa: Colin Lindsay.

Wilkinson, P. (1995). Terrorism: Motivations and causes. *CSIS Commentary, No. 53.* Ottawa: https://www.csis.gc.ca/pblctns/cmmntr/cm53-eng.asp

INDEX

A
affectivity, 145, 166, 220
Afghanistan, 1, 3, 10, 22, 25, 39, 40, 48, 64, 65, 94, 95, 107, 116, 117, 126n103, 127n110, 132, 137, 140–3, 145, 146, 157–61, 194, 201, 203, 211, 212, 224
al-Awlaki, Anwar, 18, 19, 34n87, 145, 188
Al-Maqdisi, Abu Muhammad Asim, 18, 34n87, 101–2, 113, 124n57
al Qaeda, 3–5, 7, 11, 14, 15, 17–20, 23, 25–7, 29n13, 29n18, 33n74, 34n87, 60, 64, 65, 95, 99, 100, 108, 133, 134, 136, 149n18, 150n29, 215, 227
Althusser, Louis, 19, 155, 184
  displacement and condensation, 37–84
anti-Muslimism, 39, 40, 52, 74n9
  Islamophobia, 38, 40, 124n46
Anti-Terrorism Act (ATA), 64, 153, 162, 163, 169, 172
as-Salim, Muhammad bin Ahmad, 102

ATA. *See* Anti-Terrorism Act (ATA)
Aziz, Abdul-Qadir Ibn Abdul, 101

B
Bosnia, 60, 134, 140, 141

C
Canadian Security Intelligence Service (CSIS), 56, 57, 95, 97, 138, 153, 154, 164, 167, 169, 171—6, 178n1, 182n60, 196, 198, 224
Chechnya, 60, 116, 132, 137, 140, 141, 187, 194
Cox, Kevin
  network of scales, 118–20
  spaces of dependence, 118
  spaces of engagement, 118, 119
Cresswell, Tim
  In Place/Out of Place, 87
  transgression, 88, 89
CSIS. *See* Canadian Security Intelligence Service (CSIS)

D

defamiliarization, 16, 33n74
discursive formations
  dominant, 73, 89, 90–110, 118
  subversive, 40, 73, 89, 90–110, 118

E

11 September 2001, 1, 2, 5, 14, 18, 27n7, 32n64, 38, 40, 43, 51, 52, 54, 55, 58, 59, 61–6, 68, 71, 78n64, 81n97, 83n116, 87, 93, 96–8, 107, 114, 124n46, 131, 146, 154, 154, 162, 164, 167, 175, 183, 213, 214, 224

F

Fanon, Frantz, 155
fardh ayn/fardh kifayah, 186
Foucault, Michel, 182n69
  power/knowledge, 182n69
Fukuyama, Francis, 41
  end of history, 41

G

Gramsci, Antonio
  common sense, 11, 177
  war of manoeuvre, 20
  war of position, 20
Guantanamo Bay, 1, 2, 107, 137, 145
Gulf War, 14, 49

H

halaqaat/halaqah, 102, 145, 202
homo Islamicus/homo terrorismus, 87
Huntington, Samuel, 41, 46, 80n87, 211
  clash of civilizations, 41, 80n87, 211

I

ideological closure, 209–11
insecuritization, 98, 99, 108, 123n46
Integrated National Security Enforcement Team (INSET), 138, 172, 196
Iraq, 1, 3, 10, 22, 49, 107, 130, 137, 140–2, 145, 157, 175, 201, 203, 212, 229
  Abu Ghraib, 1, 3, 108, 137
Islamitic extremism
  Domestic Islamitic Extremism, 22, 23, 87, 111, 165, 177
  Transnational Islamitic Extremism, 22, 23, 62, 64, 87, 111, 162, 165, 176–7

K

Kashmir, 20, 60, 140
Kenya, 14, 55

L

Lacan, Jacques, 113

M

Massey, Doreen, 85
  place, 85

P

Pakistan, 1, 8, 17, 34n92, 78n60, 86, 108, 116, 140, 198
Palestine, 132, 140, 194
participant observation, 215, 216
  observer-as-participant, 216
Poulantzas, Nicos, xxx

R

Royal Canadian Mounted Police (RCMP), 96, 97, 164, 169, 171–6, 196, 199, 206n34

S

Said, Edward, 11, 42, 45, 59, 71, 85, 112, 213
 Orientalism/Orientalist, 11–16, 71, 112, 113
Saudi Arabia, 23, 49, 55, 63, 116, 117
security certificates, Canadian, 165, 180n35
Somalia, 20, 108, 140
spatial agony, 210, 211
spheres of influence
 group, 209, 211
 state, 110, 119, 148, 150n45, 153–82, 209
 transnational, 119, 129–51, 178, 209
state intellectuals/state intellectualism, 5–6, 13, 41, 74n2
suspect community, 2, 28n9, 166, 173, 180n35

T

Tanzania, 14, 55
terrorism studies
 critical approach, xln47
 problem-solving approach, xix, xx
Toronto 18
 Mississauga Group, 18, 26, 138, 142, 161, 194, 200, 204, 211, 224–6
 Scarborough Group, 26, 134, 136, 139–41, 159, 188, 194, 200, 201, 204, 225, 226
typologies, terrorism, 5

W

war of terror, 1, 11, 60, 63, 65, 72, 81n103, 96, 108, 146, 157, 158, 180n35, 183, 192, 208, 213, 221

Y

Yemen, 1, 14, 24, 55, 101, 108

Z

Zizek, Slavoj, 91–3
 master signifier, 92